THE GREAT REBELLION

Books by Earl Schenck Miers

GETTYSBURG (WITH RICHARD A. BROWN)

THE GENERAL WHO MARCHED TO HELL

THE WEB OF VICTORY

THE LIVING LINCOLN (WITH PAUL M. ANGLE)

ROBERT E. LEE

THE AMERICAN STORY (EDITOR)

WHEN THE WORLD ENDED: THE DIARY OF EMMA LECONTE

A REBEL WAR CLERK'S DIARY (ABRIDGED)

THE GREAT REBELLION

The

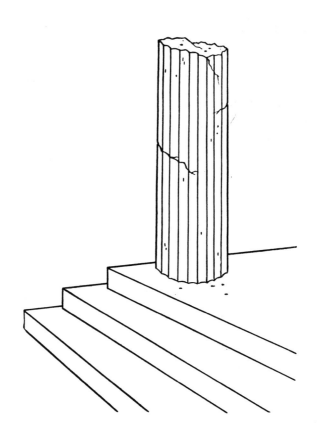

EARL SCHENCK MIERS

Great Rebellion

THE EMERGENCE OF THE AMERICAN CONSCIENCE

THE WORLD PUBLISHING COMPANY

CLEVELAND AND NEW YORK

Published by THE WORLD PUBLISHING COMPANY
2231 West 110th Street, Cleveland 2, Ohio

Published simultaneously in Canada by
Nelson, Foster & Scott Ltd.

Library of Congress Catalog Card Number: 58-9407

FIRST EDITION

WP758

TO THE AFFECTIONATE MEMORY OF

Benjamin P. Thomas

WHO SLEEPS NOW ON A HILLSIDE ACROSS

FROM LINCOLN'S TOMB

AND WHO LIVES ON IN THE HEARTS OF

HIS MANY DEVOTED FRIENDS

Contents

CONTENTS

THE GREAT REBELLION

Prologue

THIS is a book about the American people and what happened to them during one Christmas week, as the result of a tragic Thursday, and on a Palm Sunday. It is a book of love and hate, of faith and fear, of tormented loyalties and unyielding principles, of passion and patience and greed and sacrifice. It is a book of some moments that took years to crystallize and of other moments that were clear and complete in the winking of an eye. It is a book about persons so well known in history and legend that we speak their names as though they were honored kinsmen and about others who rest today beneath crumbled, forgotten tombstones.

They were all related, these people—the great and the unknown, the friend and the foe; and although they traveled many roads they reached the same valley, and, crossing over, rested beneath the same trees. Their tragedy they called the American Civil War; their victory they called Freedom.

There are no great battles in this book—no Bull Run or Shiloh, no seven bloody days on the Peninsula, no Fredericksburg and Chancellorsville and Gettysburg and Vicksburg, no Missionary Ridge, no Atlanta, no ghastly Wilderness, no butchery at Cold Harbor—and the fighting that is described is indecisive, unnecessary, futile, as so much fighting is. Yet the will to fight, to bleed and die, to sustain this war is here; for the conflict, in terms of human aspiration, was too deeply rooted in eternity to be denied, and once the struggle began there could be, in terms of human aspiration, but one ending.

The world watched this war. It belonged to people everywhere, a thing terrible and yet grand, as old in a way as man himself and as new as the unborn children in his dreams. Many historians have tried to describe this war and to say what in essence it was, but none has succeeded quite so well as a Midwestern professor named Denton Jacques Snider, who years ago wrote a curious and passionate book. Professor Snider compared the war to the *Iliad* and observed:

> . . . But now a restoration is to take place far deeper than the Grecian or that of Helen; the mighty struggle is now not for the ideal of beauty but for the ideal of freedom, though its bearer be not the most beautiful woman of the world but the homeliest mortal of God's creation, the black African, most un-Grecian as to nose and feature and foot and form. . . . As the Greek during his whole national existence never could get rid of the eternal pother over Helen, but had to re-enact her and hers in his art, in his poetry, even in his history and religion, with the ever-recurring conflict between Greece and Asia from Troy till Rome, so the American seemingly cannot bring to an end the eternal pother over the Negro after hundreds of trials, but has to spend his thought, his treasure and his blood, till this humblest and by nature most servile of the races of men be transformed and re-generated into a free being, capable of free institutions. . . .

One man knew this as a truth burned upon his soul. Once he said, "I love the sentiments of those old-time men," meaning Washington and Jefferson and George Mason and John Marshall and the other great patriots of the first generation of American statesmanship who had believed all men were created equal and had conceived of a government that was the image of this faith. Once he said, "Such a man the times have demanded, and such, in the Providence of God was given us," meaning Henry Clay, with Calhoun and Webster a towering symbol of the second generation of

American statesmanship that compromised its jealousies and clung to the faith of its fathers. Then, midway in the third generation of American statesmanship, came the new and fearful crisis, when brothers quarreled, when the faith became obscured in conflicting interests, and again the times demanded a man and found it in Abraham Lincoln.

For it was always Mr. Lincoln's War. Where others around him quavered, he stood firm—during that Christmas week in 1860. He decided that the war must be fought, for good or evil, and so on a Thursday in 1861 old John Brown arose from his grave. Lincoln decided how on the battlefield it should be fought—setting the destruction of Lee's army as the objective; and how in the heart of humanity it must be fought—and he alone decided to issue the Emancipation Proclamation. Always he fought one war, and on July 4, 1861, in a special message to Congress, he said:

> This is essentially a People's contest. On the side of the Union, it is a struggle for maintaining in the world, that form, and substance of government, whose leading object is, to elevate the condition of men—to lift artificial weights from all shoulders—to clear the paths of laudable pursuit for all—to afford all, an unfettered start, and a fair chance, in the race of life.
>
> I am most happy to believe that the plain people understand, and appreciate this. It is worthy of note, that while in this, the government's hour of trial, large numbers of those in the Army and Navy, who have been favored with the offices, have resigned, and proved false to the hand which had pampered them, not one common soldier, or common sailor is known to have deserted his flag.

Again, dedicating a national cemetery, he described the lasting meaning of the war: ". . . that from these honored dead we take increased devotion to that cause for which they gave the last full measure of devotion—that we here highly resolve that these dead shall not have died in vain—that this nation, under God, shall have a new birth of freedom—and that government *of* the people, *for* the people, *by* the people, shall not perish from the earth," and the italics, which are the author's, indicate where Lincoln placed the emphasis.

So Lincoln was the fulcrum; and the basic tenet of his faith—that, among a free people, what diminishes one man diminishes all men—led irresistibly to the Palm Sunday in 1865. But always the people were there too, torn between ideal and private necessity, living day by day, sometimes meanly, sometimes nobly, sometimes selling their birthright for a mess of pottage, sometimes astonishing in the tragic splendor of their selflessness. They all belonged to Mr. Lincoln's America then. They all belong to Mr. Lincoln's America today.

This story could begin anywhere in America. It could begin, for example, somewhere on "the southern boundary of Iowa," where Cyrus Jones, who styled himself "The Pioneer Trapper," turned over in his mind a letter he intended writing to Horace Greeley, that newspaper fellow in New York:

> I am but a plain frontier hunter and trapper, and very seldom handle much paper money. And lately a great deal I do get is refused by the storekeeper and shoemaker, and so I concluded it would also be refused by you; I therefore thought I would send you a prime mink skin, which I thought would bring a premium, instead of being discounted in your city, for which I desire you to send me your Weekly Tribune for as long a time as the pay will last.
>
> . . . I hear a great deal said about the danger our country is in, and I wish to keep informed about it. But if at any time it is necessary, I will abandon my traps, and with my good rifle I will be one to march to my country's call, wherever it may be necessary. . . .*

Unhappily history knows nothing more of Cyrus Jones; this is his document, terse but eloquent. So, arbitrarily, this story begins on a Sunday afternoon in Washington, D.C., matching strides with a stroller whose many moods and movements endure. . . .

* New York *Tribune,* February 14, 1861; the letter's authenticity must be taken on faith.

PART I

Christmas Week, *1860*

I

"We Did It Glory to God"

THE slouching, slender figure walked briskly, for after the season's first snow the weather had turned damp and chilly. Across the Potomac drifted mists that threatened, before evening descended, to enshroud Washington in fog and rain and spoil the promise of a white Christmas. Many who glimpsed the ungainly wayfarer on this Sunday afternoon in 1860 doubtless mentioned the fact at dinner. In a city where minding one's own business had become a lost art, some had to say, "The Governor is dining with the Adamses"; and perhaps one or two remembered that not long ago there had been good odds in Washington the Governor would be called Mr. President by now.

But William Henry Seward had learned to live with that disappointment. He carried proudly, even jauntily, the head that reminded young Henry Adams of a "wise macaw." Beaked nose and shaggy eyebrows, disorderly hair and hoarse voice, offhand manner and perpetual cigar—in such phrases young Adams described the Governor, confessing that he loved this man who "though sixty years old, had the youth of his sympathies." A Yankee instinct in Henry Adams that drove him to grub some profit from every experience almost failed in the case of the Governor. Let the politicians label Seward as unconventional for his western New York simplicity—and let Bostonians, by habit, pronounce the non-Bostonian provincial—but Henry Adams found "charming" a man who was "never petty or personal" and whose talk was "large." The Governor "never seemed to pose for statesmanship"; and what was more unusual—young Adams, on second thought, believed the quality "almost singular and quite eccentric"—was the Governor's "means, unknown to other Senators, of producing the effect of unselfishness."

The fog spread thin patches along the street; the rain could begin falling at any moment. If Seward's spirits grew depressed, another cause could have been the brightness of his prospects so short a time ago. The Governor possessed no memory more triumphant than his visit to Europe the previous summer. England especially had welcomed him warmly and not alone for the fact that he could have been a character out of the pages of *Pickwick Papers*. When Lord Palmerston had entertained Seward at his Piccadilly home and Lord Granville had invited him to weekend at Chiswick, both had been motivated by considerations quite aside from a curiosity to observe this American whose angular spindle-shanks pushed awkward knee knockers into his oaken-colored pantaloons, who sat gracelessly with the skirts of a long-tailed coat hanging in limp dejection at his sides, and whose lofty collar, black stock, and white ruffled shirt emphasized his huge ears, small, womanish neck, and sagging shoulders. For Lord John Russell dining Seward at Pembroke Lodge or the Duke of Sutherland exhibiting him at Stafford House, it was the Governor's prominence as an antislavery leader and author of the doctrine of "irrepressible conflict" that made him so attractive in these citadels of the British intelligentsia.

Even so, it became difficult to imagine in Queen Victoria any taste for a bizarre figure or any patience with the mid-nineteenth century equivalent of an egghead. After three years as secretary of the American legation in London, Benjamin Moran noted with disapproval that Sir Edward Cust had applied for permission to present Mr. Seward at the coming ball. "I don't think it will be granted, as it is clearly wrong," fretted Moran, and next day his diary recorded with satisfaction that the request had been refused: "It is against practice." The surprise came a week later: "It seems the Queen is disposed to be very civil to Mr. Seward. She has invited him specially to a Concert at the Palace ... The Concert is an honor unusual, and the presentation is remarkable." The whole business was over Moran's head, but the Queen acted on shrewd political advice. William H. Seward, ex-Governor of New York, she could ignore; William H. Seward, next President of the United States, she must receive.

Now of course Seward could relate other memories—one in February and another in May. The first concerned the excitement over Lincoln's Cooper Union speech; privately Seward called Lincoln "that prairie statesman," intending no compliment. His eyes had crackled when he read the nonsense written by Joseph Medill, Washington correspondent for the Chicago *Tribune*. Great God, Lincoln a Presidential possibility—Seward summoned Medill to his office and, in the journalist's phrase, "blew me up." Unless the Republicans gave him the nomination, Seward stormed, "he would shake the dust off his shoes, and retire from the service of an ungrateful party for the remainder of his days." Didn't Medill know that he, William H. Seward, "was the chief teacher of the principles of the Republican party before Lincoln was known other than as a country lawyer of Illinois"? Medill could go. They were no longer friends.

By May Seward's anger had cooled and in May the Republican National Convention assembled in Chicago, a city now of one hundred and ten thousand inhabitants, fifty-six churches, and one thousand saloons and grogshops. To the New York delegation Chicago's balance between godliness and gaiety provided a happy discovery. Ever since leaving the good old Empire State, these loyal backers of Seward-for-President had been sopping up the heady elixirs of certain victory. Led by such a keen student of the American conscience as Tom Hyer, the celebrated fisticuffer, the New Yorkers had tumbled off the trains as drunk as lords and, at least one witness vouchsafed, singing songs not found in hymn-

books. Marching along the plank walks from the depot to Seward's
headquarters at the Richmond House, Hyer's hawklike eyes must
have observed a few of the eighty "ballrooms" that were also a
Chicago feature. At home in Auburn, New York, at that moment
Hyer's hero strolled the quiet streets and nodded agreeably to
neighbors. In their admiring glances he discerned what his heart
told him: here passed a man of destiny.

Yet both the sober Seward and the glowing Hyer had misread
the signs. Now in damp December, living with the disappointment, the Governor could understand some of the reasons why
fate had betrayed him; but other reasons he would never comprehend, and neither would friends as close to him as the Adamses.
The brutal truth remained (as much so in December as in May)
that all sorts of ideals, ambitions, prejudices, frustrations, greeds,
and jealousies had produced the Republican Party in this, its sixth
and merriest year. Old Whigs who had nowhere else to turn without defaming the memory of Henry Clay, scowling partisans of
Know Nothingism seeking a new shoulder on which to rest their
chip, Free Soilers who recently had done well in New Hampshire
shouting "Land for the Landless and Homes for the Homeless
without money and without price" were among the dissidents
who had descended on Chicago, determined to break the rule of
the Democrats and set the country on the highroad to industrial
revolution.

Long before the Convention settled down to drafting a platform
that would serve as a catchall for victory in November, the boys
who knew their political p's and q's (an appropriate figure in
Hyer's case since it was derived from the pints and quarts on which
Colonial America had drunk itself groggy) realized the peculiar
assortment of qualifications a successful candidate must have. The
planks that went into that platform amounted really to a series of
tightropes upon which the Republicans, playing to local audiences,
could captivate constituents with facile twists and dazzling turns.
A firm stand must be taken against the extension of slavery, but
the antislavery vote wasn't going to swing the Convention or win

the election. What the Irish in New England and the Germans in the Midwest wanted was free land; Pennsylvania's ironmongers didn't give a damn about buying freedom for the slaves or passage to recolonize them in Africa* but a sound tariff was worth almost any price; Vermont intended to make political capital out of Buchanan's veto of Justin Morrill's bill to promote agricultural education through Federal grants to the states; and a Pacific railroad stretched the appeal of Republicanism from ocean to ocean. At the Richmond House the ebullient Hyer bought another round of drinks, believing the Convention would break wide open when New York threw its seventy votes behind Seward. And at the nearby Tremont House a group of Illinois lawyers and politicians dispatched a telegram on the day before the Convention opened:

> To A Lincoln
> We are quiet but moving heaven & earth. Nothing will beat us but old fogy politicians. The heart of the delegates are with us.

Both Hyer and Seward would have been better prepared for the coming shock had they possessed the prescience of young Murat Halstead, up from Cincinnati to report Convention proceedings for the *Commercial*. Halstead shouldered his way through the crowded halls, listened to the "thousand rumors afloat," and awakening to noisy gaming for gin cocktails before breakfast guessed the truth. Before the balloting started, the movements in behalf of Edward Bates of Missouri, old Judge McLean of Ohio (for all that abolitionists loved him after his dissenting opinion in the Dred Scott Case), Simon Cameron of Pennsylvania, and Nathaniel P. Banks of Massachusetts already had "gone down like lead in the mighty waters." Salmon P. Chase of Ohio had no chance; he didn't know it, but Halstead did. Only one contest counted—either Seward or Lincoln would emerge as "the representative of the conservatism, the respectability, the availability,

---

* To an honest Pennsylvania Republican in 1860 Africa was the Deep South east of the Mississippi.

and all that sort of thing" that could save the Union for right-minded Republicanism.

In fancying himself "the chief teacher" of the party, in believing he could not be forsaken, Seward overlooked one fact. The spring elections in Connecticut and Rhode Island had taught the Republicans something, too. The cautious businessman was beginning to run this political show, and with good reason the canny Lincoln had made four speeches in behalf of that ultraconservative shipowner, Ichabod Goodwin of New Hampshire. What was required to insure victory at the polls and in the Convention was a safe, affable, pliable middle-of-the-roader who could cement into a single force all the moods of dissent that troubled the American conscience. No one faced the tragic truth: that south of the Mason and Dixon line and east of the Mississippi there was very little American conscience in the Republican sense, or that Republican victory in November might very well bring secession in December, or that secession meant war. No one said in so many words that in the decade of torment that had followed the Compromise of 1850 neither the North nor the South could exert a compelling influence without striking a political bargain with the Midwest, but such was the American reality well demonstrated by Stephen A. Douglas who in the heated assertion that he cared not whether slavery was voted up or down had lost the whole game. Lincoln was no fool; he recognized his assets even though he knew he would not be "the *first* choice of a very great many" at the Convention; and shrewdly he advised his supporters: "Our policy, then, is to give no offense to others—leave them in a mood to come to us, if they shall be impelled to give up their first love."

Seward would be neither the first nor last to find costly the price of underestimating Lincoln. And that May, while Seward strolled the streets of Auburn in an agreeable mood, the fact in Chicago had been that he could not win on any pre-Convention tally sheet unless he carried Pennsylvania, Indiana, and Illinois. The Lincoln men, sounding out the Pennsylvania delegates, were not disheartened. The favorite son of the Keystone State, the ex-

Democrat and ex-Know Nothinger Simon Cameron, might like Seward personally, but Cameron's ear was to the ground listening for the rumble of the winning bandwagon. If there had been any doubt about Cameron's scruples, Pennsylvania's Governor Andrew Curtin settled that question. Cameron had none. A deal was possible, especially for a moderate who was sound on the tariff. So Lincoln's foot was thrust into the Pennsylvania door, but what of Indiana? The Hoosiers divided almost evenly between anti-slavery and proslavery. A workable Fugitive Slave Law, protection for industry without monopoly, a generous homestead law—with such planks Hoosiers banged together their platform. The Seward men were lavish with promises of money for the Indiana canvass, but Seward had been a long time in public life, blowing hot, blowing cold. He was more an old love than a first love.

The Convention opened with Tom Hyer in an alcoholic heaven and with that wheel horse of New York Republicanism, Thurlow Weed, striving to ignore the "damned old ass"—meaning Horace Greeley, who, denied a place with the New York delegation, had wheedled a proxy to represent the territory of Oregon. Whenever the Oracle of the New York *Tribune* appeared, an amused Murat Halstead observed, "the crowd became as dense as possible, and there is the most eager desire to hear the words of wisdom that are supposed to fall on such occasions." Not since the days of Ben Franklin's *Almanack* had rural America learned to value next to the Bible any publication like Greeley's *Tribune*; and to ignore the Oracle amounted to denying that the sun shone upon the earth. Greeley had neither forgotten nor forgiven the political support Seward once had given to Henry J. Raymond, editor and proprietor of that upstart sheet, the New York *Times*. Greeley had come to Chicago for one purpose—to bury Seward. Weed, on the other hand, believed in what money could buy and Weed had the money. To the sounds of brass bands, carefully packed galleries, hysterical delegates, a hoarse Weed and hoarser Greeley, voices in smoke-filled rooms and torchlight parades, an American tragedy began. After the third ballot another telegram thrummed over the wires to Lincoln in Springfield: "We did it glory to God."

Waiting for Mr. Seward, young Adams decided that "John Adams was better off in Philadelphia in 1776 than his great-grandson Henry in 1860 in Washington." Events swirled with cyclonic force around him. Hardly more than a month and a half had passed since, returning from Europe, he had "dropped back on Quincy like a lump of lead." He had decided on the same day to begin the study of law and to vote for Mr. Lincoln; thinking back forty years later, he realized that "although no one believed in civil war, the air reeked of it, and the Republicans organized their clubs and parades as Wide-Awakes in a form military in all things except weapons." Henry had reached home in time to see the last of these processions, "stretching in ranks of torches along the hillside," and, he decided afterward, "let them pretend what they liked, their air was not that of innocence." With the Democrats hopelessly split between the Southern faction for Breckinridge and the Northern faction for Douglas, Lincoln had won by the accident of political passion.

Now, only hours old, was the fearful news—South Carolina had seceded. The bumbling Buchanan, playing out the last feeble weeks of his sorry Administration, Henry Adams thought, gave the government "an air of social instability and incompleteness"; to state the case bluntly, "secession was likely to be easy when there was so little to secede from." Forty years later, the conviction remained:

> . . . Not one man in America wanted the Civil War or expected it or intended it. A small minority wanted secession. The vast majority wanted to go on with their occupations in peace. Not one, however clever or learned, guessed what happened. Possibly a few Southern loyalists in despair might dream it as an impossible chance; but none planned it.

Thus wrote Adams, forty years later, wise only in personal insight. At the time, for all that he was "tossed into space by an unknown energy which played with his generation as a cat plays with mice," he would not have missed a moment of it. It was great luck to be a Congressman's son and to be in Washington as his private secretary; it was great luck, too, to have Mr. Seward an old friend of the family. If the secession of South Carolina disturbed Mr. Seward, his attitude said, rather comfortingly, that time heals all wounds. So, too, did his lips, judging by his remarks the day before at the New England Dinner in New York's plush Astor House. Was there value in fraternity which is compelled, the Governor had asked, answering brightly: "All I have to say on that subject is, it was so as long ago as the time of Sir Thomas More, when he discovered it and set down the discovery in his writings. You will find it there; that while there were a very great many schoolmasters, and that while there were a very few that knew how to instruct children, there were a very great many who knew how to whip them."

At the table, among friends, said Henry Adams, the Governor "threw off restraint." The tenor of his remarks at the Astor House had been that the election of Mr. Lincoln, an "unexceptionable" candidate, had been a shock—certainly to South Carolina if not to Mr. Seward. What, under even less restraining circumstances, he may have said to the Adamses is too risky to conjecture. Washington knew by now that Mr. Seward had accepted a place in Mr. Lincoln's Cabinet as Secretary of State; knew it in some quarters with not a little apprehension, fearing that Seward would dominate the President and amount to a "Prime Minister." Seward, talking conciliation, scarcely appealed to the old masters in the radical wing of the Republican Party—not to Pennsylvania's club-footed war horse, Thaddeus Stevens, seeing in conservatism a "vile ingredient . . . worse than secession"; nor to Michigan's Zack Chandler, held together by whiskey, believing that without "a little blood-letting" the Union wouldn't "be worth a rush"; nor to Ohio's Ben Wade, who thought all along that to follow Seward's leadership would leave the party "in the wilderness longer than the children of Israel under Moses." With Seward on one side and the radical party stalwarts on the other viewing Mr. Lincoln as a Simple Susan, to be discounted before he reached the White House, well might young Henry Adams decide to accept "the wishes of Mr. Lincoln as orders" in the belief that "the new President was likely to need all the help several million young men would be able to give, if they counted on having any President at all to serve." Underestimating Mr. Lincoln that Christmas week reached almost the proportions of a national pastime. Even in Springfield, Illinois, a few indulged in the game, but those close to Mr. Lincoln had a tendency, after a time, to wonder if maybe they shouldn't re-evaluate the fellow.

2

"God Will Keep Lincoln Right"

HENRY VILLARD recalled an incident in 1858 when he had reported four of the Lincoln-Douglas debates for a German-language newspaper, the New York *Staats-Zeitung*. Mr. Lincoln—"a lean, lank, indescribably gawky figure," in Villard's eyes, with "an odd-featured, wrinkled, inexpressive, and altogether uncomely face"—had confessed that Mary Lincoln insisted he was going to be both a Senator and President of the United States. Arms locked around his knees, Lincoln burst into a roar of laughter, exclaiming to the journalist, "Just think of such a sucker as me as President."

Now two years later Villard had come to Springfield to report for readers of the New York *Herald* the activities of the President-elect. He told of "one garrulous old lady" who remembered Mr. Lincoln as a boy in Kentucky. The woman couldn't conceal her astonishment that he had been elected to the highest office in the land. "Why," she declared, "he was the gawkiest, dullest-looking boy you ever saw." Yet she admitted that he had possessed one remarkable trait: "He could always remember things better than any other boy in the neighborhood."

But what manner of man was Mr. Lincoln? America wondered. Certainly he could not be so bad as the "outrageous cartoons" of *Harper's Weekly* had made him. The Reverend Galusha

Anderson of St. Louis remembered the "grotesque and monstrous misrepresentations"—of Lincoln drunk in a barroom, of Lincoln frightened by ghosts, his shocky hair standing on end—so that it became credible for stump speakers to call him "an idiot, a buffoon, a baboon, the Illinois ape, a gorilla." But what were the intrinsic qualities of Mr. Lincoln? Senator Henry Wilson of Massachusetts sought an answer from Lincoln's law partner.

"I know him better than he does himself," Billy Herndon began his reply to Wilson. Billy supposed that the assertion "seems a little strong," but Billy looked around the office that he had shared for more than sixteen years with the President-elect. The old sofa, where Lincoln liked to rest while gazing at the ceiling, had been pushed against the wall for support; the two windows, giving a view of the back yard, needed washing, which was nothing new. In the pigeonholes of the old-fashioned secretary were filed, without much system, the firm's papers, but Mr. Lincoln kept a pile of papers on top of the desk in which he had inserted a note: "When you can't find it anywhere else, look in this." Yes, Billy Herndon knew Lincoln—knew most of his stories a hundred times over; knew him in the long, coarse, yellow-flannel shirt in which he slept at night, a ridiculous garment that reached halfway between his knees and ankles and made him the "ungodliest figure" on earth; knew him in those reflective moods when "melancholy dripped from him as he walked"; knew him as a man who rarely read a book but who could sit for hours with his long nose in the pages of a newspaper; knew him as a critic of Herndon's own ardent abolitionism: "Billy, you're too rampant and spontaneous"; knew him as the indulgent father who paid no heed while young Willie and Tad Lincoln "bent the points of all the pens, overturned ink-stands, scattered law-papers over the floor, or threw the pencils into the spittoon"; knew him as a tall, ungainly man who stopped along the street to play with a little dog or kitten; knew him by the wince in his eyes when Mary Lincoln had been scolding; knew him in court when Billy would grow so restless at his slow move-ments and speeches that in exasperation Billy would cry, "Speak with more vim and arouse the jury—talk faster and keep them awake."

Yes, Billy Herndon knew Lincoln—knew, perhaps better than anyone, how the Lincoln of the debates with Douglas, of the speech at Cooper Union, the Lincoln who was President-elect of a troubled, divided country had begun to emerge during the summer and fall of 1854. Five years had passed since Lincoln's one term in Congress—years in which Lincoln had seemed to draw back from public life. But the Kansas-Nebraska Bill extending slavery into territory where it had been prohibited since the Compromise of 1820, had stirred Lincoln, and suddenly he had taken once more to the stump, carrying his protest in speeches to farmers and storekeepers in town after town—Winchester, Carrollton, Jacksonville, Bloomington—and speaking at last to the crowd at the State Fair in Springfield on a crisp October afternoon. Billy himself had written the editorial that appeared afterward in the Springfield *Journal*: ". . . He felt upon his soul the truths burn which he uttered, and all present felt that he was true to his own soul. . . . He quivered with emotion. The whole house was as still as death. . . . Women waved their white handkerchiefs in token of woman's silent but heartfelt assent. Douglas felt the sting; the animal within him was roused because he frequently interrupted Mr. Lincoln. . . . At the conclusion of this speech every man and child felt that it was unanswerable. He took the heart captive and broke like a sun over the understanding."

The speech was as good as Billy said—as good as any speech Lincoln ever made, a part of the heart of the man revealed, as true to Lincoln in 1860 as it had been in 1854. For this was the Lincoln who hated slavery "because it deprives our republican example of its just influence in the world . . . because it forces so many really good men amongst ourselves into an open war with the very fundamental principles of civil liberty." Yet he spoke without prejudice against the Southern people: "They are what we would be in their situation. If slavery did not now exist amongst them, they would not introduce it. If it did now exist amongst us, we should not instantly give it up." It was a measured, thought-ful speech that destroyed any historical basis for the extension of slavery. It was a speech that pricked at the conscience of the South, seeing the "institution" not as between black man and white but as between one white man and another:

> . . . you have amongst you, a sneaking individual, of the class of native tyrants, known as the "slave-dealer." He watches your necessities, and crawls up to buy your slave, at a speculating price. If you cannot help it, you sell to him; but if you can help it, you drive him from your door. You despise him utterly. You do not recognize him as a friend, or even as an honest man. Your children must not play with his; they may rollick freely with the little Negroes, but not with the "slave-dealers'" children. If you are obliged to deal with him, you try to get through the job without so much as touching him. It is common with you to join hands with the men you meet; but with the slave-dealer you avoid the ceremony—instinctively shrinking from the snaky contact. If he grows rich and retires from business, you still remember him, and still keep up the ban of non-intercourse upon him and his family. Now why is this? You do not so treat the man who deals in corn, cattle or tobacco. . . .

It was a speech disputing the contention that the extension of slavery involved the principle of self-government, and with strong Midwestern undertones it was a speech that spoke for plain people: "Slave states are places for poor white people to remove *from,* not to remove *to.* New free states are the places for poor people to go to and better their condition. For this use, the nation needs these territories." It was a speech that scorned fear of the ex-tremist, abolitionist, or slaveholder: "Stand with anybody that stands *right.* . . . Stand *with* the abolitionist in restoring the Missouri Compromise; and stand *against* him when he attempts to repeal the fugitive slave law. . . . To desert such ground, be-cause of any company, is to be less than a Whig—less than a man—less than an American." Fundamentally, it was a Lincoln of Jeffer-sonian traditions and ideals, of a belief in the American past and a concept of American destiny he would never surrender, who spoke that October day in Springfield:

> Let us turn slavery from its claims of "moral right," back upon its existing legal rights, and its arguments of "necessity." Let us return it to the position our fathers gave it; and there let it rest in peace. Let us re-adopt the Declaration of Independence, and with it, the practices, and policy, which harmonize with it. Let North and South—let all Americans—let all lovers of liberty everywhere—join in the great and good work. If we do this, we shall not only have saved the Union; but we shall have saved it, as to make, and to keep it, forever worthy of saving. We shall have so saved it, that the succeeding millions of free happy people, the world over, shall rise up, and call us blessed, to the latest generations.

Yes, Billy Herndon knew Lincoln—the practical politician and prairie philosopher, and to Senator Wilson he wrote: "Lincoln is a man of heart—aye, as gentle as a woman's and as tender— but he has a will as strong as iron. He therefore loves all mankind, hates slavery and every form of despotism. Put these together— love for the slave, and a determination, a will, that justice, strong and unyielding, shall be done when he has the right to act, and you can form your own conclusions. Lincoln will fail here, namely, if a question of political economy—if any question comes up which is doubtful, questionable, which no man can demonstrate, then his friends can rule him; but when on justice, right, liberty, the Government, the Constitution, and the Union, then you may all stand aside; he will rule then, and no man can move him—no set of men can do it. There is no fail here. This is Lincoln, and you mark my prediction. You and I must keep the people right; God will keep Lincoln right."*

That same day Lincoln also composed a letter, addressing it to the Hon. A. H. Stephens and writing at the top of the page, "For

* In later years Wilson wrote Herndon: "These words of yours made a deep impression upon my mind, and I came to love and trust him even before I saw him."

your own eye alone." This Georgian had first impressed Lincoln a dozen years ago, during the President-elect's first year in Congress; after listening to Stephens denounce the Mexican War as an aggression against the Mexican people, Lincoln had written Billy Herndon: ". . . Mr. Stephens of Georgia, a little slim, pale-faced, consumptive man . . . has just concluded the very best speech, of an hour's length, I ever heard. My old, withered, dry eyes, are full of tears yet." Again Alexander H. Stephens had delivered a speech that affected Lincoln. Georgia's fire-eaters had started a cry for secession even before there had been an official count of ballots in the Presidential canvass. Spurred by Governor Joseph E. Brown, who asked the Legislature to summon a special convention and appropriate a million dollars for Georgia's defense, secession fever raced across the state. From town and city, hamlet and crossroad poured in resolutions upon the capital at Milledgeville, damning Lincoln, damning Black Republicanism. Against the swirling, thundering tide of passion Stephens dared to plunge his finger into the dike. His moods, Stephens once had admitted, probably stemmed from "some physiological derangement," and with the agony he suffered with his bowels and liver, neuralgia and migraine, that was small wonder. He had convinced himself that he was sexually impotent and had never married; yet his mind was quick, incisive, often brilliant and his nervous energy was drawn in no small part from his belief that "the secret of my life has been revenge . . . Oh what I have suffered from a look! What have I suffered from the tone of a remark . . . But each . . . such pang was the friction that brought out the latent fires."

In mid-November Stephens had addressed the Georgia Legislature. Why was there all this fuss over Mr. Lincoln? "The President of the United States," admonished Stephens, "is no Emperor, no Dictator—he is clothed with no absolute power. He can do nothing unless he is backed by Congress. The house of Representatives is largely in the majority against him." In moderate tones, Stephens counseled: "Good government can never be built up or sustained by the impulse of passion." And again: "If all our hopes are to be blasted, if the Republic is to go down, let us be found to the last moment standing on the deck, with the Constitution of the United States waving over our heads. Let the fanatics of the North break the Constitution, if such is their fell purpose." And again: "The greatest curse that can befall a free people is civil war."

He was happy to send Mr. Lincoln a revised copy of the speech in response to his "short and polite note," Stephens wrote; he was surprised that the press had given it such extensive circulation. "The Country is certainly in greal peril," Stephens added, "and no man ever had heavier or greater responsibilities resting upon him than you have in the present momentous crisis." Lincoln disputed neither the nation's peril nor "the weight of the responsibility on me"; but his heart asked what his mind could not understand: "Do the people of the South really entertain fears that a Republican administration would, *directly,* or *indirectly,* interfere with their slaves, or with them, about their slaves?" There was no cause for such fear—no more danger now than in the days of Washington. But two days before church bells had tolled in Charleston; South Carolina had seceded. "You think slavery is *right* and ought to be extended; while we think it is *wrong* and ought to be restricted. That I suppose is the rub."

Lincoln knew. He could confess to an old friend: "The political horizon looks dark and lowering." And he could cling still to the one faith of his political lifetime: "The people, under Providence, will set all right." What more could he say? What was left to explain or deny? Two years ago, in those moments when his debates with Douglas were ending, he had tried with all the simplicity of his very simple being to define "the issue that will continue in this country when these poor tongues of Judge Douglas and myself shall be silent":

> . . . It is the eternal struggle between these two principles—right and wrong—throughout the world. They are the two principles that have stood face to face from the beginning of time; and will ever continue to struggle. The one is the common right of humanity

and the other the divine right of kings. It is the same principle in whatever shape it develops itself. It is the same spirit that says, "You work and toil and earn bread, and I'll eat it." No matter in what shape it comes, whether from the mouth of a king who seeks to bestride the people of his own nation and live by the fruit of their labor, or from one race of men as an apology for enslaving another race, it is the same tyrannical principle. . . .

How could the South misunderstand him? He had never contended that the Southern people did not possess a right to a workable Fugitive Slave Law; he had consistently denied the legal right of Congress to interfere with slavery where it now existed. He simply had resisted the extension of slavery, for that corrupted the intent of the Constitution and endangered the freedom of the whole people. If the South would use its eyes to read, its mind to reason, its heart to believe, there could be no misunderstanding.

The trouble with Mr. Lincoln, Henry Villard felt compelled to inform readers of the New York *Herald,* was neither "his wrongly imputed hostility towards the South, nor the alleged aggressiveness of the party that elected him." Rather the weakness that Villard detected in the President-elect was "his good nature." Mr. Lincoln was too uniformly kind, too untiringly patient, too willingly compliant to all requests—qualities, Villard conceded, that were "good and pleasing" in private life and "an effective means of popularity in public spheres"—but could "so high-stationed a personage as the President of the United States" afford to be "the very embodiment of good temper and affability"? Villard thought not; once Mr. Lincoln occupied the White House, "His ears and eyes must learn to be closed at certain times. His lips must be trained to less ready and unqualified responses. If not, the crowd will unbalance and overwhelm him." In an earlier dispatch Villard had written: "What his executive abilities are we still must learn." In these days of America's torment, the journalist was certain on this point: "Mediocrity will no longer do." What was required now was the highest statesmanship—without illusion, capable of looking boldly and squarely in the face of all difficulties. Villard gave his readers a comforting belief: " . . . there are dormant qualities in 'Old Abe' which occasion will draw forth, develop and remind people to a certain degree of the characteristics of 'Old Hickory.' "

Yet with South Carolina already out of the Union, with Georgia and Mississippi, Florida and Louisiana summoning conventions for the same grim purpose, with no one able to say what, if anything, a frightened President Buchanan intended to do about the Federal forts and arsenals in these states, was Villard simply whistling in the dark to bolster his own courage? At rock bottom, what could be said for the untested Lincoln? He was "a strong debater," and what more? "A good dialectician," Villard thought, adding "a well informed politician and a sound lawyer." There the catalogue of Lincoln's demonstrated abilities ended for Villard, who recognized the gentleness but not the iron will that Herndon knew. More close-mouthed than Villard ever suspected, Lincoln wrote Peter H. Sylvester, an old Whig friend in upstate New York, that twenty-second of December: "If Mr. B. surrenders the forts, I think they must be retaken."

In effect, Mr. Lincoln was telling his old friend that if secession meant war, he would risk it. This was the biggest news story of a century and Villard's journalistic nose had not even sniffed it.

Meanwhile, in New York, the Oracle spoke. Let the Cotton States go, decided Horace Greeley, reasoning editorially:

"If the Declaration of Independence justified the secession of three millions of Colonists in 1776, *we do not see why it should not JUSTIFY the secession of five millions of Southerners in 1861.*"

3

The Revolt of the Ancients

CHRISTMAS week brought clear, sparkling weather to Charleston. Secession was now a fact and war a hope. The jubilant giddiness that swept the city, the exultant old men awakening in a world where the fondest dreams of their youth had come true, the red sashes and guns and swords that replaced poinsettias and mistletoe as Yuletide decorations knew no parallel anywhere in America. Neither Seward in Washington nor Greeley in New York, no Adams Christmas-shopping in Boston nor Lincoln in Springfield possessed any realistic comprehension of this phenomenon. No Lee in Virginia understood it.

South Carolina had marched out of the Union to the hoarse cries of its ancients, who, carrying the recent elections, bragged that they were insensible to fear. "There never was such a resurrection of the dead and forgotten," Mary Boykin Chesnut wrote in her diary, aghast at the truth. Yet remembering "the time of the nullification row" when her father had been governor, Mrs. Chesnut knew why the old men had carried the day: "South Carolina had been rampant for years . . . the torment of herself and everybody else. Nobody could live in this state unless he were a fire-eater. . . . South Carolinians had exasperated and heated themselves into a fever that only blood-letting could ever cure. It was the inevitable remedy. So I was a seceder."

A seceder, yes—even a "ready and willing" one—but Mrs. Ches-

38

nut could not keep from herself a feeling of "nervous dread and horror" at this break "with so great a power as the United States." She had been visiting in Florida when she learned the news of Lincoln's election. A fellow traveler declared: "That settles the hash!" And in more ways than one, Mrs. Chesnut might have added, since almost immediately her husband had resigned his seat in the United States Senate. If she had stayed in Washington, she might not have been able to prevent his action, but she certainly would have tried. It was too late afterward for anything but journeying back to South Carolina to join him. One after another, "some old fossil who was ages ago laid on the shelf," was forgetting the birthday of the Prince of Peace and winking boldly at the God of War. Call it insanity, but in South Carolina it was rational.

A new kind of Greek civilization based on black slavery and flowering here among the magnolias—the dream was as old as living memory; as old as the Convention which, repealing the Ordinance of Nullification of 1833, adopted a resolution that declared the *allegiance* of a citizen of South Carolina belonged exclusively to his state, and only *obedience* was due the Union. The knife thrust of the tariff issue had twinged for decades in the Southern back. Whither had the accumulated savings of a century in South Carolina gone except into slaves and a slave system that cared for its own? Why must that economy be weakened and endangered to pay tribute to a central government for "internal improvements" that South Carolina neither wanted nor felt were anyone's business except that of each state? Herein resided the beginning of the struggle between the agrarian South and the industrial North, between States Rights and the Union. In the Free States, with their factories and vast territory to attract the immigrant, the white population increased by bounds; but in the Slave States, the Negroes multiplied more rapidly than the whites. Unless slavery could be extended into the territories, what promise did the future hold for the Southern civilization?

The dream was born of that phrase—the Southern civilization.

It was distinct; it was better. Travelers went North, observed the textile mills in places like Lowell, Massachusetts, and returned shouting that the feudalistic industrialism of New England was cruel beyond the wildest imagination of the Southern planter. The factory system used up its "wage slave" then threw him aside, not caring if he starved or went homeless; whereas the plantation system nurtured the young, healed the sick, protected the aged. When Mrs. Stowe came along with her *Uncle Tom's Cabin*—this "moral scavenger," poetized South Carolina's William J. Grayson, who

> Snuffs up pollution with a pious air,
> Collects a rumor here, a slander there;
> With hatred's ardor gathers Newgate's spoils,
> And trades for gold the garbage of her toils

—the instinct to counterattack produced a rash of proslavery novels with such provocative titles as J. W. Page's *Uncle Robin in His Cabin in Virginia and Tom without One in Boston*. In "this game of the pot and the kettle," as Vernon L. Parrington has observed, "the exploitative root of both systems was nakedly exposed," but only in the degree that each, believing it supported the lesser evil, lived with the better conscience. And in South Carolina, with its peculiar homogeneity full-grown in the years since the early nullification struggle, it was in completely good conscience that the Greek ideal became the happy, workable compromise, making the white, wealthy or poor, the master class.

The revolt of the ancients, which Mrs. Chesnut found sweeping reason before it in Charleston, was no mysterious triumph to one, like herself, who was "of necessity a rebel born." And it was no surprise either, in this fulfillment of an ideal that honored the patriarchs, to find the young men of Charleston exuberantly following the oldsters—willing lambs to the slaughter, if such must be the consequence. Shouting disunion and independence, for without both the dream would be dead. Gay wearing their blue cockades. Loving the drilling, marching, parading. And the girls waiting under the live oaks. Had Christmas week ever been so exciting? A day in Charleston proved as much as Mrs. Chesnut could endure; wisely, journeying on, she carried a bottle of morphine for her racking headache.

Strollers crowded the city. Planters grown wealthy from rice and cotton watched from the verandas of their three-story town mansions. Sometimes the strollers were a boy and a girl—secession might end interest in normal business pursuits, but tender sentiment remained—and often a dozen youths, arms locked, swung down the street with martial sprightliness. They wore their French military caps jauntily, and their long gray overcoats were trimmed at cuffs and collar with red worsted. The drilling Home Guardsmen frequently were elderly men, and to one visitor they seemed to fall into a type with "bald crown, sandy side-locks, reddish whiskers, sanguineous cheeks, and blue eyes . . . luminous with confidence." Resolutely the old fellows practiced the simpler military evolutions, grim in their resolve to keep "a strong hand over the Negroes," who in turn leaned against trees and fences, listlessly observing these stern maneuvers.

A favorite meeting place was the Battery, always a delightful discovery for the stranger in Charleston, with its plots of clover that seemed a wonder in this "grassless land." Neatly fenced promenades, covered with broken shells, led beneath palmettos and old oaks waving streamers of Spanish moss. A handsome bronze lantern, standing twenty-five feet high, served as a beacon; and the long and solid stone quay was the finest sea walk along the Atlantic coast. Beyond, the Ashley and Cooper rivers joined to give Charleston its excellent harbor before flowing on, the natives joked, to form the Atlantic Ocean. In the harbor, looking seaward, to the left rose the fortress Castle Pinckney, defender of the city, and to the right the massive, commanding red-brick walls of Fort Sumter, defender of the sea lanes. Distantly between the two on clear days the Charlestonian glimpsed with surging pride the yellowish walls of old Fort Moultrie, where during the Revolution South Carolinians had fought behind ramparts of palmetto logs and turned back a British fleet that had come to capture the port. Old

Moultrie, enshrined in sacred memories—that Federal troops should occupy these honored ramparts, now that South Carolina had declared herself, was an outrage, sir. A damned outrage.

Captain Abner Doubleday's opinion of Moultrie was based on military principles rather than sentiment. Arriving with his wife during the summer when the baked-in heat of Charleston had turned day and night into the same limp, dampish experience, Captain Doubleday had assumed his duties at the fort as second in command to Colonel John L. Gardner. Doubleday found Moultrie a discouraging outpost. The walls of the old place were so weak and full of cracks that soldiers used the crevices to climb to the top. Sea breezes heaped sand hills upon the shore front and so dominated the parapet that only one word described Moultrie. The fort was "untenable." And to Doubleday the Federal force stationed here approached the ridiculous—sixty-one enlisted men, seven officers (whose Southern feelings were obvious), thirteen musicians in the regimental band.

Doubleday soon considered himself the black sheep of the garrison since he alone favored the election of Mr. Lincoln, and presently he heard rumors from within the city that if Doubleday was that sort of confounded abolitionist, it would be a pleasure to hang him. No doubt, Doubleday thought. And not in effigy. From July on, all Charleston appeared to turn giddy-headed from toasts drunk in derision of the national flag flying over Moultrie. On October fifth Governor William H. Gist sent a letter by secret agent to the chief executives of other Cotton States. "The great probability, nay almost certainty" of Mr. Lincoln's election, Gist contended, called for "concert of action." If no other state would take the lead in secession, Gist declared, then

> . . . South Carolina will secede (in my opinion) alone, if she has any assurance that she will be soon followed by another or other States; otherwise it is doubtful. If you decide to call a convention upon the election of a majority of electors favorable to Lincoln, I desire to know the day you propose for the meeting,

that we may call our convention to meet the same day, if possible. If your State will propose any other remedy, please inform me what it will probably be, and any other information you will be pleased to give me.

Five governors responded before October ended—documents, perhaps, that reveal why the successful conspirator should beware of the written word since it so often spoils the perfect crime. "Our people are very far from being agreed as to what action the State should take," admitted North Carolina's chief executive, but he added: "I could not in any event assent to, or give my aid to, a political enforcement of the monstrous doctrine of coercion." Whereas Alabama would not secede alone, her governor believed that "if two or more States will cooperate with her, she will secede with them; or if South Carolina or any other Southern State should go out alone and the Federal Government should attempt to use force against her, Alabama will immediately rally to her rescue." Louisiana's governor would not advise secession nor did he believe the people of his state favored it; still, he would "recommend that Louisiana meet her sister slaveholding States in council to consult as to the proper course to be pursued, and to endeavor to effect a complete harmony of action." From the moment Mississippi knew that "the Black Republicans have carried the election," her governor replied, she would counsel with the other states and secede, if such became the common will; and Georgia's chief executive, accepting the same strategy, added that "events not yet foreseen" might lead to "action on the part of Georgia without waiting for all the Southern States, if it should be found necessary for her safety."

To accept the contention of Henry Adams that no one planned the Great Rebellion requires ignoring this correspondence. The political murder of the Union then has more the appearance of boyish manslaughter. The people of the South then seem less willfully led to the violence of executive passion. In view of this correspondence, how pathetic became the later voice of Alexander Stephens, pleading only for time so that tempers could cool and calmer judgments prevail and experience disclose whether Mr. Lincoln's proffered hand of friendship actually possessed a black and villainous palm! There was no time. Emotions were ripe. Even before Gist heard from his fellow governors, on October twelfth he called the Legislature into session for the ostensible purpose of naming Presidential electors. Three days earlier in the "October states" of Pennsylvania and Indiana voters had delivered their majorities to Mr. Lincoln; Gist, forewarned, called his session for November fifth, the day before the almost certain election of the Republican candidates.

On November seventh, when there no longer existed any doubt of Mr. Lincoln's victory, the crowds now so common on the streets of Charleston began to appear. From the upper window of the office of the Charleston *Mercury* streamed the banner of the Palmetto and the Lone Star, and people, seeing it, broke into cheers and wiped eyes misty with emotion. A stranger asked an eight-year-old boy: "What is your country?" Quickly, proudly, came the answer: "South Carolina, sir!" The *Mercury* exhorted: "The tea has been thrown overboard—the revolution of 1860 has been initiated"—perhaps forgetting that the Boston of the tea party was also the Boston of Garrison and *The Liberator*. On the tenth of November the Legislature called for the convention in December that everyone knew would sanction secession; Charleston celebrated with fireworks, parades, a mass meeting at Institute Hall, and on the twenty-first of November devoted itself to prayers that God would find it in His heart to don a long gray overcoat and march to whatever battles must come. Yet underneath there was the gnawing fear among many that the other Southern states might prove unwilling to follow South Carolina out of the Union. As one speaker told Charlestonians, three thousand million dollars worth of property rights were involved in this game—this was no child's play. If Virginia, Alabama, Georgia, North Carolina, Mississippi failed South Carolina, what then? By God, sir, shouted the fire-eaters, the cause wasn't lost. There was always France. South Carolina could become a French protectorate.

Like a foghorn droning over Charleston rose the voice of Robert Barnwell Rhett—stormy editor of the Charleston *Mercury,* six terms a Congressman and one a United States Senator, lawyer and churchman and father of twelve, advocate of restoring the African slave trade, foe of any Union sympathizer and friend of any foe of the Union. Today there is no statue of Rhett in Charleston; then, he was the spirit of this city-state—Rhett proclaiming boldly: "The secession of South Carolina is not the event of a day. It is not anything produced by Mr. Lincoln's election, or by the non-execution of the Fugitive Slave Law. It has been a matter which has been gathering head for thirty years"; Rhett, heckled by a voice in the crowd declaring that the ordinary people didn't know what was happening, snapping back: "But who ever waited for the common people when a great movement was to be made?"; Rhett, learning that the father of Lincoln's running mate had named four of his sons Europe, Asia, Africa, and America, and drawing the biting conclusion about the origins of any family that would name a child Africa: "Hamlin was a mulatto." Could any decent South Carolinian tolerate a Negro Vice-President?

All notes blended into the tune of this Pied Piper, leading his children to calamity. Occasionally Rhett was fooled, and the most violent spokesman for disunion on the *Mercury* staff was planted there by Greeley to send Charleston news to the *Tribune,* for the Oracle was a man of many ruses. Yet Rhett was on firm ground with old Edmund Ruffin, who came down from Richmond to help spread the gospel of secession. A brilliant agriculturist whose discovery of marl as a fertilizer had made millions for Southern farmers, Ruffin had forgotten his venerable years and marched with a cadet corps from V.M.I. to witness the hanging of John Brown. Afterward he had forgotten his conscience as well, handing out pikes that he declared had been captured with Brown at Harper's Ferry and spreading the spurious story that the pikes had been intended for arming revolting slaves. Ardent organizer of disunion lodges, believer in the inherent inferiority of the black race, Ruffin possessed the kind of mind to which the extremist

George Fitzhugh appealed so strongly when in *Sociology for the South* he ridiculed the Declaration of Independence and the doctrine that all men were created equal: "Some were born with saddles on their backs, and others booted and spurred to ride them, —and the riding does them good." With the rising fervor for secession and war, business in Charleston threatened to grind to a standstill; large property owners, fearing that the brunt of the expense for military preparations must fall on them, grumbled crossly; but Rhett and Ruffin were equal to every emergency. The merchant who suffered now would be richly repaid when Charleston, becoming a free port, outstripped New York in trade and wealth. And what would be the result of reopening the African slave trade? Negroes at thirty dollars a head, sir. Even a poor laboring man, at those prices, could become a rich slaveowner and cotton planter!

Cooped inside Moultrie, Captain Doubleday came to suspect everyone. Buchanan's Secretary of War, John B. Floyd, he considered an outright traitor, or why would he send seventeen thousand muskets to South Carolina when he knew Charleston had become "a hot-bed of sedition"?* The kindest description Doubleday could give of his superior was the observation that Colonel Gardner, strongly pro-Southern in sympathy, was "ill fitted to weather the storm that was about to burst upon us." One afternoon a small party from the fort rowed across to the United States Arsenal on the banks of the Ashley River to secure forty muskets and a supply of cartridges. Word of the maneuver reached the city's Vigilance Committee and "an excited mob" turned back the soldiers. It did not surprise Doubleday that Gardner abandoned further efforts to obtain weapons or ammunition from the Arsenal; nor was he surprised when Gardner proposed "removing the garrison to Smithville, North Carolina, having received permission to do so, in case the yellow fever, which had proved so disastrous the previous year, should break out again."

Early in November one hundred and fifty masons arrived from

* The story was false.

Baltimore to strengthen the forts in the harbor; Doubleday conceded that they were good workmen but "regretted that they were not also good Unionists." Early November likewise brought to Moultrie "crowds of excited countrymen, wearing secession cockades" who "formed in procession and marched around" but "did not offer any violence." Doubleday, clearly on edge, cast a jaundiced eye on Major Robert Anderson, arriving on the twenty-first of November to take command of Moultrie. Courteous, honest, intelligent, thoroughly versed in his profession—in such terms, Doubleday admitted that Anderson was a gentleman and a gallant soldier who had been brevetted for services in the wars against the Seminole Indians and the Mexicans—yet a reservation remained: "In politics he was a strong pro-slavery man." The seed of doubt lingered in Doubleday's mind.

With December, the signs of ill-boding multiplied for the defenders of Moultrie. Hostile cannon now had been planted to guard the channel and oppose the approach of any vessel bringing reinforcements to the fort. "Lines of countervallation," Doubleday added, "had been quietly marked out at night, with a view to attack the fort by regular approaches in case the first assault failed." Meanwhile "two thousand of the best riflemen in the State" occupied adjoining sand hills and rooftops, "the intention being to shoot us down the moment we attempted to man our guns." On the eleventh the secessionists were reported building batteries at near-by Mount Pleasant and on the upper end of Sullivan's Island, and, Doubleday learned, "ladders had been provided for parties to escalade us." Two "enemy" steamers patrolled the harbor, discovering that the low and once visibly yellow walls of Moultrie now were almost hidden by a glacis thrown around them.

Inside the city grew a new conviction, nourished on the unshakable belief that all Republicans were abolitionists—March fourth, Lincoln's inaugural day, had been set as a signal for a slave insurrection. Military preparations quickened under this dreadful fear, and Charleston, neglected to the point where not one-third the usual shipping was seen in its harbor or one-fourth the accustomed cotton on its wharves, took on a dirty and shabby look, its brick-work and stucco wanting repair, its houses needing paint. Yet there was still a plentiful food supply, and Northern papers that declared beef had soared to thirty-five cents a pound exaggerated the facts—good beef could be bought by the pound for ten or fif-teen cents. Under the walls of the Arsenal were half a dozen cannon—perhaps twenty-four-pounders—and the few Negroes who passed an idle day hanging over the fences and staring at the horsemen within were in turn observed by a few whites, pond-ering the rumors of the March fourth uprising. There were guns along the Battery, too, an eighteen- and twenty-four-pounder, one or two that seemed like a thirty-six; neither passing police nor idlers appeared to understand much about them, or just why they were there.

Under the growing discomfiture of what his ears could hear and his eyes could see, Doubleday noted on December eleventh the arrival at Moultrie of Major Don Carlos Buell, sent by the War Department in Washington "to examine and report on our con-dition." Doubleday, touchy toward everyone, did not spare Buell: ". . . he did not appear to sympathize much with us, for he ex-pressed his disapproval of our defensive preparations; referring particularly to some loop-holes near the guardhouse, which he said would have a tendency to irritate the people." Doubleday thought the remark "strange"; after all, " 'the people' were pre-paring to attack us."

But Doubleday misjudged Buell. Two weeks hence events would prove that, in writing, Buell had provided Anderson with broad discretionary power. Recognizing that the "smallness" of Anderson's force would not permit him to occupy more than one of the forts in Charleston Harbor, Buell instructed the com-mander to regard "an attempt to take any one of them" as "an act of hostility," whereupon Anderson was authorized to put his force "into either of them which you may deem most proper to increase its power of resistance." In later years of the war Don Carlos Buell might not always seem the man for the moment; but now, as Assistant Adjutant General, doubtless aware that possible treason riddled the office of the Secretary of War, Major Buell added a sentence that was manly, direct, and sweeping in the confidence it placed in Anderson: "You are also authorized to take similar steps whenever you have tangible evidence of a design to proceed to a hostile act."

Buell needed only to use his eyes and ears to know that the "tangible evidence" existed. A tight-lipped Welshman from Ohio, like Anderson a graduate of West Point and a veteran of the wars against the Seminoles and Mexicans, Buell didn't allow politics to warp either his honor or judgment as a soldier. In Charleston St. Michael and the Dragon were lying down in an uneasy peace. The defenses at Moultrie had been partially improved by filling up the crevices, digging to the foundations of the walls, and throwing up the surplus earth as a glacis so that these barricades now rose to a height of sixteen feet. A sloping picket fence, erected as an obstacle against an escalading party, was worth little more than the sarcastic comment of one Charleston editor: "Make ready your sharpened stakes, but you will not intimidate freemen."

Again needing no more than to use his eyes, Buell could understand the advantage of Sumter over Moultrie. Situated on an artificial island of large blocks of stone at the edge of the channel, Sumter dominated the narrowest part of the harbor. A mile distant from Moultrie, the gloomy, prisonlike brick walls of Sumter were designed for three tiers of guns. At the moment workmen labored in Sumter at the direction of the Secretary of War mounting guns and, Doubleday believed, the moment this work was finished, "the rebels would seize the fort, and turn its powerful armament upon us." What Buell may have said to Anderson about Floyd's motives remained a secret between them; so, presumably, as far as Floyd was concerned, did Buell's written orders that left Anderson free to move where—and when—he liked.

Charlestonians generally enjoyed their Christmas dinners, although there were a few whom Rhett's *Mercury* ridiculed as "the young and thoughtless" who wanted to gain their independence and forts by argument but whose ardor was quickly dissipated by any thought of bloodshed. Rhett's most uncomfortable moment had come when he confronted stubborn Judge James L. Petigru, a lifelong friend and one of the best lawyers in Charleston.

"Are you with us?" Rhett asked.

"I should think not!" blazed back Petigru. "South Carolina is too small for a republic and too large for an insane asylum." Pointing to the Baptist Church, where the secessionists had convened, Petigru said: "It looks like a church, but . . . go right there and you will find one hundred and sixty-four maniacs within."

But Petigru, daring to speak out, was almost a lone exception. Closer to the spirit of Charleston was Judge A. G. Magrath, tearing off his robes of office "in rage and disgust" when informed of Lincoln's election, an act so dear to Charlestonian hearts that a painter had been commissioned to preserve the Judge in this glorious moment. To Mrs. Chesnut the result seemed "the frightfullest signpost-style of painting" but the likeness now hung on numerous streets and "in vivid colors" captured "a countenance flaming with contending emotions—rage, disgust and disdain."

For years William Gillmore Simms, the one fine novelist South Carolina had produced, had been treated with chilly disdain as a plebeian who might better learn his place in the hierarchy of Charleston gentry, but the December issue of *De Bow's Review* devoted a long article to Simms, not certain whether his "genius, character or literary labors" deserved the greatest admiration and deciding that "his harp sheds a various, soothing and inspiring melody." Coupled with the impulse to glorify every spokesman of secession was a deep conviction that the North had no backbone for war. Even that bloodiest of abolitionists, Horace Greeley, had thrown in the sponge, telling his *Tribune* readers to let the South go and call the deed good riddance—"unexpected views," Doubleday insisted, that "strengthened the hands of the Disunionists" and influenced "the fearful and wavering" to join "the clamorous majority."

Inside Moultrie, Major Anderson ate his Christmas dinner in quiet contemplation. So many army men grew beards and hid their youthfulness; Anderson, a clean-shaven man, was now fifty-five. Born near Louisville, Kentucky, he supposed that he had come by his proslavery attitudes naturally; environment shaped a man's mind. But the army—a belief in the Union—that too was environment. Soldiering, faith in the old flag, were really the only life he knew; and in a way, through his translation from the French of *Instruction of Field Artillery, Horse and Foot,* and *Evolutions of Field Batteries,* he had made some impression upon the army by which he would be remembered. Perhaps his older brother, Larz, choosing Harvard instead of West Point and going into business, had made the wiser decision; today Larz was called a "capitalist." Well, Larz could think one way and he another. He was a soldier facing a soldier's problems that required a soldier's solutions. At least he knew what he would do. Quietly. Unexpectedly.

That Christmas Day Captain Abner Doubleday began to sense the change. Walking along the parapet with Anderson, Doubleday heard the major ask, "Captain, what is the best course to take to render gun-carriages unserviceable?" Many methods would work, Doubleday answered, but one seemed best: "Heap pine-knots around them, and burn them up." Anderson said no more, but Doubleday knew then: "The question was too suggestive to escape my attention."

4

Cranks and Prophets

WASHINGTON, Springfield, Charleston . . . each a thread being woven into a tapestry of tragedy during this week when the lips and hearts of men, women, and children sang anew of peace on earth, good will toward men. Across the nation kitchens smelled of gingerbread, plum puddings, fruitcakes, and molasses cookies; in butcher shops chickens and turkeys hung on hooks in the windows; children dreamed at night of dolls and hunting guns, popguns and stockings by the chimney; and yet, beneath the festive spirit, there spread across the land a whisper, disturbing, filled with evil meaning, difficult to identify, but *there*.

In Cleveland, Ohio, a correspondent who signed himself as "G. A., a Wide Awake," wrote to Mr. Lincoln, urging the President-elect to believe that "no Spiritualist" penned this letter. G. A. lived in the same dwelling with a young girl who was "a Sonambulist, a Clairvoyant (not a Spiritualist), in a very highly developed State." Arriving home the previous evening, G. A. had found the girl "in a trance." Voices warned her "that a conspiracy existed, to murder your Excellency," and, G. A. cautioned, it had been "resolved to employ poison, to effect your death, and if no other opportunity presented itself, to bribe your domestices, to consummate the deed" at the time of Mr. Lincoln's arrival in Washington. G. A. spoke for his friend in the trance: "She counsels complete secrecy and circumspection, and begs your Excellency, that You should on feeling the slightest indisposition, drink hot milk in Large quantities—in order to frustrate the diabolical plot."

Such letters, reaching Springfield, sometimes were shown Mr. Lincoln. From Fillmore, Louisiana, Pete Muggins wrote the President-elect: "God damn your god damned old Hellfired god damned soul to hell" and some twenty "god damns" or "god damnations" later, plus one "double damn" managed to convey his contempt for Mr. Lincoln. A "young creole" warned: "You will be shot on the 4th of March 1861 by a Louisiana Creole we are decided and our aim is sure"; from Washington "Vindex" declared that "a sworn Band of 10" had "resolved to shoot you from the south side of the Avenue in the inaugural procession—on the 4th March 1861"; three correspondents, Joseph Bradley, Joseph Roints, and Mike O'Brien, not identifying their city, boasted that "there is a club of 100 young men in this place who have sworn to murder you"; and in New Albany, Indiana, J. D. Cromwell directed Mr. Lincoln to "Read immediately, Sixth Chapter, Second Volume, Macaulay's History of England, character of King James." The estimable "Hinchaway Beeswax" and "Eagle-eyed Carbuncle" pursued another tack:

> Deformed Sir, The Ugly Club, in full meeting, have elected you an Honorary Member of the Hard-Favored Fraternity.—Prince Harry was lean, Falstaff was fat, Thersites was hunchbacked, and Slawkenbergius was renowned for the eminent miscalculation which Nature had made in the length of his nose; but it remained for you to unite all species of deformity, and stand forth the Prince of Ugly Fellows. In the bonds of Ugliness—Hinchaway Beeswax, President. Eagle-eyed Carbuncle, Secretary of the Ugly Club.

The wild curses, the cruel buffoonery, the threats born of hatred . . . a few wrote, many muttered. The subconscious mind of America was clearly, acutely disturbed; and plain people, trying to understand, wondering what had happened and what it would mean to them and the country, expressed themselves as cranks, as self-anointed prophets, as bewildered fathers and mothers and husbands and wives, as patriots and traitors. The full range of a nation's emotions was in the mail that came to Springfield. G. A., the Cleveland Wide-Awake, and Hinchaway Beeswax each struck out, in his own way, against an unknown torment.

There was something there, in the dark. It haunted them. Hennibeek Hives in Somerset County, Maine, told Mr. Lincoln: "May God preserve and keep you, to save a wicked nation, from its many sins!" The West Wisconsin Conference of the Methodist Episcopal Church, electing Mr. Lincoln a life member of its missionary society, moved the Reverend Peter S. Mather to proclaim: "We are indeed the true children of *Abraham*." George P. Bissell of Hartford, Connecticut, advising Mr. Lincoln when he left for Washington, "If you say the word, I will be there with from twenty to one thousand men, or one hundred, (any reasonable number) *organized & armed*," was echoing the thoughts of Colonel David Hunter, writing from his army post at Fort Leavenworth, Kansas: "Would it not be well, to have a hundred thousand Wide Awakes, wend their way quietly to Washington, during the first three days of March: taking with them their capes and caps? By a *coup-de-main* we could arm them in Washington."

Lincoln, emptying his mail pouch, could see the pulse of a troubled nation throbbing before his eyes. A Rhett in Charleston, a Greeley in New York, a Seward in Washington, a G. A. and his girl friend in her Cleveland trance, the alliterative Hennibeek Hives of Somerset County, Maine, each told him something. So, too, did the goddamning Pete Muggins and the bloodthirsty "young creole." If Buchanan gave up the Federal forts to the secessionists, Lincoln would retake them. Against the flood of emotions swirling upon him, doubted and damned and threatened and compromised, he had made the historic decision. Meanwhile he worked and prayed to save the imperiled peace.

5

The Oracle and the Copperheads

HORACE GREELEY wouldn't back down. On the twenty-second of December, seated in his drafty office in the Tribune Building at the corner of Nassau and Spruce, the Oracle stared at windows so begrimed that unless he raised them he couldn't see the clock on City Hall. "I have yours of the 19th," Greeley wrote Lincoln. "Let me try to make my views a little more clear."*

Since South Carolina's ordinance of secession many readers of the *Tribune,* like Mr. Lincoln, must have wished that Mr. Greeley would make his views "a little more clear." One day the Oracle declared, editorially, that the nation was not "seriously disturbed" by South Carolina's rebellion; and the next James Shepherd Pike, the *Tribune's* Washington correspondent, opined that "the National government may have to *show* its teeth, but it is not at all likely that it will have to *use* them." Let the South go, advised Mr. Greeley; but within a week when Ohio's Senator "Bluff Ben" Wade, growing more profane by the minute, shouted that there should be no compromise with the South, Mr. Greeley applauded this "calm, luminous and authoritative statement of the Republican party." Apparently the Oracle was more impressed by Wade than Lincoln as the party's spokesman; to the extent

* No letter from Lincoln to Greeley under this date appears in *The Collected Writings of Abraham Lincoln.*

that he had been for Lincoln by being against Seward, he expected the President-elect to heed his wishes and his counsel. Greeley always had an ace up his sleeve, or a joker. Where else, except in the *Tribune*, could one learn that a straw vote among the inmates of Auburn State Prison had given 682 ballots to Douglas, 200 to Breckinridge, 0 to Lincoln?

"Able but queer," said a contemporary, not too far wrong in capturing the essential character of Greeley. Scotch-Irish, the son of a poor farmer who had fled New Hampshire to escape imprisonment for his debts, Greeley had learned early to take hard knocks cheerfully. He was precocious and bookish almost from the cradle, learning to read at the age of three before he could talk plainly. In his teens he was apprentice printer and virtual editor of the East Poultney, Vermont, *Northern Spectator,* exhibiting even then a passionate interest in politics. He reached New York City in 1831, at twenty a gawky, seedy, eccentric fellow with his clothes in a bundle on a stick and ten dollars in his pocket. His employment as a printer on the *Evening Post* ended when the proprietors decided that they wished "at least *decent looking* men at the cases." But Greeley at heart was an editor and soon was publishing *The New Yorker* on a shoestring and making it the best literary weekly to be found in America. James Gordon Bennett offered him a partnership in the *Herald,* but Greeley refused, wanting to run things more his own way. Two adventures in political journalism with *The Jeffersonian* and *The Log Cabin* showed the gift of the man; twenty thousand copies of the first issue of *The Log Cabin* were printed and Greeley's backers cried that he was crazy. Where were there that many Whigs who cared to pay to read about Harrison? Greeley's answer was to go back on press; forty-eight thousand copies of his first issue were sold and by the time the campaign ended his circulation grew to between eighty and ninety thousand.

"You don't humbug enough," an early partner complained of Greeley; it was a fault he learned how to correct. His *Tribune,* a penny paper, began in 1841 with a circulation at the end of the first four weeks of six thousand; then the *Sun* tried to use strong-arm methods to keep Greeley's paper off the streets and within the next four weeks public sympathy helped to double his circulation. Why Greeley should obtain the solid success that he did in New York defied explanation—the city stood for free trade and Greeley was a lifelong screaming protectionist; the city was extremely orthodox in its religious outlook and Greeley championed Universalism; the city carried on a large trade with the South and Greeley was an abolitionist thoroughly despised in the South; the city clung to conservatism and Greeley, convinced that his was an age destined to experience a great social revolution, embraced such radical fads as Fourierism and, with tongue in cheek, spiritual rappings. Vegetarianism led him to the girl who became his wife, and since she was as nervous and as full of isms as he, they made a good pair. Greeley never let anyone question that he was a man of strong opinions. The tariff, jobs for women, Irish repeal were causes he embraced; suffrage for women, theaters, easy divorce, drink were all targets of vigorous Greeley campaigns. This was the man, a fuzz of white hair encircling his balding crown, spectacles sliding down on his nose so that he looked like the Oracle, who now proposed to teach the political facts of life to Mr. Lincoln.

All right, the Oracle conceded—no single state had a right to secede "any more than a stave may secede from a cask." But what if seven or eight states should come to Washington, saying they were tired of the Union and wished to withdraw? Greeley knew how he'd respond: "I should say, 'There's the door—go!' and I think they would have a *right* to go, even though no one recognized it." On the other hand, if one or more of the seceding states should "go to fighting and defying the laws—the Union yet being undissolved, save by their own say so—I guess they will have to be made to behave themselves." It was a grudging admission; "I am sorry for this," Greeley added. The threat of secession was what put the Free States at a disadvantage; and plainly in a bad mood, Greeley warned:

The Cotton States *are going*. Nothing that we can offer will stop them. The Union-loving men are cowed and speechless; a Reign of Terror prevails from Cape Fear to the Rio Grande. . . . You will be President over no foot of the Cotton States not commanded by Federal Arms. Even your life is not safe, and it is your simple duty to be very careful of exposing it. I doubt whether you ought to go to Washington via Wheeling and the B. & O. Railroad unless you go with a very strong force. . . .

"I fear nothing, care for nothing," Greeley exhorted, "but another disgraceful backdown of the Free States." A little less than cavalier, he asserted: "Let the Union slide—it may be reconstructed; let Presidents be assassinated—we can elect more; let the Republicans be defeated and crushed—we shall rise again." Since many people entertained "a violent prejudice" against his handwriting, Greeley had indulged Mr. Lincoln by having his letter copied "to save you trouble in deciffering it."

Within four days, writing to Billy Herndon, Greeley changed his tune. The South would be pacified, the Oracle informed Billy, only when "we are in position to *use* daggers as well as *speak* them." Nor was Greeley's seeming inconsistency mysterious, if one troubled to probe for motives. Conciliation had begun to make strange bedfellows. Seward's chief political bedfellow, Thurlow Weed, wrote in the Albany *Argus*, that the "rights" of the South had been "invaded," its "feelings . . . insulted," its "interests and honor assailed," and said for the secessionists: "We think that all the instincts of manhood rightfully impelled them to resort to a separation from the Union." Closer to home, the New York *Herald* moved into Greeley's camp, insisting that "coercion, if it were possible, is out of the question." Then Greeley's arch enemy, William H. Seward, arrived in New York to address the New England Dinner at the Astor House. Seward oozed soft phrases: "Brethren even in the same family must differ . . . I believe that secession was stronger on the night of the 6th day of November, when a President and Vice-President who were unexceptionable were elected, than it is now. That is now some fifty days since. I

believe that every day that has set since that time has set upon
mollified passions and prejudices; and if you will only give it
time, sixty more suns will give you a much better and more cheerful atmosphere." Greeley, maintaining his own pipe lines into the
heartland of Secessia, knew that Seward was talking through his
hat—to Greeley, nothing new. Later events certainly influenced
in part Greeley's complete about-face; but after Seward's "sixty
more suns" had set, the *Tribune* appeared each morning with its
masthead blazing:

> NO COMPROMISE!
> NO CONCESSIONS TO TRAITORS!
> THE CONSTITUTION AS IT IS

The phenomenon of war—of this "people's contest," as Mr.
Lincoln would call it—was a strange, involved affair. New York
City, giving Lincoln some thirty-five thousand votes or one-third
of its Presidential canvass, approached the issue of Union or Disunion with tormented indecision. Although in 1860 the city map
extended to One Hundred Thirty-seventh Street, there were only
scattered farms north of Fifty-seventh Street; Croton Reservoir
stood on Forty-second Street, and from its high walls New Yorkers
saw shipping in both rivers and the green, pleasant country that
now has become Harlem, Yorkville, and Manhattanville; the fine
homes were along lower Fifth—Stuyvesant Square, Madison
Square, and Gramercy Park—and not many steps beyond were
slums, poverty, and vice. Where Pearl, Worth, Baxter, and Water
Streets intersected sprawled the notorious Five Points section; and
between Second Avenue and the East River and Tenth Street and
Fourteenth Street was Mackerelville, so named since in those
days a "mackerel" was a procurer. A two-hour stroll revealed the
human mixture that made up the city—the wealthy riding in their
carriages, the laboring men homeward bound with their kettles of
beer, the pimps and whores who were more a dim glitter than a
bright sparkle along the sidewalks of Mackerelville, the brass-
knuckled toughs at Five Points. When Mr. Greeley left his

quarters in Printing House Square he could approach quickly City Hall surrounded by its splendid eleven-acre park; a block north stood the elegance of the Astor House, where Seward had spoken; and nearby were the theaters, Barnum's Museum, the fine eating places, the great, bustling stores.

New York, America's gateway to the world, stood for many moods, many ambitions, many dispositions, many tensions, and Mr. Greeley could not represent them all. New York was the city of the Dutch farm boy turned steamboat czar, Commodore Cornelius Vanderbilt; of very rich William B. Astor, earning one million dollars a year from real estate and tenements; of the merchandising genius, A. T. Stewart, growling that "the refusal at Washington to concede costs us millions daily"; of Barnum and Tom Thumb, Henry Ward Beecher and Walt Whitman, Tom Hyer and Dan Sickles and the other Tammany stalwarts. And it was also the city of those remarkable, unsavory brothers, Ben and Fernando Wood.

Of Fernando, mayor of the city, Greeley commented, not without cause, that he "evidently wants to be a traitor; it is lack of courage only that makes him content with being a blackguard." Fernando had made a quarter of a million from politics, by conservative estimates—made it by selling two supreme-court judgeships at five thousand dollars apiece, made it by ignoring a bid lower by eighty-four thousand dollars to award the "right" party a street-cleaning contract, as examples. In Five Points, in Mackerelville, the Wood brothers were well known—they owned the lotteries and licensed the gamblers who pinched the pennies from the whores and pimps, the saloon keepers, the luckless but hopeful who frequented these districts. Insofar as these enterprises operated on charters from Southern states, it perhaps surprised no one that Ben's newspaper, the New York *Daily News,* became almost as secessionist as the Charleston *Mercury.*

Occasionally the mayor and his brother dropped in at the Astor House for a drink and a chat. The sight of Fernando with his ear tilted to Ben's lips should have been a chilling experience, under normal circumstances; that Christmas week circumstances were hardly normal. Shrewdly, Ben and Fernando calculated what war should mean. The country would fall apart. California? With her sister states, the Wood brothers believed, California doubtless would "set up as an independent Republic and husband their own rich mineral resources." And the Western states, "equally rich in cereals and other agricultural products"? To the Wood brothers, wish becoming mistress to reality, the complete "dissolution" of the Union had become "inevitable." God knows, they hoped so. To carry New York City out of the Union, making it a free city and disrupting "the bands which bind her to a venal and corrupt master" (meaning the State Legislature with its plundering "speculators, lobby agents, and Abolition politicians") —ah, what a dream, what a chance!

Time obviously was of the essence and Fernando must make his move to carry New York City out of the Union at the first January meeting of the Common Council. The "recommendation" itself must be a telling document—one, in other words, that employed Ben's literary talents. Neither Ben nor Fernando hesitated to present his own view of the Constitutional question involved in secession: "Being a Government created by *opinion,* its continuation is dependent upon the continuance of the sentiment which created it." The grudge that the Wood brothers held against the State Legislature was revealed in the complaint that "even the common right of taxing ourselves . . . has been yielded," and, considering what such a right could mean in the game of politics as Fernando and Ben played it, need more be added? To the carriage trade in Stuyvesant Square, Madison Square, and Gramercy Park the appeal in New York as a free city could be stated succinctly: "Thus we could live free from taxes, and have cheap goods nearly duty free." Only free love in Mackerelville was omitted.

Yet Greeley was right; Fernando (and Ben as well) lacked the courage to be anything better than a blackguard. Each wanted freedom—but without violence. "The redress can be found only in appeals to the magnanimity of the people of the whole State" was how Fernando finally put it, himself hardly an example of magnanimity on any level. And the Wood brothers had read the national signs badly. California had no intention of forsaking the Union; true, the Cincinnati *Gazette* would report that agents from the Gulf States were trying to organize a Confederacy of Northern and Southwestern states, "to cut off New York, Pennsylvania, New Jersey, and all the New England States, which are so wedded to a protective tariff,"* but this was no more than an early example of a Copperhead movement that hissed louder than the malignancy of its bite warranted. Of all such activities, now and later, Fernando and Ben were well informed; three years hence they would have their violence in the bloody Draft Riots when, for the sake of sweet freedom, a band of white men used pistol butts to beat a seven-year-old Negro boy to death, among other niceties spawned by such affairs; but as yet the Wood brothers were just sensing the dislocations that threatened their political power and gambling enterprises. With their heads bent together that Christmas week, the bold, grandiose gesture—double or nothing, on one roll of the political dice—was their best instinct. Within a year Fernando would be out of the mayor's office but elected to Congress; Ben, through the *Daily News,* would be skating the thin ice of sedition.

It was sometimes difficult to say what motivated a Copperhead. Self-interest, certainly; for some, an idealism that made peace worth any price; for the Wood brothers, a sense fundamentally of the undersurface of this city—a sense of the rowdies and toughs and large immigrant population, each resenting its inevitable competition with the Negro; a sense of businessmen who feared what saving the Union could cost; a sense of how Black Republicanism threatened Tammany. Lincoln said, "The people, under Providence, will set all right." But the Woods knew people in different terms than Lincoln, understanding their latent hatreds, their desperate fears and frustrations, the immediate and future meagerness of life in the slums, the avarice that squeezed tribute

* The report is identified as circulating during "the winter of 1860."

from dirty tenements. So they took one gamble and Lincoln another.

Whereas not every city along the Atlantic seaboard could boast the novelty of a mayor like Fernando Wood, secession first as a threat and then as a reality played upon the nerves of the conservative, business-minded city dweller and made him susceptible to all varieties of "peace feelers." December brought municipal elections in Boston and other New England cities, where the results disclosed a sharp cutback in Republican support; and even in the little upstate town of Hudson, New York, a similar trend prevailed. On December third a Beacon Street crowd, shocked by what Garrison's abolitionism had done to a jittery Boston stock exchange, broke up a meeting in Tremont Temple that tried to commemorate the anniversary of John Brown's execution. When the well-known abolitionist, George William Curtis, wished to speak in Philadelphia, the owners of Concert Hall canceled the contract for its use, making no secret of their concern for what a riot might do to their property. These Eastern activities were more a reflex action, the pulling back of the hand from the hot stove, than the symptom of any deep-rooted Copperhead sentiment as in the case of the Wood brothers.

Generally that disloyalist movement flourished in the valley of the Ohio River and made its inroads more into Indiana, Illinois, Wisconsin, and Iowa than it did east of the Alleghenies. In re-creating how America moved forward, torn and baffled, frightened and despairing, toward the bloodiest civil war the world ever would know, the search among the widely divergent emotions is for the common truth that links a Horace Greeley and a Fernando Wood though they seem as wide apart as Stuyvesant Square and Mackerelville. In a society of free men, perhaps what the psychologist labels the illusion of individuality constitutes the great peril, for even the extremist does not stand alone. Yet freedom itself is nourished upon extremes—God opposed to the devil, learning opposed to ignorance, equality opposed to slavery. America's torment, Lincoln said in concluding his debates with Douglas, was as old as the conflict between right and wrong. The political disruptions, even the bloody battles that these produced, were merely symptoms of the deeper struggle between individuality and ideal. Whither bound was ambivalent America? South Carolina had one answer and Massachusetts another, the West had one answer and the Border States another. Within the complex individuality of these regions rested the origins of the Great Rebellion, and each contributed to the war and to the triumph of the America that yet endures. Nor were any of these regions truly unified, except in the illusion of individuality. Each, groping toward the social ideal that America represented, was betrayed by its own emotions.

Certainly the South of Rhett was not the South of Robert E. Lee, and yet the illusion of both men—Rhett the segregationist and Lee the Virginian—endangered the nation. Lee had the more difficult choice; and it began that Christmas week of 1860 when Lee, now fifty-three years of age and a colonel in the army, was stationed in Texas. How does Lee stand now, and where does he differ from Grant in Illinois or Herman Melville in Boston or Sam Clemens piloting a steamboat upriver to St. Louis? Perplexed and even agonized were the hearts of each of these men, and none could see himself yet as a figure who would symbolize in heroic proportion this troubled week when in large measure America made its bitter choice. Least of all did Lee know where his future led.

6

Lee's Lonely Debate

IN A depressed mood, on the nineteenth of December, Lee left
San Antonio to join the Second Cavalry at Fort Mason. Since
the third of the month, when in spite of the hardheaded opposition of Governor Sam Houston secession fever spread like a growing plague across Texas, Colonel Lee had reacted stormily to the
"convulsion" of the Southern states. The prospect of going to Fort
Mason where, as he wrote his son Custis in Virginia, he would be
"farther from you all" made Lee so pensive that intimate friends
used phrases like "grave," "cold dignity," and "prudential reserve"
in describing his manner. "My little personal troubles sink into
insignificance when I contemplate the condition of the country,"
a letter told Custis, "and I feel as if I could easily lay down my life
for its safety. But I also feel that would bring but little good."
Again, father told son: "If this Union is dissolved, which God
in his mercy forbid, I shall return to you." Did Lee go to Fort
Mason because he believed war was not yet inevitable? The as-
sumption squares perfectly with Lee's simplicity of intellect, his
complete naïveté of political judgment, and a background that
could be catalogued under Virginia, West Point, and the army.
For Lee every tradition and circumstance of a lifetime had ruled
out almost any necessity for wrangling in the dark with the great
dilemmas of his age. The closest he had come to such inner torment was in 1856 when, writing to his wife, he called slavery "a
greater evil to the white man than to the black race," and con-

tended that even under slavery the Negro was "immeasurably better off here than in Africa, morally, socially, and physically." Lee believed that the subjection of the Negro must continue as long as it was "ordered by a wise and merciful Providence"; and he added testily: "Is it not strange that the descendants of the Pilgrim Fathers who crossed the Atlantic to preserve the freedom of their opinion have always proved themselves intolerant of the spiritual liberty of others?"

So Lee had dismissed the issue, more or less; but now the "irrepressible conflict" nibbled at his conscience and for the remainder of his life, there were to be many lonely debates for Lee. After early December, 1860, Lee's letters home would be filled with the emerging struggle—almost the resentful struggle, reading between the lines. It became a torment, his wife one day remarked, that cost him "tears of blood." At the outset he did not conceal from Custis his dismay over Southern extremism, referring to those " 'Cotton States,' as they term themselves" that were eager for "the renewal of the slave trade," a plan to which he was opposed "on every ground." Hoping for the best, he reported to Fort Mason and there soon heard the bitter news—hotheaded South Carolina had seceded. In his own angry phrase, the country stood between "a state of anarchy and a civil war"; and a note of rising despair was in his entreaty: "May God avert us from both."

For Lee the debates within himself, and with himself, quickened thereafter. Soon friends would speak of him as seeming disturbed to the point of illness; and what was maturing in his mind, slowly, painfully, were the ideas reflected in a frank letter to Markie Williams, a distant cousin living in the North:

> . . . I only see that a fearful calamity is upon us, and fear that the country will have to pass through for its sins a fiery ordeal. I am unable to realize that our people will destroy a government inaugurated by the blood and wisdom of our patriot fathers, that has given us peace and prosperity at home, power and security abroad, and under which we have acquired a colossal strength unequalled in the history of mankind. I wish to live under no other

government, and there is no sacrifice I am not ready to make for the preservation of the Union save that of honour. If a disruption takes place, I shall go back in sorrow to my people and share the misery of my native state, and save in her defence there will be one soldier less in the world than now. I wish for no other flag than the "Star spangled banner" and no other air than "Hail Columbia." I still hope that the wisdom and the patriotism of the nation will yet save it.

At Fort Mason Lee was happy to secure a copy of Nicholl Everett's *Life of Washington*—that great man "by nature" the most loyal "to order and law." A dissolution of the Union, he would say again, reflecting on the example of the Father of the Country, "would be an accumulation of all the evils we complain of." To avoid such a war, he told Custis as he informed Markie Williams, he would sacrifice everything "save honour."

A Virginian's honor, Lee meant, for Lee was in no sense the representative man of the South, if any such being existed in late 1860. In this region, so different from the rest of the nation, so confused between myth and reality, if in time Lee emerged as the symbol of the pure South and Rhett fell before the later fashion to damn the fire-eaters for losing to passion the great ideal of the South, that fact was significant. Lee always had been destined for legend and Rhett for history; the selflessness of Lee, the lack of ambition, the inner torment gave him the better dimension, the wholeness of a hero. Lee stood above and beyond the average man of the South so that he could with impunity even voice criticism of the "peculiar institution" whereas if a man of the cloth should seek the same privilege he might, like the Reverend John G. McFee of Kentucky, be twenty-two times attacked by a mob and twice left for dead.

No Southerner could have been born under a brighter star than had shone on Robert Edward Lee from cradle to manhood; his father was "Light Horse Harry" Lee of Revolutionary fame, his mother was a Carter, his father-in-law the adopted son of George Washington. If Lee's courtship for Mary Anne Randolph

Custis—a name that sang the poetry of Virginia's past glory—
had its fractious moments when Mary's father, recalling the later
years of old "Light Horse Harry" and his inept land speculations
fretted over the financial instability of the Lee clan, the "unspoiled"
daughter took matters in her own hands, deciding on a June
wedding and letting the nasty gossips wait to see how wisely she
had chosen. Thirty happy years of marriage had passed since then;
as an army officer, engineer, and superintendent of West Point
her Robert had demonstrated his capability and steadiness; and as
a sensitive husband and devoted father who would tell his children stories while they tickled his feet she measured Robert at his
affectionate best. "No tickling, no story," she heard him tease the
children when, engrossed in his tale, they forgot his pleasure; and
the laughter, the gentleness, the love he brought to the beautiful
mansion at Arlington Heights her father had left them were
always her richest heritage.

Lee had come home to Virginia to settle affairs after the death
of his father-in-law when on an October morning, a year ago,
a young cavalry lieutenant named J. E. B. Stuart had caught up
with the handsome colonel on a shopping trip to Alexandria. Lee
was needed at Harper's Ferry, Stuart said; that old fool, John
Brown, had seized the armory, arsenal, rifle factory, and bridge
across the Potomac and only God knew what Brown and his hellbent abolitionists thought they could do next; so Lee hastened to
Harper's Ferry, took command of a marine corps, stormed the
fire-engine house where the insurgents had barricaded themselves,
and helped thereby to place John Brown in the grave where ever
since he had rested so badly. Lee had returned to Texas, compre-
hending nothing of what Harper's Ferry portended. He had
captured "a fanatic or madman," in his own estimation; it was a
job well done, he believed, journeying back to San Antonio; but in
New England at that moment Longfellow's diary hailed John
Brown as bringing on "a new revolution, quite as much needed
as the old one," and Louisa May Alcott gushed girlishly over
"Saint John the Just."

Young Henry Adams attended Harvard while Lee's son Rooney was there, a circumstance for which the Southerner owed the New Englander little thanks in later years. Rooney, said Adams, had been a tall, handsome boy possessing "the Virginian habit of command" and taking "leadership as his natural habit"; and added Adams, without a blush for his own priggishness, "No one cared to contest it. None of the New Englanders wanted command." For a year Rooney was, Adams believed, the most prominent and popular man in his class, but seemed "slowly to drop into the background." At Harvard, after all, the habit of command—"and the Virginian had little else"—was not enough. Remembering Rooney Lee, Adams commented: "He was simple beyond analysis; so simple that even the simple New England student could not realize him. No one knew enough to know how ignorant he was; how childlike; how helpless before the relative complexity of a school. As an animal, the Southerner seemed to have every advantage, but even as an animal he steadily lost ground."

By 1918, when the Massachusetts Historical Society published *The Education of Henry Adams,* trying to piece together the Southern mind and the Civil War which it helped to produce was reviving as a national fascination. Others would come along to take different sides—W. J. Cash supporting Adams, John Peale Bishop to defend the older image of the South—and yet Adams, for his very closeness to the age, retained validity in his recollections of Harvard:

> The lesson in education was vital to these young men, who, within ten years, killed each other by scores in the act of testing their college conclusions. Strictly, the Southerner had no mind; he had temperament. He was not a scholar; he had no intellectual training; he could not analyze an idea, and he could not even conceive of admitting two; but in life one could get along well without ideas, if one had only the social instinct. Dozens of eminent statesmen were men of Lee's type, and maintained themselves well enough in the legislature, but college was a sharper test. The

Virginian was weak in vice itself, though the Bostonian was hardly a master of crime. The habits of neither were good; both were apt to drink hard and live low lives; but the Bostonian suffered less than the Virginian. . . . When a Virginian had brooded a few days over an imaginary grief and substantial whiskey, none of his Northern friends could be sure that he might not be waiting, round the corner, with a knife or pistol, ready to revenge insult by the dry light of *delirium tremens* . . .

So speaks Henry Adams, retaining the full color of his prejudices; and in answer, one hears the voice of John Peale Bishop—descendant on his mother's side from the Tidewater Virginia of the seventeenth century, yet no guardian of the South of "moonlight and wet lawns" so dear to "a few old ladies and Mr. Joseph Hergesheimer":

> . . . The Confederacy, for all the brevity of its formal existence, achieved more surely the qualities of a nation than the enduring Republic has been able to do. There were more emotions shared; its soldiers knew how to speak to one another or without speaking to arrive at a common understanding. Their attitude toward life was alike, and when they faced death it was in the same way. This makes for integrity, as it certainly makes for a sounder emotional life.

W. J. Cash, a descendant of the good upcountry farmers who helped to build South Carolina into a vigorous state in ante-bellum days, adored the South no less than Bishop, though, choosing between the two, the South has tended to adore Cash the less. A newspaper man and free-lance writer in the heyday of H. L. Mencken, Cash was satisfied to publish a single book (1941) that achieved the dimensions of a classic. In looking back on the South of his ancestors, Cash saw "a world in which horses, dogs, guns, not books and ideas and art, were his normal and absorbing interests"; a world in which "to be a Yancey or a Rhett ramping through the land with a demand for the sword—this was to be the very heart of one's time and place, was, for the plantation youth, full of hot blood, the only desirable career"; a world in which "the defense of slavery ... eventuated ... in a taboo on criticism" and "set up a ban on all analysis and inquiry, a terrified truculence toward every new idea, a disposition to reject every innovation out of hand and hug the whole of the *status quo* with fanatical resolution"; a world in which "the evangelical ministers ... had almost complete control of the schools, in which ... they established an iron wall with an effectiveness which went well beyond even its American average"; a world in which both Virginian and *nouveau* "developed no need or desire for intellectual culture in its own right—none, at least, powerful enough to drive him past its taboos to its actual achievement."

Each generation brings its own needs to history and an Adams at the close of World War I, a Bishop in the years of the depression, a Cash tormented by the fears of the early 1940's, each seeks something for himself. What all find is valid, to that degree at least; and if in late 1860 one had asked, "What is the mind of the South?" what then would one have found?

The answer—rather the answers—would depend on where one turned, and the Census of 1850 could have been a legitimate starting point. These figures would have shown that less than 8,000 Southerners owned 50 or more slaves; some 165,000 Southerners owned less than 50 but as many as 5 slaves; 105,683 Southerners owned from 2 to 4 slaves; and 68,820 Southerners owned 1 slave. The total white nonslaveholding population was about 4,250,000; the slave population nearly 3,500,000. Statistically, the South's "peculiar institution" appeared to rest upon very shaky ground, but emotionally and economically quite the reverse was true. The one Southerner who tried to reason in light of the statistics, seeing that a few and not the many were the beneficiaries of the Southern system, became as thoroughly hated as William Lloyd Garrison or Harriet Beecher Stowe.

Hinton Rowan Helper, born to a poor farm family in North Carolina, hating a system that ground him under its heel, believing that slavery was wrong "both in principle and practice" and that "the first and most sacred duty of every Southerner, who has the honor and interest of his country at heart, is to declare himself an unqualified and uncompromising opponent of slavery," shocked the South when in 1857 he published *The Impending Crisis*. Helper argued that slave labor had made the South so dependent on the free labor of the North—in infancy Southerners were "swaddled in Northern muslin" and at death "entombed with a Northern spade, and memorized with a Northern slab"—that the South in its relation to the North "now ranks more as the dependency of a mother country than as the equal confederate of free and independent States." And Helper warned:

> . . . Nothing short of the complete abolition of slavery can save the South from falling into the vortex of utter ruin. Too long have we yielded a submissive obedience to the tyrannical domination of an inflated oligarchy; too long have we tolerated their arrogance and self-conceit; too long have we submitted to their unjust and savage exactions. Let us now wrest from them the sceptre of power, establish liberty and equal rights throughout the land, and henceforth guard our legislative halls from the pollutions and usurpations of proslavery demagogues.

The North hailed Helper's arguments as incontestable proof that slavery produced a bitter bondage for the poor white as well as the Negro. So at least ran the heated debates that disrupted Congressional tempers as Helper's book was defended and damned on the floor of the House. So at least reasoned Horace Greeley, who made *The Impending Crisis* the campaign book of the Republican Party in 1858. But in the South to circulate Helper's book became a crime; the Cotton Curtain was dropped and poor Helper, never recovering from the experience though by 1909 he had lived to be eighty, finally took his own life crying, "There is no justice in this world."

If Helper had pleaded his case in 1815 when the South had produced 150,000 bales of cotton, his reception might have been entirely sympathetic; but by 1859 the figure became 4,500,000 bales. In 1820 Helper would have been helped by the fact that the antislavery societies in the South had outnumbered those in the Free States; but by 1837 not a single antislavery society remained in the South. The Yankee inventiveness of Eli Whitney, giving the South its cotton gin, had been one catalyst of change; and another had been the perfection in England of machinery for spinning fine and even thread. The later fashion was to blame the Northern abolitionist for the changing attitude of the South, but without the gin or the improvements in British mills, would that change have occurred? The Jeffersonian democracy of Virginia in which Lee had been reared always had seen slavery as an institution that must succumb to a natural death in time; but suddenly Virginia and Virginian gentleness lost its leadership to South Carolina and Texas, Georgia and Alabama, Mississippi and Louisiana—the so-called Black Belt—and Negro exploitation became the passionate doctrine of economic necessity. From the title of David Christy's book, published in 1855, came the rallying cry of this Second South—*Cotton is King!* Indeed, Cotton became king over Southern thought, morals, politics, and diplomacy; Cotton preached in Southern pulpits and taught in Southern schools; and Cotton invented a myth of the master race as vicious as any the world would ever know.

The mid-1850's, when Cotton ascended to its Southern throne, brought forth a flurry of racialistic literature that the South read, discussed, and accepted far too uncritically. Dr. Josiah C. Nott of South Carolina, soon to become professor of anatomy at the University of Louisiana, was not only willing to proclaim in *Types of Mankind* that the Negro was destined to remain forever an intellectual inferior, but Dr. Nott also helped to edit an English edition of the work of Count Joseph Arthur de Gobineau, the Frenchman whose theory of "Aryanism" served so well the evil ends of Adolf Hitler. From a New Yorker, Dr. John H. Van Evrie, came the prime contribution, however; and by 1853 the bulk of his work, *Negroes and Negro "Slavery,"* was being read in the South. The small size of the Negro's brain, his eccentric posture, his linguistic habits were all seized upon by Dr. Van

Evrie to demonstrate "scientifically" that what little the Negro gained from life was everything he deserved; and to Dr. Van Evrie the abolition of slavery by the British constituted an effort by English "shopocracy" to "deface humanity." Jefferson Davis could not deny that he was impressed by Dr. Van Evrie. "An able and manly exposure of a fallacy," Davis said.

Meanwhile in Southern churches clergymen of the Methodist, Baptist, and Presbyterian sects, interpreting every word of the Bible to be literally true, recited Sunday after Sunday the scriptural defense of slavery. Doubtless there was more than a little truth in the delighted conclusion of the Reverend B. F. Stringfellow of St. Louis that whereas there were two hundred and two Unitarian and two hundred and eighty-five Universalist churches in New England, only one Unitarian and seven Universalist churches could be found in the South—proof to Stringfellow that Southerners avoided running after "strange gods." Yet it was a gentleman of similar name—the Reverend Thornton Stringfellow of Culpeper County, Virginia—who gave to the Southern clergy the substance of the familiar scriptural apologia for slavery. Drawing on the Bible to show how God had decreed hereditary slavery for the posterity of Canaan, and had recognized Abraham as the owner of slaves "he had bought with his money of the stranger," and then turning to the New Testament and drawing on the passage wherein Jesus had ordered his gospel to be published among slaveholding Romans and also had ordained that "the legislative authority, which created this relation in that empire, should be obeyed and honored as an ordinance of God," the Reverend Stringfellow asked:

> This being the case, as will appear by the recorded language of the Bible . . . of what use is it to argue against it from moral requirements? They regulate the duties of this and all other lawful relations among men—but they cannot abolish any relation, ordained or sanctioned of God, as is slavery.

In the Black Belt churchgoers said "Amen" and went home to their Sunday dinners.

To read Helper, Van Evrie, Stringfellow (B. or T.) provided part of the insight into the mind of the South in 1860 that Lee scarcely shared or understood, but it was a Northerner, Frederick Law Olmsted, to whom one had to turn to gain telling comprehension of what had happened in this diversified yet strangely unified land where Cotton was King. Disgusted both by the "red-hot abolitionists" and "the deluge of spoony fancy pictures" emanating from the South, Olmsted was determined to see and judge for himself life and times in the Cotton Kingdom. Originally Olmsted intended his observations for travel letters to appear in the New York *Times* but three books resulted—*A Journey in the Seaboard Slave States* (1856), *A Journey through Texas* (1857), and *A Journey in the Back Country* (1860)—and at the instigation of a British publisher the three books subsequently were combined into *The Cotton Kingdom: a Traveller's Observation on Cotton and Slavery in the American Slave States* (1861).

An exuberant fellow—his wife described him as "fond of arguments" and "full of life and fun"—already successful as an agriculturist, Olmsted liked travel, people, ideas. "This is exactly what we wish all well-disposed and well-behaved Northern people, who desire to know something of the South, would do," complimented the *Southern Literary Messenger* when the first of Olmsted's letters were published; but later Southern criticism would grow sharper and *De Bow's Review* would speak of Olmsted as "abounding in bitterness and prejudice of every sort." The charges that Olmsted was a bitterly biased witness of the South seem unjustified in the view of history; and in 1860 he was still, as James Russell Lowell believed, possessed of a "quiet power" that made it possible to learn more about the South from Olmsted's books "than from all the others put together."

Olmsted rarely failed as a sprightly chronicler, whether describing Richmond as seen "through a dull cloud of bituminous smoke, upon a lowering winter's day" or a Negro funeral: "Lord Jesus, have marcy on us—now! you Jim—you! see yar! you jes lay dat yar shovel cross dat grave—so fash—dah—yes, dat's right." He reported on slaves working in the tobacco fields of Virginia, lumbering in the Great Dismal Swamp, and rolling cotton bales in the Carolinas. He saw the rice plantations, large and small, around Savannah. At Claiborne in Alabama the cotton warehouse stood on a bluff above the river, and the bales were shot down a plank to the boats, a reckless business—but he learned why Irishmen were hired for this labor when the boat's mate told him: "The niggers* are worth too much to be risked here; if the Paddies are knocked overboard, or get their backs broke, nobody loses anything!"

In New Orleans he attended a Negro church service and captured the part religion played in the dreams of the enslaved: " . . . Henceforth [the preacher said] there is laid up for us a crown of immortal glory—(Ha! Ha! HA!)—not a crown of wild olive leaves that begin to droop as soon as they touch our brow, (oh! oh! oh!) but a crown of immortal glory! That fadeth not away! Never begins to droop! But is immortal in the heavens! (Tremendous uproar, many of the congregation on their feet, and uttering cries and shrieks impossible to be expressed in letters.)" He traveled the Emigrant Road into Texas, sensing the "inexorable destiny . . . that drags or drives on, always Westward, these toil-worn people," and in a magnificent passage he described these families from Alabama, Georgia, or the Carolinas as the expansionist hunger of King Cotton propelled his subjects toward new land (and war):

> . . . Before you come upon them you hear, ringing through the woods, the fierce cries with which they urge on their jaded cattle. Then the stragglers appear, lean dogs or fainting Negroes, ragged and spiritless. An old granny, hauling on by the hand, a weak boy—too old to ride and too young to keep up. An old man, heavily loaded, with a rifle. Then the white covers of the waggons, jerking up and down as they mount over a root or plunge into a rut, disappearing, one after another, where the road descends. Then

* This word is used here and elsewhere only as it occurs within historical context.

the active and cheery prime Negroes, not yet exhausted, with a joke and a suggestion about tobacco. . . . As you get by, the white mother and babies, and the tall, frequently ill-humoured master, on horseback, or walking with his gun, urging up the black driver and his oxen. . . . We passed in the day perhaps one hundred persons attached to these trains, probably an unusual number; but the immigration this year had been retarded and condensed by the fear of yellow fever . . .

He read the signs on a slave mart in Houston: "A likely negro girl for sale . . . Two negroes for sale . . . Twenty negro boys for sale." Always he heard bitter talk about uncaptured runaways, and most violent was the abuse over Mexicans who considered runaways as free and would not let them be taken back: "But that's stealing, sir. Why don't our Government make them deliver them up? What good is a Government to us if it don't preserve the rights of property, sir? Niggers are property, ain't they? and if a man steals my property, ain't the Government bound to get it for me? Niggers are property, sir, the same as horses and cattle, and nobody's any more right to help a nigger that's run away than he has to steal a horse." In Mississippi, on one of the large cotton plantations, he watched an overseer strip and beat a disobedient slave girl while the master's young son of fifteen looked on: "I glanced again at the perfectly passionless but rather grim business-like face of the overseer, and again at the young gentleman, who had turned away; if not indifferent he had evidently not the faintest sympathy with my emotion. Only my horse chafed."

Olmsted visited on plantations where life was lived graciously— where, indeed, there was much of the "moonlight and wet lawns" dear to the hearts of historical novelists—where the master fretted over the morals of his sons, with the girls in the slave quarter so handy, and so sent the boys North to school—where truly Cotton was king and wealth and leisure and privilege and gentility. But the eye of the reporter came back irresistibly to the slave quarter, recognizing here the beating heart that kept King Cotton alive. He realized the studied, good-humored indolence of the slave, making his labor more costly than master or overseer admitted. The image of the South that he created was of a restless, toiling land, closer to frontier traditions than to the background of Virginia—a South where much of what Helper wrote applied, where there was no hope for the Negro and little for most whites and so their dignity depended desperately on a belief in racial superiority, where no cities existed that could compare with the cultural and economic importance of a New York or Philadelphia or Boston, where the myth of the South was very different from the reality of the South.

One of Olmsted's letters to the *Times* dealt with "Slavery in Its Effects on Character, and the Social Relations of the Master Class." Olmsted declared: "The calculating, indefatigable New-Englander, the go-ahead Western man, the exact and stern Englishman, the active Frenchman, the studious, observing, economical German would all and each lose patience with the frequent disobedience and the constant indolence, forgetfulness and carelessness, and the blundering, awkward, brute-like manner of work of the plantation-slave." In contrast, the Southerner tended to disregard what he saw in the same manner that he tended not to hear what he did not like. His social hospitality was beyond reproach, Olmsted admitted; to no man did good manners come more naturally; yet he was "greatly wanting in hospitality of mind." The Northerner, who found rest offensive—who, in Olmsted's opinion, would find heaven "dull and stupid to him, if there is no work to be done in it"—would not understand the Southerner, this passionate man, who labored passionately and fitfully, "with the energy and strength of anger, rather than of resolute will." If an evil could not be passed by unnoticed, "it is immediately declared to be constitutional, or providential, and its removal is declared to be either treasonable or impious"—and Olmsted, himself a passionate man, could inflict a wound and throw salt upon the sore. Olmsted's admiration for the true Southern gentleman was deep and abiding, but he found many among the *nouveau*—the Cotton Snobs—who, well-dressed and gentle in the presence of ladies, still among themselves were "unable to converse upon anything that is not either grossly sensual or exciting, such as street rencounters, filibustering schemes, or projects of disunion or war." This was angry talk, and Olmsted deleted it from his books, but he told the readers of the *Times*, in a final outburst of feeling:

They call themselves Democrats, and sometimes Democratic Whigs. Call them what you will, they are a mischievous class,—the dangerous class at present in the United States. They are not the legitimate offspring of Democracy, thanks to God, but of slavery under a Democracy.

Yet Olmsted's wrathful outcry was not far removed from the conflicting emotions that seethed in the heart of Colonel Robert E. Lee during Christmas week of 1860 at Fort Mason, Texas. He always had disliked slavery, believing it "a moral and political evil." Neither the sprawling South that Olmsted saw nor the pinched, hard South that bedeviled Helper was part of his consciousness. Boyhood years spent at Stratford, the old Lee mansion, and later in Alexandria, four cadet years at West Point, courtship and marriage in the handsome Custis mansion at Arlington Heights, the War with Mexico, a dozen army posts—these were the horizons, physical and spiritual, of Lee's world. He belonged to the quiet lawyer-culture of the Old South that stemmed directly from the Virginia of George Wythe and Thomas Jefferson. Wherever roads between larger towns offered a central meeting place, a little courthouse would be built, with a tavern, a store, a few houses close by, and here the orderly system of a life founded on reason, justice, and experience was maintained. Orange Court House, Culpeper Court House, Spotsylvania Court House—these were the sleepy villages that were the stalwart guardians of the Southern ideals that Lee knew and loved. In the mountains, on the road between Richmond and Lynchburg, another was called Appomattox Court House.

There is record of a slave ship which, after leaving Africa for

America, had both its human cargo and its crew fall victim to the disease of ophthalmia. A blind ship adrift on a blind sea—the image is Homeric in symbolizing the historical tragedy inherent in slavery. In some such measure, Lee also may be viewed at Fort Mason in December of 1860. And among what Olmsted called the "go-ahead" Westerners the one man who would come forward to contest with Lee in the final struggle perhaps was no more perceptive.

7

The Man Who
Journeyed Through Hell

ULYSSES S. GRANT may often have misjudged his friends,
but he rarely misjudged himself. The strength of Grant was
his deep streak of intellectual integrity. In the last desperate, can-
cer-ridden weeks of his life, it was within his character to seek
for the truth and to see wherein he had failed his age. "The cause
of the great War of the Rebellion against the United States," he
decided then, "will have to be attributed to slavery. For some
years before the war began it was a trite saying among some politicians that 'A state half slave and half free cannot exist.' All must
become slave or all free, or the state will go down. I took no part
myself in any such view of the case at the time, but since the war
is over, reviewing the whole question, I have come to the conclusion that the saying is quite true."

In any evaluation of the forces at play in 1860 leading the American people to war, the danger is that one forgets how much
younger the country was then. A glance at the map showing where
frontier settlement ended and Indian territory began usually pro-
duces surprise. This was still the golden age of the steamboat.
The shortest route east from California was by land across the
Isthmus of Panama. Whereas the wires of the magnetic telegraph
stretched across the continent, the news of Lincoln's election was
carried to Nevada by express rider. That there were two Souths,
one stemming from the germinal center of Virginia and another

from South Carolina, that there were Border States yet different in need, temperament, and influences, that the West was something very much apart from these sections and even more so from New England was not surprising. Environments were isolated; attitudes and customs grew up as necessity required. Actually America was groping, hesitant step by hesitant step, toward a national character. That this phenomenon must contribute to bringing on a war was regrettable but nonetheless true; a national character required a national conscience.

A Lincoln sensed this fact clearly, a Grant did not, and yet both belonged to the same Illinois in 1860. It awaited a later if not wiser Adams than young Henry to grasp the peculiar nature of the country that produced these two principal architects of the ultimate victory. "Only in the Middle States and the West," wrote James Truslow Adams, "were men living intensely in the moment but looking joyously forward and allowing themselves to float, for better or worse, on the full flood of American life." Even Anthony Trollope, a more perceptive observer than his mother or Charles Dickens, recognized this truth. Trollope might feel repelled personally by the "dirt, dishonesty and morning drinks" that were the vices of the West, yet in 1861 he must admit: " . . . there is a certain manliness about its men, which gives them a dignity of their own. It is shown in that very indifference of which I have spoken. Whatever turns up the man was still there,—still unsophisticated and still unbroken. It has seemed to me that no race of man requires less outward assistance than these pioneers of civilization. They rarely amuse themselves. Food, newspapers, and brandy-smashes suffice for life; and while these last, whatever may occur, the man is still there in his manhood." Trollope was remembering incidents of travel in Missouri and Illinois when he penned these lines. During 1860 Ulysses S. Grant called both states home.

River pilots, approaching Galena, Illinois, with its "curious Swiss look" as it perched along bluffs and slopes two hundred feet above the water, often recalled that great terraced city on the lower Mississippi—Vicksburg. On an April day in 1860 the steamer *Itasca* tied to the levee and a stumpy man, wearing a faded blue coat, strode down the gangplank with a couple of chairs in each hand. The alert, little woman, bouncing at his heels, was Julia Dent Grant; the four children were Fred, 'Lyss, Jesse, and Nellie. A good dock lounger in those days heard about news before it happened: "That's Captain Grant—Jesse Grant's oldest son—he was in the Mexican War and he's moving here from St. Louis."

Almost the first thing Galena learned about Grant was that he was a quiet man who went about his own affairs and kept pretty much to himself. Not that the gossips didn't keep busy. The Captain, they said, had drunk too much in California and had been asked to resign from the army, which was probably true to the extent that almost everybody in the army in California had been drinking more than they should. Others said that Grant had been a failure as a farmer in Missouri and his family would have starved to death if old Jesse hadn't found a place for him in his leather business. Again there was only an element of truth in the tale. Augustus Chetlin, son of the wholesale grocer, declared he heard Grant talking to a lawyer one evening in a Galena tavern.

"Stranger here?" the lawyer asked.

"Yes."

"Travel far?"

"Far enough."

"Looks as though you might have traveled through hell."

"I have."

"Well, how did you find things down there?"

"Oh, much the same as in Galena—lawyers nearest the fire."

Sooner or later most people discovered one thing about Grant; he was quiet and gentle, but he could take care of himself. He gave his own reason for leaving California and the army: "My family, all this while (1852–4), was at the East.... I saw no chance of supporting them on the Pacific coast out of my pay as an army officer." Those who wished to tell another story could do so; but this was pretty much the whole truth. And if an honest, succinct account of his experiences trying to run his wife's farm near St. Louis was wanted, Grant gave it in his own straightforward way: "I had no means to stock it. A house had to be built also. I worked very hard, never losing a day because of bad weather, and accomplished the object in a moderate way. If nothing else could be done I would load a cord of wood on the wagon and take it to the city for sale. I managed to keep along very well until 1858, when I was attacked by fever and ague." What he omitted was his embarrassment when occasionally he encountered old army friends in St. Louis. His seediness, in the frayed and fading blue army coat to which he still clung, shocked them: "Great God, Grant," an officer cried one day, "what are you doing?" Grant answered simply: "I am solving the problem of poverty." He omitted, too, the Christmas in '58 when he pawned his gold watch for money to buy presents for Julia and the children. Perhaps he was a failure; still, he was doing his level best.

After years in the army, in 1856 Grant had his first chance to vote in a Presidential election. In a choice between the Republican Frémont and the Democratic Buchanan, he said, "I voted for Buchanan because I didn't know him and voted against Frémont because I did know him." His political naïveté tricked him into a misjudgment that he was still trying to explain away in his *Memoirs*:

> ... Most of my neighbors had known me as an officer of the army with Whig proclivities. They had been on the same side, and, on the death of their party, many had become Know-Nothings, or members of the American party. There was a lodge near my new home, and I was invited to join it. I accepted the invitation; was initiated; attended a meeting just one week later, and never went to another afterwards.
>
> I have no apologies to make for having been one week a member of the American party; for I still think native-born citizens of the United States should have as much protection, as many privileges in their native country, as those who voluntarily select it for a

home. But all secret, oath-bound political parties are dangerous to any nation . . . No political party can or ought to exist when one of its cornerstones is opposition to freedom of thought and to the right to worship God "according to the dictates of one's own conscience" . . . Nevertheless, if a sect sets up its laws as binding above the State laws, wherever the two come in conflict this claim must be resisted and suppressed at whatever cost.

Phrases like "native-born citizens" and "those who voluntarily select it for a home" echo emotions that were intense along the border in those years when the American was becoming a composite of many blood streams. Yet Grant's political experiences were of slight moment under the pressure he still faced in holding skin and bones together. From farming he turned to a partnership in real estate with Harry Boggs, a cousin of Julia Grant; the business was too young and too small to support two families, and Grant withdrew, accepting the reality that "there was no more than one person could attend to." He announced himself a candidate for the office of county engineer, "an office of respectability and emolument," and again there is an echo of deepening Middle Border prejudice in the observation: "My opponent had the advantage of birth over me (he was a citizen by adoption) and carried off the prize." Since early boyhood he had hated his father's tannery and leather business, but now there was no choice. He packed up belongings and family and boarded the *Itasca* for Galena.

Quickly in Galena Grant appeared to get his feet on the ground. His brothers, Simpson and Orvil, were happy to welcome Ulysses into the firm; poor Simpson hacked and coughed with consumption and tried to accept the fact that his years now were briefly numbered and Orvil's conceit had earned the rebuke that he was "an uninhibited sharper," so that Ulysses' calm, easygoing, pleasant disposition was an asset to the business. "There was no bossing by Simpson or Orvil," a nephew-in-law of Jesse's recalled; both brothers accepted 'Lysses as "an older man and a soldier" who "knew much more than we in matters of the world." The brothers each drew six hundred dollars a year, but they were satisfied: profits went into a trust fund for their three sisters. Julia was satisfied also in the two-story brick house where the Grants now lived at 121 High Street. To the rear was a graveyard and she could see the tombstones from the back door. But what did she care? 'Lyss, as she called Captain Grant privately, seemed to find a new serenity; she saw him after rainy days sailing boats with the children along the gutters of the streets, or heard him tell them stories of his war experiences in Mexico, or saw him in the evening reading his newspaper and placidly smoking a pipe. When he came home from the store, three-year-old Jesse invariably waited with the same taunt:

"Mister, do you want to fight?"

"I'm a man of peace," the Captain answered, "but I'll not be hectored by a person of your size."

Had he added, "or of any size," he would have described his character perfectly.

Years before, the Galena River had been called La Fevre, in honor of an early French trader who had come into this part of northwestern Illinois when Fox and Sac Indians had pitched their tepees along its bluffs, but the name on Western lips sounded like "fever," suggesting a constant frontier worry, and so it was changed. But fevers traveled upriver to Galena nonetheless: the milk-sick, typhoid, and in late 1860, politics, secession, and the dark prospect of war.

Sharp-tongued Orvil was the dedicated Republican, rallying his friends around the stove in the store and enjoying the hearty sport of damning the Democrats and the Slavocrats. Captain Grant kept aloof from these heated sessions, having the excuse when argument threatened that since he hadn't yet lived in Illinois a year he couldn't vote. His personal choice was Douglas, "who had no chance of election"; between Breckinridge, the candidate of the proslavery Democrats, and Mr. Lincoln he favored the Republican for the same reason that he would make a natural choice between "minority rule and rule by the majority." Orvil of course was hip-deep in drilling Wide-Awakes, torchlight parades, speeches, insults; some Galena Republicans tried to convince the Captain that he had a right to vote but Orvil squelched that idea since "he wouldn't vote for our ticket." With Lincoln's election Orvil reached heights of ecstasy, and the Captain helped him serve raw oysters and liquor to the exuberant Wide-Awakes.

Captain Grant was solemn that night. It was no surprise to him when Christmas week brought the news of South Carolina's secession. Within his own mind he had wrestled long with this problem, conceding that "the right to revolution is an inherent one," and yet equally convinced that "if the right of any one State continued to exist at all after the ratification of the Constitution, it certainly ceased on the formation of new States, at least so far as the States themselves were concerned." Southern men, meeting in Convention at Vicksburg in 1859, had voted 40 to 19 in favor of reviving the slave trade; Orvil not only asked what choice had existed except to slap down this kind of evil conspiracy but also added, mocking the vaunted boasts of Southern Chivalry, that the "Chivs" would never fight. Captain Grant, who understood how a person reacted if he were "hectored" long enough, told a friend in Galena: "The South will fight." Since he was a veteran of the Mexican War, everyone in Galena sought his opinion on what to expect, what to do, and, to the surprise of some he began to speak of "his debt . . . to his country, and . . . the capacities of the North to raise troops." Buchanan's ability to handle the crisis gave no comfort to the Captain, who wrote a friend in St. Louis: " . . . with the present granny of an executive, some foolish policy will doubtless be pursued which will give the seceding States the support and sympathy of the Southern States that don't go out."

"So suicidal an act" as secession, Grant said in the same letter, he found "hard to realize." The leather business forced him to travel across Illinois, Wisconsin, and Iowa. His war record found people seeking him out everywhere. Were the "Chivs" really serious? "Each side underestimates the other and over-estimates itself," he said. He was glad to return home to Galena, except that letters from his own father lambasted secession and those from Julia's father, a former slaveowner, praised it. Apparently all calmness in the South and in the West had flown out the window. The Captain put on a brave front for Julia and the children, not wanting to spoil Christmas. This year at least he had not needed to pawn his watch to buy presents for them. To count one's small blessings from day to day was about the only refuge the times left a sensible man.

Yet Grant was no more the representative man of the West than Lee was of the South. To the extent that Lee was a descendant and Grant an ancestor, they both symbolized the age and youth of the two sections in national terms. The population of Chicago in 1840 had been less than five thousand; in 1860 it was past the hundred thousand mark and climbing rapidly. The New England fashion was rather to look down its nose at the West, believing neither good taste nor a vital culture was developing here, but as the national character emerged it would embrace with enduring affection the legends of Davy Crockett and Mike Fink that the West was creating. At least one New Englander grasped this truth, and in *Israel Potter* Herman Melville described Ethan Allen as "a curious combination of a Hercules, a Joe Miller, a Bayard and a Tom Hyer. He was frank, bluff, companionable as a Pagan, convivial, a Roman, hearty as a harvest. His spirit was essentially Western; and herein is his peculiar Americanism; for the Western spirit is, or will yet be (for no other can be) the true American."

As Charleston was the spiritual head of the Black Belt and Boston of New England, so had Chicago begun to emerge in the West. Not all British travelers, drawn irresistibly by the magnetism that the West exerted, came to write books like Dickens and the Trollopes. John Henry Vessey, here in 1859, was an English gentleman who came only to satisfy his own curiosity and to keep a journal for the edification of his friends and family. Unsettled by the bustle and zeal of Chicago, Mr. Vessey could only feel that "the rakings of hell get out here"; yet he had to admit that "the enterprise of these people is marvellous" though he was forced to tell a story that jibed at what he considered their essential weakness:

> ... An Englishman passing through an American town noticed four churches and asked a Yankee on the omnibus to what denomination each belonged. "That," says he, "is a Methodist"; "And what is next?" "Episcopalian"; the next Presbyterian; "But what is that?" says the Englishman, "it appears to be shut up." "She was a Baptist but they don't use her now. I guess she don't pay."

From mere trading post to the Empire City of the West within a span of three decades made Chicago, in Mr. Vessey's opinion, "one of the wonders of America," already "the centre of more miles of railway than London" and boasting of "houses, stores, public buildings and streets that would not disgrace that or any other city." Mr. Vessey was in Chicago but a few days, and lacked the advantage of realizing the Chicago that the proud Chicagoan liked to show off. The Prince of Wales, who would follow Victoria to the throne as Edward VII, would see Chicago the following September with its best foot forward and its Western pride bursting at the seams. Accompanied "by the Mayor, Consul Wilson, &c." he visited one of the great grain elevators where 750,000 bushels were stored in large bins "with long shoots leading down to the vessels beneath"; from the cupola of the Court House he gazed down on streets "broad, well-lighted, and provided with central railways"; and a note of astonishment remains in the observation that "we saw one *entire* house being transported along the street." Before the Prince retired to his suite in the Richmond House, where in May the lusty Tom Hyer had drunk 'em down for Seward, he observed "a large theatre-like building called a 'wigwam,'—a kind of 'political machine' where conventions are held."

Next day the Prince shot prairie chickens and quail, growing

quite enraptured by "the grand breezy expanse of soft rich meadows"; and he beheld the splendor of a prairie sunset that transformed "the whole ocean of meadow into a sheet of gold which
seemed to blend with the great firmament of reds and pinks, pale
rosy orange hues, and solemn-looking crimson clouds above till
not only the sky but all the land around was steeped in piles of
colour as if the heavens were reflected from below, or as if the
sinking sun shone through the very earth like mist, and turned it
to a rainbow." Earlier lightning had started a prairie fire; the grass
broke into flame in three different places, then joined; and so the
Prince and his party viewed "a scene as nothing but a prairie fire
can show":

> . . . a sea of red smoldering ashes, glowing for miles in all direc-
> tions, while the deep white ridge of flames ahead mount the
> slopes with awful rapidity, and flap their heavy tongues up in the
> air with a hoarse roaring voice that fills you with astonishment
> and almost with terror . . . the mass of red sultry ruins grows and
> grows each minute, till your eyes are painted and heated with its
> angry glare and you almost dread the grand, fierce sheet of fire,
> which has swept all trace of vegetation from the surface of the
> prairie.

Elemental beauty, strength, struggle—these were the essence
of the young, frontier West, building its own empire, growing the
grain that filled the great elevators in the proud city on the shores
of Lake Michigan—this was the force that drew Swedes into Minnesota and Germans into Wisconsin to build their own traditions,
and, yes, would soon send their sons to fight against the Randolphs
and Lees, the Beauregards and Stuarts in a war that gave them
their share in forging the national character. Day by day, living on
lonely farms, pushing back the forests, grubbing for their future,
their existence seemed mean and meager; Mr. Vessey saw it as
such, visiting in rural Michigan. "A man wants to be badly off
indeed in the old country to better himself here as a tiller of the
soil," he observed; but in the next breath he admitted: "Undoubt-
edly their children, bred and born there and knowing nothing

better than a squatter's life, will as the population increases and
land improves in value, be better off than they would have been
in England."

Here in Illinois and Michigan, Wisconsin and Minnesota lived
the spiritual sons of Jackson and Harrison and Clay. And of Lincoln. These were the Free Soilers, obtaining their acres of land for
the faith they were willing to invest in them. The war in which
they joined the New England literary historian delights in calling
a disruption of America, but it was quite the reverse. America
already was disrupted. If nothing else, the war created a fresh
opportunity to get ahead with the nation's business.

Knowing the spirit of these people as a thing of his own heart
and conscience, in September of 1859 Mr. Lincoln journeyed to
Milwaukee to speak at the Wisconsin State Fair. The address was
billed as nonpolitical, but the times were highly political. Mr.
Lincoln quoted Pope: "Happiness is our being's end and aim";
and "in some sort a politician, and in no sort a farmer" attacked
the "mud-sill" theory that divided the laboring class between the
hired and the enslaved. Not forgetting he once had been a hired
hand, Mr. Lincoln spoke for Free Soilers: "They hold that labor is
prior to, and independent of, capital; that, in fact, capital is the
fruit of labor, and could never have existed if labor had not *first*
existed—that labor can exist without capital, but that capital could
never have existed without labor." Again it was the essence of the
Free Soiler's faith that he reduced to a sentence: "Men, with their
families—wives, sons, and daughters—work for themselves, on
their farms, in their houses and in their shops, taking the whole
product to themselves, and asking no favors of capital on the one
hand, nor of hirelings or slaves on the other." And again, pounding hard at the mudsill theory, Mr. Lincoln said:

> ... it is assumed that labor and education are incompatible; and
> any practical combination of them impossible. According to that
> theory, a blind horse upon a treadmill, is a perfect illustration of
> what a laborer should be—all the better for being blind, that he
> could not tread out of place, or kick understandingly. According

to that theory, the education of laborers, is not only useless, but pernicious, and dangerous. In fact, it is, in some sort, deemed a misfortune that laborers should have heads at all. Those same heads are regarded as explosive materials, not only to be safely kept in damp places, as far as possible from that peculiar sort of fire which ignites them. A Yankee who could invent a strong *handed* man without a head would receive the everlasting gratitude of the "mud-sill" advocates.

Free Soilers knew what Lincoln meant; States Righters, in solid opposition to any use of the Congressional power to tax for the general welfare, had fought legislation that could foster growth of state universities. Mr. Lincoln moreover believed what he said and proved it early in his Administration with the passage of the Morrill Act of 1862. That act granted to each state, for each Senator or Representative, thirty thousand acres of land (or its equivalent in scrip) from the public domain, and the money realized was to promote education in the "agriculture and mechanic arts." Today in all forty-eight states the land-grant college exists as the greatest single contribution American democracy has made to higher education; farmers, listening to Mr. Lincoln at the Wisconsin State Fair in 1859, heard the vision described:

> . . . Every blade of grass is a study; and to produce two, where there was but one, is both a profit and a pleasure. And not grass alone; but soils, seeds, and seasons—hedges, ditches, and fences, draining, droughts, and irrigation—plowing, hoeing, and harrowing—reaping, mowing, and threshing—saving crops, pests of crops, diseases of crops, and what will prevent or cure them—implements, utensils, and machines, their relative merits, and how to improve them—hogs, horses, and cattle—sheep, goats, and poultry—trees, shrubs, fruits, plants, and flowers—the thousand things of which these are specimens—each a world of study within itself.

It was heady talk like this that turned a Robert Barnwell Rhett so dead against Lincoln; and Mr. Lincoln believed he knew why the born-and-bred "mud-siller" disliked him, telling the farmers in Wisconsin: "Even in all our slave states, except South Carolina, a majority of the whole people of all colors, are neither slaves nor masters."

Fifteen months had passed since then, and almost three since the future Edward VII had viewed the awesome spectacle of a prairie fire. Now the threats of secession were like scattered flames leaping up in the grass, and if they joined, the result might well fill one "with astonishment and almost with terror." Home for Christmas in Galena, Captain Grant scarcely knew what to believe or to expect, an unhappiness he shared with Colonel Lee in Texas. From Springfield at that moment a letter sped to Senator Lyman Trumbull in Washington. The President-elect had heard that Buchanan intended to surrender the Federal forts in South Carolina, and declared: "I can scarcely believe this; but if it prove true, I will, if our friends at Washington concur, announce publicly at once that they are to be retaken after the inauguration. This will give the Union men a rallying cry, and preparation will proceed somewhat on their side, as well as on the other." As Anthony Trollope observed of the Westerner, "Whatever may occur, the man is still there in his manhood."

One of the great tragedies of ante-bellum America was the little heed given to its true spokesmen. In this respect, Lincoln was luckier than most—far luckier than Walt Whitman, his sensitive heart torn apart by the furious tug-and-pull of a turbulent democracy that he could see and touch and taste and smell and hear; far, far luckier than poor Herman Melville, who had achieved a masterpiece that neither New England nor America would recognize until the second decade of the twentieth century. Melville, gazing down at the Charles River from his Boston room that Christmas week, was now forty-two and broken in health. He sensed the coming conflict as clearly as anyone in New England; but he sensed too his utter physical unfitness to be a real part of it. Was it perhaps a stroke of genius of the creative subconscious that had led him in this generation to seize upon the legend of the albino whale for the source of his masterpiece? The question is entirely rhetorical. He would be in New York during the bloody Draft Riots of 1863 and write:

> Were men but strong and wise,
>   Honest as Grant and calm,
> War would be left to the red and black ants
>   And the happy world disarm.

Yet in late 1860 the paradoxes of the South were difficult, almost next to impossible even for a Lee to comprehend; the hopes, the dreams, the compelling impulses of the West were rather simpler, for they all were earth-bound; but New England, more adrift in the American mainstream than it possessed the courage to confess, as self-enclosed as a Brittany or Provence, had to face up also to the national tragedy: humanity opposed the White Whale and could not yield its burdens to the red and black ants.

8

The Evil of Whiteness

IN THE best Calvinistic tradition the New England conscience, as the celebrated *New England Primer* proclaimed, was nourished on spiritual milk "sucked from the breasts of both Testaments." The result, at least in Massachusetts, was not altogether satisfying to Emerson, who grumbled that "from 1790 to 1820 there was not a book, a speech, a conversation, or a thought in the State." Thereafter "the Channing, Webster and Everett era" began, and, said Emerson, "we have been bookish and poetical and cogitative since." What Emerson observed was true with one important qualification: the "cogitative" New Englander looked toward Europe rather than over the whole United States. He had so little feeling for the great impulse to national unity that when he encountered it in a Webster during the Compromise of 1850, in his great surprise and pique the New Englander failed to understand how his bad behavior helped to send Webster to his grave. New England, busy with its own flowering, almost forbade to other sections of the nation any access to the secrets of pollination; on this side of the Atlantic it seemed to own all the intellectual bees.

A deep, driving force in New England became its wish to escape from reality. The genius of William Ellery Channing, aside from his nobility of character, rested in the fact that his Unitarianism discarded the old Puritan concept of personal guilt and vileness for a belief in man's essential goodness. Utopia became obtainable and New England groped toward it. Emerson was ever the incurable optimist; Bancroft, the historian, loved "to observe the bustle of the world" but detested "mixing in it"; and the statue of "Apollo Belvedere" that stood in the home of Edward Everett was suitably draped. Art like life became nicer if one did not look at it too candidly. Was it really surprising that at Gettysburg Mr. Everett could speak for two hours and not tell the world as much as Mr. Lincoln did in two minutes?

Nor should it have astounded even Melville that New England tended to shudder at *Moby Dick* with its overpowering arguments that evil was a force inherent within the structure of the universe and that man, if he were to save his soul, was destined through all eternity to fight this force with tooth and nail. In an age when white supremacy was the excuse for black slavery, when the peculiar institution required a peculiar morality, a peculiar Christianity, and a peculiar politics to support it, perhaps it was sheer luck in terms of historical symbolism that led Melville to write his magnificent chapter on the very whiteness of his whale.

Melville sees white as the cold color, the hue of terror and despair, the white shark lurking in the warm green sea, the elemental shade of nature's brutality and harlotry. Thus "the palsied universe lies before us like a leper"; thus we are "like wilful travellers in Lapland, who refuse to wear coloured or colouring glasses upon their eyes, so the wretched infidel gazes himself blind at the monumental white shroud that wraps all the prospect around him." The White Whale captures the heart of Captain Ahab; it eats away his feeling for humanity and we hear him tell his first mate: "Some men die at ebb-tide; some at low water; some at the full of the flood;—I feel like a billow that's all one crested comb."

That Melville believed at least part of intellectual New England was old in this sense we know from his criticism of Hawthorne, harping on human sin and ignoring the profound depth of evil— or, as Melville said, broadening the slash of his critical sword, the "great mistake" among all who "fancy he will come in the costume of Queen Elizabeth's day" and write dramas "founded upon

old English history or the tales of Boccaccio." There was no Utopia
in Melville for a New England desperately in need of Utopia;
for a New England that, strolling the pleasant Merrimack in the
spirit of Thoreau, came suddenly face to face with textile mills
and the underside of the industrial revolution; for a New England,
as Parrington states the case so lucidly, that was endeavoring "to
struggle free from the chains of the eighteenth century, only to
be bound by new chains."

Elusive Utopia! If there seemed little room here for Melville,
there was even less for William Lloyd Garrison, whom Parrington
captures in a telling phrase as "an agitator fashioned in the ancient
Hebraic pattern," perhaps borrowing an idea from Edmund
Quincy who in 1843 wrote that Garrison "wrapped up" a debate
"in some of his favorite Old Testament Hebraisms by way of
vehicle, as the apothecaries say." If the South detested Garrison,
it must be remembered that the Boston Tory loved no more this
spawn of a shiftless, drunken father. But his mother was Irish,
fearless in her bitter effort to raise her fatherless brood of three,
and in William that streak of the tenacious tigress endured. The
New England conscience among the intellectuals in Boston and
its spiritual suburbs of Cambridge and Concord tended to be soft
and yielding as they looked backward; but the less "cogitative,"
flinty Yankee tended to strike fire from the hard rock of his day-
by-day struggle for survival, and therein rested the essence of
Garrison's character.

His early career was about what one would expect—a drive of
passion that offset his lifelong ignorance. Garrison's early achieve-
ments were all small—apprenticed cobbler, carpenter and cabinetmaker, apprenticed printer and village editor—but in his protest
against the inhumanity of man and nature, this evil with which
he had lived since birth, he was of heroic dimension. That statement does not imply that he used his power wisely or justly; but
the power he both possessed and exerted. Remembering his
father's example, temperance was his first cause, and as a cold-

water crusader he marched until he chanced upon a copy of Benjamin Lundy's *Genius of Universal Emancipation.* Suddenly he was transformed; happily he went to jail for naming a Newburyport merchant he discovered trying to make a dollar in the coastal slave trade; and with a borrowed font of type he began *The Liberator,* informing his public that on the subject of slavery "I do not wish to think, or speak, or write, with moderation." He was then about twenty-six, and the year 1831; he died in 1879 without ever breaking that promise.

A little of the ascetic, dogmatic, arrogant Garrison comes close to being the sum of him, for he was that dedicated and primitive. "I will be heard," screamed the first issue of *The Liberator* in capitals, and indeed he was—shouting at a Philadelphia meeting in 1838, "Sir, slavery will not be overthrown without excitement, a most tremendous excitement"; denouncing the Constitution as "A Covenant with Death and an Agreement with Hell" and burning it in full view of everyone on Boston Common; defying all who would stone and degrade him—a Bowery mob in New York or shocked Bostonians in Faneuil Hall. Bold and perhaps even vulgar, an anarchist in the name "of God's dear Son," inflamed with his crusade to drive the moneychangers out of God's temples and the market places of human slavery, his was a power so great that in the end it resurrected John Brown from the grave. To understand New England in Christmas week, 1860, when the ferment of the nation had come to full strength in this holiest of Christian holidays, the croaking voice of Garrison must be heeded, just as one must remember why Webster disappointed New England so deeply, and why Harriet Beecher Stowe was impelled to write her novel.

Old "Black Dan," the country called Webster, sometimes with affection, sometimes with scalding annoyance. In either case, Webster learned in time to wear a mask over his own emotions, a true son of the granite slopes of New Hampshire. Among those rock-strewn foothills to some of the finest mountains in America,

Webster's life had turned on a February day in 1797. Riding in a carriage to the hillside village of Boscawen, the farmer-father who scraped from dawn to dusk to support his numerous family announced the momentous decision. He had been thinking about young Dan, Ebenezar Webster confessed; a boy who could make a passing teamster stop or a farmer pause with sickle in hand, listening to him recite verses of poetry and passages from the Bible, deserved his chance. So they were coming to Boscawen where Dan could study under the Reverend Wood and prepare for college. By some hook or crook, Ebenezar Webster grumbled, he'd find the money; and a warmhearted, emotional boy laid his head on his father's shoulder and wept.

New England for years adored Webster, for he seemed so sound, so consistent. Love of country, the grandeur of American nationality, fidelity to the Constitution, the nobility of the Union . . . in such terms Webster, a student at Dartmouth College, spelled out his faith in a Fourth of July oration to the townspeople of Hanover. The same faith, much the same Webster rose in the United States Senate a bit more than a quarter of a century later to reply to Robert Y. Hayne of South Carolina during the acrimonious debate on the tariff that produced the first threat of secession. On this day the Webster who once had caused farmers to pause with sickles in hand earned his laurel wreath as the American Demosthenes. Perhaps Webster departed at times from the strict letter of history—as certainly Hayne distorted the record to fit his case—but Webster was nonetheless masterful in the superb Attic simplicity with which he appealed to the common sense of his countrymen to reject the revolutionary doctrine of nullification. Schoolboys, committing to memory Webster's "Reply to Hayne" sometimes forgot the cussedness of that chore; in unpretentious sentences whose meanings shone like bayonets in the sunlight they beheld and responded to the fervid patriotism of Webster.

"Webster the great orator," praised Everett of the draped "Apollo," remembering that March day in 1850 when "Black Dan"

sat at his desk in the Senate, quietly taking the measure of a
hollow-eyed Clay and a scowling Calhoun. For the last time the
three old giants of the Senate, each moving in the shadow of
death, were crossing oratorical swords. The same old sputtering
fuse of slavery had turned the Senate (and the country) into a
sizzling powder keg whose staves were the states of Texas and
California, Utah and New Mexico. The nation sensed the drama
and Webster sensed the danger. Content to conserve his strength,
he watched and listened, quietly, thoughtfully, while the mind
that for a generation had dazzled Senate galleries with its eloquence turned over phrases: "I wish to speak . . . not as a
Massachusetts man, nor as a Northern man, but as an American."

Behind the mask of composure, "Black Dan" judged his men.
Clay he knew well—Clay whose passionate responses often made
him resemble a Mussulman rallying to the defense of his prophet
—"Clay the great leader," as Everett estimated this square-jawed
Kentuckian-by-adoption whom Kentucky-born Lincoln revered
as "*the* man for a crisis." Clay's illness showed in his eyes, but that
hadn't stopped him from coming out of retirement at the age
of seventy-three for one last effort to save the Union. Some
called Clay "the champion of the civilized world, and of all
tongues and kindreds and people" whose name had "mingled
with the battle-cry for freedom" when the Greeks rose against
the Turks and whose speeches Bolívar had read to South American armies casting off the bonds of Spanish domination. Webster
measured Clay in simpler terms; written into the Missouri Compromise of 1820 had been a restrictive clause imposing upon the
Missouri Legislature the duty of passing laws to prevent free
Negroes or mulattoes from coming into the state. The House of
Representatives had flatly refused to admit any territory as a
state under such a constitution; so the issue had come back to a
Senate committee, with Clay as chairman, and out of those
deliberations had emerged the resolution that forbade Missouri
ever to make any law prohibiting as settlers within its boundaries
any description of persons who then or thereafter might become

citizens of the Union. In no small measure, that resolution had been Clay's triumph.

Webster shifted his glance. Sheer intensity of will seemed to keep alive the man of whom Everett said: "Calhoun the great thinker." Beneath flannel-wrappings Calhoun's tubercular body wheezed miserably; at times the tip of his tongue moistened dried, feverish lips. Only weeks separated this devoted South Carolinian from the Abode that knew no disunion, and in this respect his old antagonists, Clay and Webster, who would live another two years, held him at a disadvantage. The courage of John C. Calhoun had never been doubted by Webster, nor had he ever denied the genius so closely akin to that of a John Stuart Mill in this man through whose veins the full flood of Southern passion had flowed for the past two decades. No one ever had been readier to defy the devil and Daniel Webster. When South Carolina had passed its ordinance nullifying the tariffs of 1828 and 1832, who but Calhoun had been sent to carry on the fight in the Senate as champion of this doctrine of state interposition? On a grim, chill December day Calhoun reached a hostile Washington. Both major parties opposed him, the Jackson Administration lashed out in menacing vituperation, but firm and undaunted the solitary rebel stood his ground, advancing his theory that a convention of the people of a state, under a state's constitutional compact, could declare null and void any law which it believed violated that compact, and inoperative the law must stand throughout the land until the states amended the Constitution to make valid through a new grant of power the law thus nullified by the people of a state.

Calhoun, the States Righter who belonged to neither the Democratic nor Whig Party, thus became the impulse behind that odd political courtship in America that ended in 1861 in a shotgun divorce. He stood with Democrats or Whigs, as the best interest of States Rights directed, never really confused until the War with Mexico seemed to drop "a curtain between the present and the future, which to me is impenetrable." Now he could not see the future: "It has closed the first volume of our political history under the Constitution, and opened the second, and no mortal can tell what will be written in it." Yet Calhoun had not long to wait for a glimpse of what was behind his "impenetrable curtain." The Wilmot Proviso declared that slavery should never be allowed in any territory acquired by treaty from Mexico and in two years in Congress Lincoln voted "as good as forty times" for the measure. Calhoun struck back, asserting that Congress possessed no right to enact any law which deprived any state "of its full and equal share in any territory of the United States acquired or to be acquired."

Now in 1850 Clay, whose heart had never deserted the Wilmot Proviso, proposed the speedy admission of California, the establishment of territorial governments in New Mexico and Utah without any restriction to slavery, the settlement of the boundary line between Texas and New Mexico as it substantially still stands, indemnity to Texas for the relinquishment of her claims in New Mexico, no interference with slavery in the District of Columbia, the prohibition of the slave trade in the district, and a more effective Fugitive Slave Law. Calhoun, too weak to take the floor, had his speech read by Senator Mason of Virginia: he yielded no principle.

The eyes in the Senate gallery turned to "Black Dan." Webster's "Seventh of March" speech supported Clay. By this plan, he said, the whole nation would be blanketed by compromises, and the slavery question settled. Natural conditions of soil and climate ruled out slavery for the regions west of Texas so that they required no Wilmot Proviso. But now Webster reached the Fugitive Slave Law, knowing the bitter hostility any support of this measure could stir up in the North. The law, he insisted, was simply a provision for carrying into effect a clause of the Constitution, without which that instrument could never have been adopted. With a few amendments, he accepted it—content in his own mind that slavery had been hemmed in, that the free labor of the North must win the predominant power in the nation, and that in time slavery must succumb to a natural death. No one need tell him that he spoke not as a Massachusetts man; rather, Emerson believed, Webster obeyed "his powerful animal nature" when he lashed out:

> . . . there are the Abolition societies, of which I am unwilling to speak, but in regard to which I have very clear notions and opinions. I do not think them useful. I think their operations for the last twenty years have produced nothing good or valuable. . . . I cannot but see what mischiefs their interference with the South has produced . . . everything these agitating people have done has been, not to enlarge, but to restrain, not to set free, but to bind faster, the slave population of the South.

Fighting words, these, in Garrisonian New England; Webster should have known the scorn that awaited him except, Emerson insisted, "all the drops of his blood have eyes that look downward"; and so "Black Dan" spent his last years in silent grief for the friends of his youth who had been turned from him by such "vagaries of the imagination" as abolitionism, free-soilism, transcendentalism. In the view of history the gain scarcely seemed to justify the sacrifice. On the surface the Compromise of 1850 appeared to be Clay's triumph with Webster's support, but the heavy infighting of the committee meetings revealed the extremist accepting the compromise only as an opportunity for bringing the more explosive elements in the controversy to other tests.

The decade of torment for America that ended with Christmas week, 1860, was thus begun. Dred Scott, Kansas-Nebraska, the bloody war in Kansas itself, Garrison burning the Constitution on Boston Common . . . so did the extremists force their tests and exert a will with which in the end there could be no compromise. From a Puritan mind nurtured on the electrifying Unitarian controversy and the still stormier passion of abolitionism came one of the most staggering blows. The iniquity of slavery wedded to the injustice of the Fugitive Slave Law shook every moral fiber in Harriet Beecher Stowe; pen dipped into the ink of wrath, she wrote *Uncle Tom's Cabin.*

On fields where vice eludes the light of day,
She hunts up crimes as beagles hunt their prey,
Gleans every dirty nook—the felon's jail,
And hangman's memory, for detraction's tale, . . .

So poetized South Carolina's William J. Grayson, but South Carolina's Mrs. Chesnut, in the privacy of her diary, was more shattered by Mrs. Stowe's novel than she almost dared to confess. All at once she found herself pouring out her heart:

> I hate slavery. You say there are no more fallen women on a plantation than in London, in proportion to numbers; but what do you say to this? A magnate who runs a hideous black harem with its consequences under the same roof with his lovely white wife, and his beautiful and accomplished daughters? He holds his head high and poses as the model of all human virtues to these poor women whom God and the laws have given him. From the height of his awful majesty, he scolds and thunders at them, as if he never did wrong in his life. Fancy such a man finding his daughter reading *Don Juan.* "You with that immoral book!" And he orders her out of his sight. You see, Mrs. Stowe did not hit the sorest spot. She makes Legree a bachelor.

Seven months later Mrs. Stowe's book was still on Mrs. Chesnut's mind:

> Read *Uncle Tom's Cabin* again. These Negro women have a chance here that women have nowhere else. They can redeem themselves—the "impropers" can. They can marry decently, but Mrs. Stowe revels in it. How delightfully Pharisaic a feeling it must be to rise superior, and fancy we are so degraded as to defend and like to live with such degraded creatures around us—such men as Legree and his women.

Little Evas, Mrs. Chesnut felt certain, mostly existed "in the heaven of Mrs. Stowe's imagination"; after all, "People can't love things dirty, ugly, and repulsive, simply because they ought to do so, but they can be good to them at a distance; that's easy." Three months later Mrs. Chesnut tried once more to read *Uncle Tom's Cabin,*

. . . and could not. It is too sickening. A man sent his little son
to beat a human being tied to a tree. It is as bad as Squeers beating
Smike. Flesh and blood revolt. You must skip that; it is too bad,
like the pulling out of the eyeballs in Lear.

Yet Mrs. Stowe touched something deep within Mrs. Chesnut—
"this monstrous system, a wrong and an iniquity," she would call
it on another occasion, wherein "like the patriarchs of old our
men live all in one house with their wives and their concubines."
Across the Black Belt in Mississippi the diary of young Kate Stone
would confess: "Always I felt the moral guilt of it [slavery],
felt how impossible it must be for an owner of slaves to win his
way into Heaven. Born and raised as we were, what would be our
measure of responsibility?" A Virginian noted in his journal:
"Cato born of Dinah, by some white chap on the commons,"
giving a clue to why in the Southern conscience there was no
geographical boundary to the dark thought of miscegenation. Sailing down the Red River, Frederick Law Olmsted observed
peddlers with paper-backed copies of Uncle Tom's Cabin: "They
did not cry it out as they did other books they had, but held
it forth among others, so its title could be seen." Later a planter
told of another planter who "had had a favourite, among his girls,
and suspecting that she was unduly kind to one of his men, in an
anger of jealousy he mutilated him." Didn't the incident corroborate Mrs. Stowe, Olmsted asked. "Ah," replied the storyteller,
"but then nobody would have any respect for a man that treated
his niggers cruelly." For all the cries of lies, trash, libels leveled
against the book, Mrs. Stowe's masterpiece of propaganda made
its inroads into a troubled South.

The first appearance of Uncle Tom's Cabin as a serial in a little
antislavery journal, National Era (1851), occasioned only a mild
response. With no extravagant anticipations, the Boston firm of
John P. Jewett & Company the following year risked an edition
of the novel in two somber volumes bound in black, but before
the year passed presses ran day and night to meet the demand.
Three hundred thousand copies were sold that year, and especially

popular was an edition in paper covers that could be bought for thirty-seven and a half cents. Twelve pirated editions appeared; before 1852 ended *Uncle Tom's Cabin* was selling in English and Spanish editions and the next year translations became available in French, German, Dutch, Italian, Danish, and Javanese—a few of the thirty-six languages in which Mrs. Stowe's harrowing tale ultimately could be read. In parlors across America piano racks held a flood of new songs, among them "Uncle Tom's Glimpse of Glory" with "Words written by Eliza and by her Respectfully Dedicated to Mrs. Harriet Beecher Stowe," "Little Eva, Uncle Tom's Guardian Angel" with words by John Greenleaf Whittier, and "Uncle Tom's Lament for Eva," carrying beneath its title the couplet:

> He strikes his harp immortal,
> To Eva's gentle song.

The first stage presentation was at Troy, New York, in the fall of 1852; Chicago playgoers had their first chance to weep for Uncle Tom and Little Eva at Rice's Theater that December, and their sea of tears was shared in New York and London and by January, 1853, in Paris where *La Case de l'Oncle Tom* wrenched hearts no less profoundly.

To scoff at *Uncle Tom's Cabin* and to call it childlike, artless, a literary monstrosity required no special critical training; and yet Tolstoy hailed its superb characterizations and intensity of incident. That Mrs. Stowe had communicated with the inner heart of humanity was not surprising—perhaps least of all to Mrs. Stowe, who insisted God had stood at her elbow while she wrote her book. She would speak of Garrison as "spiritually born of the eternal influences"—and his astral body at least must have been standing by Mrs. Stowe's other elbow as she labored over *Uncle Tom*. On meeting Mrs. Stowe, Lincoln said: "So this is the little woman who made the big war"; the historian, James Ford Rhodes, conceded that among the factors producing the Republican victory in 1860 *Uncle Tom's Cabin* was "one of the most important" and even the sober Woodrow Wilson admitted that the novel "played

no small part in creating the anti-slavery party." Damning Mrs.
Stowe became easy, ignoring her impossible.

Death at ebb tide, low water, the full of the flood . . . Captain
Ahab said to his first mate, "I am old; —shake hands with me,
man." And just as Captain Ahab was lost to his White Whale, so
was poor New England unable to escape from her own paradoxes.
She had sought pleasant Utopias so all could be as noble as Channing and as cheerily prosy as Emerson, and instead the thunderous
Garrison had led her by the nose, so to speak, down the road to
the New England Emigrant Aid Society and the Sharp's rifles
that had brought death in Kansas. She had been raised on the
ardent patriotism of Webster's "Reply to Hayne" and had seen that
patriotism turn against her in Webster's concessions on the Fugitive Slave Law. Her Edward Everett draped his "Apollo Belvedere" and a minister's daughter awakened in Southern white
womanhood tormenting thoughts of in what slave bed husband
or son was sleeping or whether, in vulgar lust on the dark commons, one or the other was responsible for "Cato born of Dinah."
Even her folk hero she failed to realize in any true dimension—
that old John Brown was crazed, that on Pottawatomie Creek
he had murdered senselessly a father and two sons dragged un-
armed from their beds, or that the widow, Mahala Doyle, had
written Brown after his capture by Colonel Lee at Harper's Ferry:
"You can now appreciate my distress in Kansas when you then
and there entered my house at midnight and arrested my husband
and two boys and took them out into the yard and in cold blood
shot them dead in my hearing. You can't say you did it to free
our slaves; we had none and never expected to own one. . . ."
New England's poets created monuments to man's goodness and
her propagandists inspired the savage impulse to war. And
through it all she felt remote, like her schoolboys arguing that if
a tree fell in a forest where no one could hear was there any sound,
except that in this instance the sound was of rifles barking in the
still and fearful Kansas night.

Troubled, disturbed, disrupted, New England certainly was in Christmas week, 1860, as the decade of torment started by Clay, Calhoun, and Webster came to its tense and bitter last hours. The evil of whiteness had crept into the green Berkshires, up the blue Merrimack, along the gray coasts of Maine. The protest in Whittier, his moralistic New England conscience shaken by Webster's "Seventh of March" concessions, rang in his verses:

And sandy Barnstable rose up, wet with the salt sea spray—
And Bristol sent her answering shout down Narragansett Bay!
Along the broad Connecticut old Hampden felt the thrill,
And the cheer of Hampshire's woodmen swept down from Holyoke
    Hill.

The voice of Massachusetts! Of her free sons and daughters—
Deep calling unto deep aloud the sound of many waters!
Against the burden of that voice what tyrant power shall stand?
No fetters in the Bay State! No slave upon her land!

Whittier, distrusting the Bostonian, spoke for the New England villager, wrapping his provincialism beneath the extra cloak of isolated hominess. "I pride myself," William M. Evarts told young Henry Adams, "on my success in doing not the things I like to do, but the things I don't like to do." For the New England youth growing up this was excellent advice; Webster, of course, applying the rule had never been forgiven, but then the mistake was in forgetting there was a New England passion as well as a New England conscience. And a New England excess. Sorry spectacle though it was to behold Charles Sumner of Massachusetts caned into insensibility on the Senate floor by Preston Brooks of South Carolina, yet the bitter, unpardonable invective that Sumner had employed in provoking the attack could not be denied. Here, New England could contend, and did contend, was the savage end to which Southern extremism led; but in doing so New England must ignore its own Reverend Theodore Parker inveighing against the South as "thriftless, idle, drunken, lewd, shrill-voiced . . . feeble bodied and ugly to look upon." Whether

the New England pot was less black than the Southern kettle
became a moot point. Thoreau could extoll the Merrimack and
Whittier the Connecticut, but did either know there was a river
in America called the Mississippi, or that on its western banks,
close to the border where the passions of North and South en-
twined, there was a robust and growing city called St. Louis?

9

Border City

S T. LOUIS in 1860 was a city of red brick. Stores, warehouses, schools, residences, churches, sidewalks, reflecting the rich clay deposits near-by, all turned ruddy cheeks to the visitor. Situated on bluffs and on terraces rising one above the other, this border city on the western bank of the Mississippi had its own character, charm, and troubles. "Trees won't grow worth shucks in a Cincinnati graveyard," declared Mark Twain's Child of Calamity, "but in a Sent Louis graveyard they grow upwards of eight hundred foot high. It's all on account of the water the people drunk before they laid up. A Cincinnati corpse don't richen a soil any."

Even the visitor to St. Louis, less learned in local lore than the Child of Calamity, retained vivid impressions—of very few front yards since most dwellings were built out to the street, of chimneys belching dense columns of black smoke that on calm autumn and winter days "hung like a pall over the city," of hot summers with "the stifling heat, swelling up like a mouse in an exhausted receiver," of a compact city that stretched six and a half miles along the river, and from three to four from it, of side-wheelers and stern-wheelers tied up at the wharves, of from fifty to sixty thousand Germans who were a sizable part of the city's 151,780 inhabitants.

Other traits made St. Louis distinctive. White males outnumbered the females by ten thousand. Coal was bought by the bushel. About fifteen hundred slaves resided in St. Louis, for this was a city where North met South—in somewhat sullen, distrustful silence after Lincoln's election. St. Louis was the home of old Tom Benton, slaveowning Senator who had growled when his son-in-law, John C. Frémont, was offered the Republican nomination in 1856; "If you accept the nomination, I'll drop you like a hot potato, sir! like a hot potato, sir!"; of the Reverend Richard Anderson, free Negro, descendant of an African chief and "very black"; of Dred Scott, voluntarily emancipated by his master, and portering in a hotel; of the Honorable R. M. Stewart, former governor of the state and stanch Bourbon Democrat, telling anyone who cared to listen, "Cotton is not king, but corn and corn-whiskey are"; of Frank Blair, Jacksonian turned Republican, whose drooping mustache and long goatee seemed to belong behind a mint julep and whose brother Montgomery became Lincoln's Postmaster General; of Edward Bates, Missouri's disappointed favored son at the Chicago Convention, who became Attorney General in Mr. Lincoln's Cabinet.

Whereas in Missouri the Presidential election settled into a nip-and-tuck contest between John Bell of the Constitutional Union Party and Stephen A. Douglas of the Northern wing of the Democratic Party—Douglas won by one-tenth of one per cent of the vote—Lincoln polled more than seventeen thousand votes, almost wholly in St. Louis, Gasconade, and Cole counties. The large German population in the city was strongly for Lincoln and the Union, for these were the soldiers who in another year would march off to war proudly singing:

> When I comes from der Deutsche Countree,
> I vorks sometimes at baking;
> Den I keeps a lager beer saloon,
> Und den I goes shoe making;
> But now I was a sojer been

To save der Yankee Eagle;
To schlauch dem tam secession volks,
I'm going to fight mit Sigel.*

St. Louis Germans made good Republican Wide-Awakes, marching to torchlights, hurrahing for Lincoln, and jeering the Douglas
supporters who called themselves Minute Men.

Down from the free soil of Wisconsin came sober, bearded,
bespectacled, Prussian-born Carl Schurz, fluent orator in German
or English, to rally his fellow countrymen to Lincoln by speaking
on "The Doom of Slavery." Thundered Schurz, who barely had
escaped to Switzerland after the 1849 revolutions in the Palatinate
and at Baden: "Imagine a future generation standing around the
tombstone of the bravest of you, and reading the inscription, 'Here
lies a gallant man, who fought and died for the cause—of human
slavery.' What will the verdict be? His very progeny will disown
him, and exclaim, 'He must have been a knave or a fool.' " Three
thousand crowded Verandah Hall to hear Schurz condemn slavery
that educated no one except as servants, that developed no domestic
industries, and demanded class privileges instead of privileges for
all. Schurz was voicing the aspirations of the first-generation
American. In free labor, in educational opportunity resided the
hope of their brave, new world. Galusha Anderson, clergyman,
loyal Lincoln man, responded to Schurz's virile, fearless speech
and believed that he "strengthened feeble knees, stiffened gelat-
inous backbones, and gave courage to the faint-hearted." Yet just
as Henry Adams in Quincy, Massachusetts, recognized that the
Wide-Awakes were "military in all things except weapons" so
Galusha Anderson in St. Louis could feel, as Schurz spoke, "the
first breath of the coming battle between freedom and slavery."

Actually that Christmas week, 1860, Galusha Anderson felt the
coming battle much more intimately than Henry Adams in Wash-

* Franz Sigel, born in Baden in 1824, came to America in 1856 and at the outbreak of the Civil War organized a regiment that served with distinction. Sigel's
rank at the close of the war was that of Major General.

ington or Horace Greeley in New York or Mr. Lincoln in Springfield. Those who had prayed for Lincoln's defeat, Anderson realized, "seemed to settle down into sullen, silent, blank despair"; those who were joyous at the Republican victory "gave little or no public expression of their giddiness, lest they might unduly vex their disappointed and downhearted neighbors"; but under the surface calm "there were clandestine, but energetic, movements that portended armed conflict." Neither the Wide-Awakes nor the Minute Men disbanded their organizations; they were openly hostile groups now, Unionists opposed to secessionists. Except at the Arsenal only one Federal flag hung in the city—and that, floating over the entrance to a dry-goods store, was there "partly, as we thought, from patriotic, and partly from mercenary, motives." No minister dared preach in behalf of the Republic. No one sang "My Country 'Tis of Thee"; no one heard played "The Star-Spangled Banner." Tense, the city waited; then, in grim and ominous uncertainty, it heard the news of secession in South Carolina. Galusha Anderson sensed the brittleness of the city:

> . . . Upon which side our neighbors, our partners in business, and often those of our own households would array themselves it was difficult to determine. Nor could we forget that the announcement of the secession of a State might lead to bloody conflict in our streets. Under such peculiar circumstances the proposed, or actual, secession of States stirred profoundly our whole city. The excitement was not noisy, it was too deep for that. Men met, and transacted their business, without uttering a word concerning the country. Many of the most thoughtful seemed to hold their breath and listen to the beating of their hearts. Not because they were afraid, but because, standing in the presence of such portentous movements, they did not yet know what they ought to do.

Where the secessionist Minute Men were obtaining arms with which to drill was anybody's guess, but the evidence seemed strong that treason had reached inside the Arsenal. In any case, the Union boys had no intention of being outsmarted or caught napping.

Nothing could have appeared more innocent or less warlike than
the public art exhibit they arranged. St. Louis agreed that the
affair was both a critical and a financial success. Boxes marked
"plaster casts," arriving from New York, aroused no one's suspicion. After midnight when the exhibit doors were closed the
Wide-Awakes gleefully unpacked these boxes. "Shining muskets
never gave more joy than these imparted to the Union men of
St. Louis," Galusha Anderson declared; and those two Copperheads, Fernando and Ben Wood, plotting treason over their
whiskey toddies at the Astor House, did not know as much about
"some patriots of Gotham" as the Reverend Galusha Anderson
and his cronies.

Nor were the Union boys satisfied with this action. A custom
each New Year's Day was to sell at public auction from the granite
steps of the Court House such slaves as must be disposed of at
their market value to settle up estates in St. Louis and St. Louis
County. On the appointed day the slave auctioneer appeared with
seven human chattels—"the thinking fag-ends of estates," Anderson called them—placed the slaves on a pedestal of one of the
great pillars of the Court House, and looked down at the crowd
around him. Never had any sale drawn better. That two thousand
Union sympathizers were there for purposes of their own was a
well-kept secret.

With bright confidence the auctioneer began: "What will you bid
for this able-bodied boy? There's not a blemish on him."

An angry roar came back from the crowd: "Three dollars!
Three dollars!" For ten minutes, fifteen, twenty, the chant continued. The auctioneer tried to take the performance as a joke.

"Now, gentlemen," he managed to say at last, in a bantering
tone, "don't make fools of yourselves. What will you bid for this
boy?"

"Four dollars! Four dollars!"

The crowd's indignant outcry, coming in waves, rolled over
the auctioneer, so that his own frantic cries, in Anderson's opinion,
"were as futile as if he had attempted to whistle a tornado into

silence." Finally a break came in the jeers and catcalls. The auctioneer began anew:

"How much will you bid for this first-class nigger?"

"Five dollars! Five dollars!"

At the end of two hours the auctioneer had not received a bid above eight dollars. Exasperated and defeated, he led his seven human chattels back to jail. St. Louis had held its last public slave auction.

But the triumph was in no sense all on the side of the Union boys. A delegation from Alabama wasn't traveling through Missouri, talking long, hard, and seriously, without the consent of Governor-elect Claiborne F. Jackson. Claib was a strong-minded old rascal; he had married in succession three daughters of the Dr. Sappington whose quinine pills were the standard frontier remedy for malaria. "I reckon you'll be back next for the old woman," growled Sappington, getting to know the measure of Claib. The Governor-elect had led Missourians into Kansas during the bloody wars there in '55, and Claib, committed to slavery, didn't intend to give up on that idea any more than on Dr. Sappington's females. If Claib was left alone to rig the Legislature, he intended to deliver Missouri to the Confederacy. Nor was Brigadier General Daniel M. Frost, in charge of the militia, any comfort to the Union men; he was hand in glove with Claib. The worry, deep and real, was that Claib would steal the government and Frost the Arsenal. Sometimes during Christmas week in St. Louis the Union boys couldn't talk about anything but this danger. Those Germans who soon would "fight mit Sigel" didn't say too much, but their angry eyes said if the secessionists tried it, blood would run in the streets of St. Louis.

In time, it did. In time, a lady informed Galusha Anderson that the first chance she got she'd shoot Frank Blair. "I have a revolver," she snapped when the minister chided her, "and I am practising with it every day in the back yard and have already become a good shot." The emotional conflict along the border was as intense and enduring as the revolt of the ancients in South Carolina. An eminent Missourian of a later generation realized this fact when he invited his mother to the White House and offered her the accommodations of the Lincoln Room. "You tell Harry," this "unreconstructed rebel" told President Truman's sister, "if he puts me in the room with Lincoln's bed in it, I'll sleep on the floor."

Yet for others in 1860 the issue was not so easily resolved. The most articulate Missourian that the Civil War generation would produce, Sam Clemens, felt the tug of divided loyalty in his own heart; as his biographer Paine points out, when in December South Carolina seceded, Sam felt "strong for the Union," but later "decided, like Lee, that he would go with his State [that part of it Claib Jackson influenced] and lead battalions to victory." In "The Private History of a Campaign that Failed," Sam recalled his personal dilemma:

> Out West there was a good deal of confusion in men's minds during the first months of the great trouble—a good deal of unsettledness, of leaning first this way, then that, then the other way. It was hard for us to get our bearings. I call to mind an instance of this. I was piloting on the Mississippi when the news came that South Carolina had gone out of the Union on the 20th of December, 1860. My pilot mate was a New-Yorker. He was strong for the Union; so was I. But he would not listen to me with any patience; my loyalty was smirched, to his eye, because my father had owned slaves. I said, in palliation of this dark fact, that I had heard my father say, some years before he died, that slavery was a great wrong, and that he would free the solitary Negro he then owned if he could think it right to give away the property of the family when he was so straitened in means. My mate retorted that a mere impulse was nothing—anybody could pretend a good impulse; and went on decrying my Unionism and libeling my ancestry. A month later the secession atmosphere had considerably thickened on the Lower Mississippi, and I became a rebel; so did he. We were together in New Orleans the 26th of January, when Louisiana went out of the Union. He did his full share of the rebel shout-

ing, but was bitterly opposed to letting me do mine. He said that I came of bad stock—of a father who had been willing to set slaves free. In the following summer he was piloting a Federal gunboat and shouting for the Union again, and I was in the Confederate army. I held his note for some borrowed money. He was one of the most upright men I ever knew, but he repudiated that note without hesitation because I was a rebel and the son of a man who owned slaves.

Sam's war experiences reached their bitterest moments when he developed a boil and spent days sitting on a pile of hay in a horse trough. A few evenings later one of the boys who shared a hayloft with him turned out to be a careless smoker. Sam aroused to a scream of "Fire!" sprained his ankle leaping down, and decided right then that he was heading north to see his brother Orion in Iowa, a Union man and an infernal abolitionist to boot. All his life Sam dreamed of making Joan of Arc his purest, greatest character, but it was out of his Missouri boyhood, as Dixon Wecter has observed, that Sam drew his "noblest creation." His Joan of Arc "turns to plaster saint," but Nigger Jim "is as vital and earth-bound as one of the lofty hickories that towered over the old farmstead" with its slave quarters where Sam spent his summers. Nigger Jim belongs to Sam's mature years when the Son of the Border berated King Leopold's brutalities in the Congo; to the Sam who spent a fortune publishing and promoting the book of one of his heroes—*Personal Memoirs of U. S. Grant.*

But in 1860, piloting his steamboat upriver from New Orleans, Sam was still the Son of the Border, confused and perplexed. A single trip carried him deep into the origins of the greater confusion and perplexity that comprised the troubled American conscience. When he sailed by Vicksburg, Mississippi, a city unsuspecting of the terrible doom that would befall it in less than three years, he was in the Black Belt of which South Carolina was the germinal center, Calhoun the prophet, Jefferson Davis the heir. Further North, passing Memphis, he reached another South, an older South, for Tennessee and Kentucky were the "intellectual heirs" of Virginia, with Jefferson the prophet and Jackson and Lincoln the distinguished political offspring. Next came St. Louis and Missouri—the fretful border, mixing North and the two Souths, and extending beyond Cairo into that part of Southern Illinois called "Egypt"—where Stephen A. Douglas, riding two horses, was the political marvel for so long.

In Washington one last great effort at compromise remained to be made. From the Old South—Andrew Johnson of Tennessee and John Crittenden of Kentucky with their stepchild, Douglas of Illinois—would come the militant leadership of that effort at compromise. Here the illusions of individuality that divided New England and the South, the Northwest and the Border States again locked in battle. Yet there was a difference now. It was not to any section that another compromise must be sold, but to Mr. Lincoln in Springfield. None of this Sam Clemens knew, steering by the China trees around a river bend.

10

Old Buck Blocks the Game

IN A BIG, old-fashioned collar with starched white choker, President Buchanan touched the heart of Mrs. William H. Gwin. The President was no frosty old bachelor to the wife of the Senator from California. She remembered gallant "Old Buck" from those pleasanter years in the friendly, overgrown village Washington had been—when at intimate dinners in the White House the President had carved his own roast, when the rock bass biting at Little Falls or the loveliness of the hyacinths in spring had been cheerful topics of conversation, when the concerts by Scala's Marine Band in the President's Park had been exciting events on Saturday afternoons. Now the election of Mr. Lincoln had changed everything, and writing to Mrs. Howell Cobb in Georgia Mrs. Gwin described the President: "He looks badly, his face indicates much unhappiness and when I see him I feel like comforting him, but you know him well enough to know no one could approach him in that way." Strongly pro-slavery herself, Mrs. Gwin was on safe ground commenting that the feeling among the Southerners in the capital "is most violent against the President, the denunciation of him is fearful. I often wonder how he can stand it. He has given up his evening walk. I think that makes him feel worse."

Yet other points of view prevailed. To many the enterprising Washington merchant who advertised, "Readers, the Union is in danger, but by buying your holiday presents at Lammond's, you *may* save it," came close to the kind of solution the President was seeking to rid the Executive Mansion of the political skeletons that, in their estimation, hung in every closet. As many more doubted that even the morning prayers to which the President faithfully attended could yield the wisdom necessary for coping with a Democratic Party which, reflecting the conglomerate of disruptive influences sweeping America, had disintegrated into a hodgepodge of hostile splinter groups. Edward A. Pollard, Richmond journalist, identified only as "a distinguished Virginian politician" the author of the remark that to see Buchanan "cowering beneath the full-length portrait of Andrew Jackson on the mantelpiece of the reception-room of the White House, munching on a dry cigar, and asking querulously what he could do, or what he should do, was more than human patience could endure, or human pity tolerate." Nor did Pollard deny his own contempt for the President, calling him "this despicable old man . . . grotesquely balancing on the question of peace and war."

Buchanan belonged to the last of the line of Presidents who for twelve years, in Walt Whitman's opinion, had filled the Executive Mansion with "deformed, mediocre, sniveling, unreliable, falsehearted men." Approaching now the age of seventy, Buchanan had been twenty-eight when his engagement to Anne C. Coleman had been broken because, fairly or unfairly, his name had been linked with that of another woman; when Miss Coleman was found dead in a Philadelphia hotel there was unsubstantiated gossip of suicide; and though Buchanan pleaded for "the melancholy pleasure of seeing her body before its interment" he was not permitted to attend the funeral.

For the remainder of Buchanan's life he went his lonely way, a bachelor, distant if not afraid of women, serving as minister to Russia and at the Court of St. James's, acquiring a personal fortune of three hundred thousand dollars, and gaining the Presidential nomination in 1856 because to Senator Slidell of Louisiana, to Virginia's Governor Wise, to New York's wealthy August Belmont he was clearly "a safe man." During the early years of the Buchanan Administration many Washingtonians wondered if the White House ever had known a more gracious occupant; Jefferson Davis compared the Executive Mansion to an elegant republican court, yet Buchanan mingled easily with the crowds that came to President's Park to hear the band concerts; and his niece, Harriet Lane, installed as hostess at the White House, achieved the solid popularity of having both a warship and a race horse named in her honor.

That a life so pleasant should suddenly be torn asunder staggered Buchanan, who misread almost every sign to the bitter end. He never came to grips with what was happening to America—not, at any rate, to the degree of shrewd old John A. Campbell of Alabama, associate justice of the Supreme Court, who blazed away:

> The truth is that the grievances complained of by the cotton States are either not material or not remediable. What guarantee will prevent the denunciation of slavery and slaveholders in the pulpit, press and academy? What will prevent the pragmatical and conceited Yankee from making foreign newspapers and magazines the vehicle of his mendacity and spite? What will prevent their women and fanatics from making petitions to Congress and their politicians from irritating the Southern representatives? Who can give self-control to Southern members or prevent them from showing that slavery is ordained by Heaven?

Buchanan didn't seek objectivity; he wanted escape. Yet he was not quite Pollard's "despicable old man"; nor did he deserve the cruel verse in *Vanity Fair* about "a White Old House with a gray old rat, fidgeting ever and blind as a bat." Some facts he understood clearly; some he ignored deliberately. Human, political, and economic forces all beat upon him, and under that shock he became rather like Lear roaring at the wild storm.

"Old Buck"—he was also "Old Venison" and "Old Obliquity" to his enemies now—had inherited a body politic covered with festering wounds, as should have been expected after a bitter campaign in which Democrats had fought Democrats every bit as viciously as they had battled Republicans. Mrs. Gwin, moving Mrs. Benjamin Fitzpatrick to the point of tearful hysterics in pleading with her husband not to throw away his political future by becoming Douglas's running mate, gave a good indication of the passions at play. Nothing, of course—not even breaking health—could stop Douglas from plunging into the campaign with incredible energy. He was like a wounded animal intent on cleaning out the entire forest—damning Breckinridge and his coterie as conspirators who wanted only to destroy the Union, and carrying this gospel to New England, to North Carolina, to the Border States, to the Middle West, and winding up in Mobile on Election Day with sufficient breath to contend that he was the one Democrat who could beat Lincoln and save the country.

What the nation had witnessed was a political phenomenon, for Douglas, denied the support of his full party, was the first candidate in American history to go to the people. There was a Vermont toughness in Stephen A. Douglas that refused to be either badgered or bluffed. Left fatherless at the age of two months, his Vermont boyhood at fifteen had consisted of the hard, cease-less toil of a farm broken during the three winter months when he attended school. Then for eighteen months he was an appren-tice to a cabinetmaker until poor health forced him to abandon this job. Deciding his mother could not support him while he studied law, he determined to seek his fortune in the Western country and the discouragements of that experience might have broken a less aggressive spirit. For four months Douglas was prostrated by fever in Cleveland, then searched unsuccessfully for employment in Cincinnati and St. Louis, Louisville and southern Illinois before he arrived in the town of Winchester one gloomy night with thirty-seven and a half cents as his worldly fortune. Here his luck changed. Three days as a clerk to an auctioneer brought him six dollars and a chance to teach in a school. Within a year he had gained a license to practice law and had won his first reputation as a political orator in support of the Jackson Administration. "I sincerely doubt whether I owe most to my friends," Douglas said at the time, "or to the violent, reckless, and imprudent opposition of my enemies." For anyone possessing the combative instincts of Douglas a pattern had been established and how far it carried him Lincoln admitted in 1856:

> Twenty-two years ago Judge Douglas and I first became ac-
> quainted. We were both young then; he a trifle younger than I.
> Even then, we were both ambitious; I, perhaps, quite as much so
> as he. With *me,* the race of ambition has been a failure—a flat
> failure; with *him* it has been one of splendid success. His name
> fills the nation; and is not unknown, even, in foreign lands. I
> affect no contempt for the high eminence he has reached. So
> reached, that the oppressed of my species, might have shared with
> me in the elevation, I would rather stand on that eminence, than
> wear the richest crown that ever pressed a monarch's brow.

Where the Republican Lincoln and the Southern extremist broke with Douglas in 1860 was on his position that slavery was a question for each territory to decide. The issue never had been more sharply drawn—Lincoln determined that there must be no further extension of slavery, and the extremists, holding tenaciously to the victory of the Dred Scott decision, stanch in their belief that Congress must protect the property rights of the slaveowner wherever he settled. If, as was entirely likely, the original bolt of the Democrats at the Baltimore Convention was simply a bluff aimed at dumping Douglas as a candidate, the stratagem was quickly out of hand. To anyone who understood the essential nature of Douglas no mystery should have surrounded the failure of later efforts to effect a reconciliation. So the Democratic Party broke apart, some adherents supporting Douglas, others Breckinridge, still others switching to Bell, and down in Texas Sam Houston ran for President on a ticket of his own.

Yet for the nation, in Shakespeare's imagery, it was not alone the acrimonious Democratic campaign oratory of 1860 that "pierced to the soul with slander's venom'd spear, the which no balm can cure." Although Douglas and Breckinridge together polled some four hundred thousand votes more than Lincoln, if all the candidates who opposed the Republican had pooled their tallies in the Electoral College they would have failed by twenty-one votes of defeating Lincoln. The will of the nation put Lincoln into office and he owed no apology for that victory.

Emotionally the South desired separate nationhood, but inherent within the campaign of 1860, for all the South rushed on toward secession, were the seeds that would produce the withered fruit of its own ultimate destruction. In those sections where the vote of the Electoral College favored Lincoln the country had pretty well recovered from the depression of 1857 and the South had not. The Middle West with bumper crops in prospect would have money to spend, a good part of the appeal to businessmen in Mr. Lincoln's candidacy. Nor was it an idle comment when the New York *Herald* advised its readers to get rid of Southern securities and to collect what Southern debts they could. By November, both North and South, banks had grown jittery over loans and in the Southern states gold was so scrupulously hoarded that except for banks in Louisiana and three banks in Alabama specie payments were discontinued. One needed only eyes to see how trade was falling off in Southern ports; one needed only to offer Southern bonds for sale in New York to feel heartsick at the heavy discount demanded; and if one owned a store in the South, one tended to reduce inventories and await developments.

The excitable arguments by which the conspiracy was nourished—the flood of rumors concerning incipient slave insurrections, the claims that Lincoln intended to fill every town in the South with a postmaster who was at least a rabid Unionist if not a free Negro—blinded Southerners to how deeply they floundered in a debtor's economy. Of an estimated twenty-five million dollars in gold in Southern banks, two-fifths of this amount was in New Orleans banks where Louisiana law then made it untouchable for any future government of seceding states. The cutback in inventories only aggravated shortages that already existed in clothing, medical supplies, coffee and sugar, leather and wool, salt, grains, iron, tin, copper, and numerous household articles. These were the grim economic facts of November that the secessionists, gathering in Washington in December, refused to see. They were hellbent to get out of the Union, and it came as an unpleasant incident to them when, as South Carolina's Keitt grumbled to Edward Pollard, Buchanan momentarily "blocked the game."

Howell Cobb of Georgia, Secretary of the Treasury, probably spoke the sentiment of the three Southerners in the President's Cabinet when he called Buchanan "the truest friend to the South that ever sat in the Presidential chair." Usually a gay and bantering fellow, Cobb was plunged into gloom by the election, the more so since "Old Buck's" first impulse was to issue some sort of soft, tongue-in-cheek statement of policy that would postpone secession at least until Lincoln's inauguration when, for all Buchanan cared, the Republicans could get out of the mess they had created. Rumors even before Election Day that South Carolina had seized the Federal forts came close to unstringing the President, who growled at Virginia's John B. Floyd, his Secretary of War, that unless those forts were held "it were better for you and me both to be thrown in the Potomac with millstones tied about our necks."

Floyd and Cobb, with help from Mississippi's Jacob Thompson, Secretary of the Interior, succeeded in allaying the President's first sick wave of alarm and the impulse to issue an immediate proclamation. Floyd especially was all soothing syrup, insisting that he had sent a very good man in Fitz-John Porter to make a personal inspection of Charleston Harbor and, really, nothing more was needed but a change in commanders. Colonel Gardner, true enough, was a proslavery man, but might not his Boston birthplace constitute a possible irritant? Men of Southern background were much to be preferred, in Floyd's opinion, and he suggested Kentucky-born Major Anderson to take over Fort Moultrie and Charleston's own Colonel Benjamin Huger to command at the Arsenal.

"Old Buck" looked almost as cheered as he often was by the fine nutty flavor of a glass of old Madeira. Congress would reconvene in December; he would handle the "situation" in his annual message. Under mounting pressure from Georgia to come home and help the secessionists, Cobb lingered in Washington, for the struggle within the Cabinet had far from abated. None of the Southerners was cheered by the opinion of Jeremiah S. Black, the Attorney General, that "the Union is necessarily perpetual" and that "it can meet, repel and subdue all those who rise against it." Cobb made certain that his counterarguments were part of the President's meditations when he sought divine guidance each morning, and Thompson appeared willing to read himself blind as he culled through the proceedings of the Constitutional Convention of 1787 for proof that the Founding Fathers had not denied the right of secession.

Buchanan's crossness increased under this tug of war. He ordered Black to write him an opinion that delved less into politics. Lewis Cass, Secretary of War, supported Black's private opinion that if "Old Buck" would show a little backbone and re-enforce those forts they could all forget the fuss over legal arguments. A recommendation from Major Anderson that the forts be re-enforced strengthened Black and Cass, but now South Carolina's William H. Trescott, Assistant Secretary of State, protested thunderously. Re-enforcing those forts would be a hostile act and he would resign immediately, not caring a snap if his resignation were interpreted by Charlestonians as a signal to storm the forts. Buchanan wished he were already home in Pennsylvania, living out his declining years in rural peace. The time had arrived, he decided, to summon to the White House to give him advice his old and dear friend, Senator Jefferson Davis of Mississippi.

Davis's solution for the problem of the forts outsyruped Floyd.

All that was required, suggested Davis, was to place the forts in the hands of ordnance sergeants as caretakers. Cass implored heaven to bring Buchanan to his senses; but Floyd assured the President that Mr. Davis was indeed a remarkably astute man, and "Old Buck," having thrust his head into the mouth of the Southern lion, decided to leave it there. A communication from the Governor of South Carolina supported Davis's contention that if no hostile act were taken, Federal property rights would be respected. How well Davis, Cobb, Floyd, Thompson, and Trescott had carried the day with the President became clear when on December third Buchanan sent his message to Congress.

Why at a time when "plenty smiles throughout the land" did discontent "now so extensively" prevail, asked Buchanan, answering huffily that "the long-continued and intemperate interference of the Northern people with the question of slavery in the Southern States has at last produced its natural effects." Yet neither the agitation to exclude slavery from the territories nor the ineffective execution of Fugitive Slave Laws, in the President's judgment, had produced "the immediate perils"; the cause, Buchanan insisted, resided in inspiring within slaves "vague notions of freedom." Swallowing every campaign report of impending slave insurrections, Buchanan blanched to think how "Many a matron throughout the South retires at night in dread of what may befall herself and her children before the morning." What if "this apprehension of domestic danger, whether real or imaginary, shall extend and intensify itself until it shall pervade the masses of the Southern people?" Buchanan could see but one result: "Disunion will become inevitable" for "self-preservation is the first law of nature."

Not Lincoln's election, the President declared in a later passage, but the personal liberty laws in the Northern states had endangered the South, and unless these laws were repealed "the injured States, after having first used all peaceful and constitutional means to obtain redress, would be justified in revolutionary re-

sistance to the government of the Union." Still later, much of the
same thought that inspired Ben and Fernando Wood, whispering
at the Astor House, emerged in this paragraph:

> The fact is that our Union rests upon public opinion, and can
> never be cemented by the blood of its citizens shed in civil war.
> If it can not live in the affections of the people, it must one day
> perish. Congress possibly possesses many means of preserving it
> by conciliation, but the sword was not placed in their hands to
> preserve it by force.

Neither confirmed secessionist nor budding Copperhead could
have stated his case more forcefully. Certainly "Old Buck" had
offended no one looking for an excuse to carry through the
conspiracy; as Keitt complained, that happy event now "must wait
for contingencies." But the President was satisfied. He had wrig-
gled off Mr. Lincoln's hook.

II

A Fretful Christmas

WITH the White House virtually flying the blue banner
of secession from its flagpole, the battle between Unionists
and disunionists shifted to the floor of Congress. Once again
Associate Justice John A. Campbell of Alabama saw the fundamental issue clearly. In objecting to a President-elect who held
"political or social opinions" contrary to their own, secessionists
had no respect "for written law or for judicial decision nor confidence that they afforded protection." What had excited these
forces, Campbell insisted, "is the agitation of tumultuous political
assemblies, and this is not within the reach of law or decision."
Tom Corwin, Congressman from Ohio, defined the difficulty
more succinctly: "Southern men are theoretically crazy. Extreme
Northern men are practical fools." Yet after hearing some of the
wild suggestions that rocked the caucus rooms—one, for example,
would have had Buchanan seize at once San Juan Island since a
neat little war with Great Britain would make the country forget
secession—Corwin's ridicule was understandable.

In the House on December fourth a Committee of Thirty-three
was organized in an effort to find some way to save the Union,
but Singleton of Mississippi declined to vote for the Committee,
declaring he had not been sent to Washington to make compromises or patch up existing difficulties; Hawkins of Florida
announced that the day of compromise had passed; Clopton of

129

Alabama, hardheaded in support of the right of secession, refused to hold out any "delusive hope"; Miles of South Carolina would make no move without instructions from home; and Pugh of Alabama made no secret of the fact that his state soon would be withdrawing from the Union and he saw no point in paying any attention to action taken in this body. When Hawkins of Florida and Boyce of South Carolina heard themselves named to the Committee they asked to be excused from this service. The House refused.

A bewildering assortment of propositions poured into the Committee's chambers. Thayer of Massachusetts wanted the spirit of the Founding Fathers reaffirmed, along with a resolution that would endorse self-government in the territories and establish the principle that no more territory ever should be acquired. Cochrane of New York was filled with motions, all stemming from his belief that the decision of the Supreme Court in the Dred Scott Case should be received as a settlement of all questions. Stevenson of Kentucky wanted the Fugitive Slave Law amended so that any resistance to it became a felony; Kilgore of Indiana thought the right of trial by jury should exist where a fugitive slave claimed to be free; McClernand of Illinois proposed a special Federal police force to execute the laws of the United States; Noell of Missouri wished to abolish the office of President and substitute a Council of Three, each elected from a district of contiguous states and each possessing the power of veto; Smith of Virginia was for declaring out of the Union every state which aimed by legislation to nullify an act of Congress. From Morris of Pennsylvania came insistence that personal liberty laws be amended to prevent the kidnapping of slaves; from Cox of Ohio a request for legislation that would punish all judges, attorney generals, executives, and other state officers who opposed execution of the Fugitive Slave Law; from Dunn of Indiana a resolution that Section 2, Article 4 of the Constitution be amended to secure the personal rights of citizens of any state, traveling or sojourning in any other state. "If the States are no more harmonious in their feelings and opinions than these thirty-three representative men, then, appalling as the idea is, we must dissolve, and a long and bloody civil war must follow," a letter from Ohio's Tom Corwin advised Mr. Lincoln.

Washington bristled with secret meetings—in the garret of the marble-fronted Brown Hotel on Sixth Street; in Breckinridge's home on Minnesota Row, where Douglas also lived; at the bar of the National on Sixth, at last living down the strange epidemic of intestinal disorders that had afflicted its patrons at the time of Buchanan's inaugural and which some Southerners had called a Republican plot to poison the stalwarts of the Democratic Party; at the staid old Kirkwood on Twelfth Street and that successful caravansary of those two Vermont brothers—Willard's at Fourteenth. New Yorkers met alone in John Cochrane's room; delegates from Ohio, Pennsylvania, and Illinois tried flocking together; Southerners tended to group into cliques, dividing the secessionist sheep from the goats. Considerably more blancmange and *pâté de foie gras,* Willard's noonday specialties, was digested than consensus of opinion obtained; Washington bartenders carried home lame arms at night, probably the first casualties that the conflict produced. A few Congressmen could remember when in 1843 with poor Sam Morse on the verge of starvation Congress had appropriated thirty thousand dollars to string a test line of the magnetic telegraph between Washington and Baltimore; now telegraph lines reached into almost every community of the country, offering a new medium for the dissemination of rumor and propaganda in the present war of nerves.

Among the first to become distinguished for perfecting "treason by telegraph" were twenty-two Congressmen representing Alabama, Georgia, Florida, Mississippi, North Carolina, Louisiana, and Texas. Only nine days had passed since the Committee of Thirty-three had been organized when this group wired their constituents: "The argument is exhausted. All hope of relief in the Union, through the agency of committees, Congressional legislation, or constitutional amendments is extinguished, and we

trust the South will not be deceived by appearances or pretence
of new guarantees." In agitating the home front, they had found
in all their secret caucusing sound reason for having tramped
back to Washington, where one of the best quips quoted Congressman Morris of Illinois. He had renamed the Committee of
Thirty-three "The Coffin."

Yet the twenty-two Congressmen with their telegram represented as much weakness as strength. In the Senate a Committee
of Thirteen worked to achieve a compromise with much less
immediate despair. The very divisions within the Democracy
that had exploded the party during the campaign now roosted on
the floor of the Senate. Those who held to the tantalizing dream
of a tight-knit, harmonious confederacy of fifteen Southern states
were finding reality something different. And at the core of this
uncomfortable awakening were the men of the Upper South,
with minds and traditions of their own and a broad streak of
cussed independence whenever they suspected the secessionists
were trying to push them around.

Among the leaders in the Senate who carried on the stern
struggle to save the Union three stood out, not only as colorful
personalities but also as symbols within the Democracy of men
who put country above party. Douglas surely was one of these
—Douglas whose very presence on the Senate floor could make the
scowling Wigfall of Texas bluster that the Illinoisian had done
more than any other to bring about "the destruction of the
country" and was "not the man to come here and preach to anybody!" Although not a member of the Committee of Thirteen,
another of the loyal Senatorial trio was Andrew Johnson of
Tennessee, who stormed into Washington with eyes blazing and
who impressed Edward Pollard as a "brave knight in season"
as he confronted the disunionists and threw "in their very faces
the rude but stalwart defiance of the patriot." If Jefferson Davis
deserved to be described as illustrating "that type of scholarly
statesmanship supposed to be nourished by the institution of

Slavery," who "was a model of deportment in the social circle, a picture of graceful and well-poised dignity in the American Senate," and who "formed his speeches with classical severity and elegance," then to Pollard the phrases to describe Johnson were "the traditional democrat, a plain, earnest man; rough, but with a face too deeply engraved with character to be accounted plebeian; scorning the pretensions of aristocracy, and yet endowed with that medium and proper dignity in public life that invites access and yet easily sustains its official position of superiority." At the age of ten, apprenticed to a tailor, Johnson had not known his alphabet but, using an old volume of speeches by British statesmen, had taught himself spelling and grammar; later his wife had read history and politics to him while he sat cross-legged plying his needle as a journeyman tailor in East Tennessee. "Sir, I do not forget that I am a mechanic," he once told the Senate. "I am proud to own it." Nor did he pretend to be the polished orator: "I have to seize on fugitive thoughts as they pass through my mind, make the best application of them I can, and express them in my own crude way."

Third of this group of Union champions in the Senate was Kentucky's John J. Crittenden, now past seventy-three, son of a Revolutionary War hero, one-time attorney general in the territory of Illinois, volunteer in the War of 1812, successful criminal lawyer, a district attorney under John Quincy Adams, Cabinet member under William Harrison and Millard Fillmore, governor of Kentucky, stormy opponent of the repeal of the Missouri Compromise and so at loggerheads with the administrations of Pierce and Buchanan, devoted friend of Henry Clay and heir to his title as the Great Compromiser, supporter in the recent Presidential canvass of Bell, six times elected to the United States Senate where he now proposed to fight savagely for the Union he loved. The proposals in the Senate upon which the great effort ultimately hinged bore his name; in essence, the Crittenden Resolutions proposed a series of permanent amendments to the Constitution whereby perpetual slavery would be guaranteed in the Slave States and the District of Columbia, the domestic slave trade would be continued and protected, slaveowners would be indemnified for runaways, and the territorial dispute resolved by extending the line of the Missouri Compromise to the Pacific on the understanding that slavery would be excluded forever north of that line.

How the Republicans stood on these proposals was a vital determinant in their life-and-death struggle. Seward, the natural Republican leader in the Senate, became suddenly a man caught in a trap. In his heart he was as stout a compromiser as the Senate claimed; moreover, his advisor and friend, Thurlow Weed, already had revealed his preference for concession in the Albany *Journal,* no doubt a trial balloon aimed toward testing Mr. Lincoln as much as anyone. The real trouble Seward faced in the Senate was his acceptance of a place in Mr. Lincoln's Cabinet; whither his heart might lead him on the Crittenden Compromise must be just so far as Mr. Lincoln wanted him to go.

Seward had not forgotten his role as "Prime Minister"; indeed, he was toiling hard at it, determined that Mr. Lincoln should fill his Cabinet with ex-Whigs who saw reality by Seward's light. John A. Gilmer of North Carolina, John M. Botts of Virginia, Randall Hunt of Louisiana, Emerson Etheridge of Tennessee, James Barbour of Virginia, compromisers all, represented the kind of men Seward wanted in the Cabinet, but the reports coming from Springfield indicated that Mr. Lincoln was flirting with Gideon Welles, Montgomery Blair, and Salmon P. Chase, who would rather sell their souls to the devil than concede anything to the Southern secessionists. To resolve his dilemma Seward called on Thurlow Weed to pack his bag and head for Springfield in the hope of bringing Mr. Lincoln around on both his Cabinet appointments and the Crittenden Compromise. In the interim Seward wondered if it were even safe for him to be seen on the floor of the Senate. There were days when he found reasons for being absent. As for the Radicals, they opposed whatever Seward wished to support. What they represented, as club-footed Thad

Stevens never let anyone forget, was the supremacy of the Constitution. Yet Seward knew he could swing the Crittenden Compromise—if Mr. Lincoln would let him.

Democratic caucuses seemed to give the Crittenden proposals a chance, at least temporarily. The doctrine of delay, so dear to the heart of Buchanan, had a claim on the loyalties of Cobb and Thompson, Floyd and Jefferson Davis. Andrew Johnson had a group meeting with him every night addressing envelopes to mail out Unionist speeches. Johnson called on J. C. G. Kennedy, Director of the Census. In these times that tried men's souls, everyone had to work overtime. Kennedy agreed and sent Johnson twenty clerks from the Census Bureau to help with the mail. Border State Democrats—Powell of Kentucky, Bayard and Saulsbury of Delaware—with Bigler of Pennsylvania gave aid and comfort to Douglas, Johnson, and Crittenden. Hope was far from dead.

Meanwhile other events clouded and complicated the Washington scene. On December eighth, no longer able to stand against the imprecations from Georgia, Howell Cobb resigned from the Cabinet. On the twelfth old Lewis Cass threw in the sponge, but with a different kind of fire in his eye—he was fed up with Buchanan's refusal to re-enforce the forts. That same day General Winfield Scott succeeded in transporting his three hundred pounds of ailing body to Washington, establishing himself in I Street in rooms rented from Wormley, the free mulatto.

"I was three years old when the Constitution was adopted," the Virginia-born old warrior, now in his seventy-fourth year, liked to tell his friends. He had commanded troops against Niagara Falls in the War of 1812, had been a gallant figure at Chapultepec, Vera Cruz, and Cerro Gordo in the War with Mexico where he had taught both Lee and Grant a good part of what they ever would know about military science, and in 1852 had been the last Presidential candidate of the old Whig Party. "What a wonderful mixture of gasconade, ostentation, fuss, feathers, bluster and genuine soldierly talent and courage is this same Winfield Scott!" a governor of Virginia once exclaimed. "A great smoking mass of flesh and blood!" Veterans of the Black Hawk War remembered that he had cured drunkenness among his troops by setting his boys to digging their own graves, a reminder of where ultimately Demon Rum deposited his victims. "Old Fuss and Feathers" was so dropsical he might nap in midsentence; a carriage groaned on its springs no louder than he when forced to hoist himself into the seat; rich food and liqueurs might be the ruination of his stomach, but Scott never forsook the loves of his youth—canvasback duck, claret, the army, the Constitution, and the Union.

Saturday, the fifteenth, brought a snowstorm to Washington. Somehow Scott struggled through the drifts to the White House and fought over what to do about the forts with Buchanan and Floyd. Scott had no more sympathy for secessionists in South Carolina now than when Jackson and he had slapped down the nullifiers in 1833. Re-enforce those forts, insisted Scott, opposed to the President's belief that politics could speak more earnestly than guns, pooh-poohing Floyd's contention that the presence of the *Brooklyn* at Norfolk which could transport three hundred men from Fortress Monroe to Charleston whenever needed constituted sensible protection. Eyes crackling, the old General plunged back into the snow, grumbling that given a day or two he'd draw up his own plan for defending Federal property. What Floyd and Buchanan may have said afterward can only be conjectured. Old Scott not only moved like a battleship, but barked like one of its gun turrets, and possibly might prove as lethal.

But the Washington stew was only beginning to thicken. On the thirteenth, when the twenty-two Congressmen were employing the magnetic telegraph as a weapon in their cold war, Jacob Thompson received an intriguing telegram from the Governor of Mississippi suggesting that the Secretary of Interior go to North Carolina, the state of his birth, and "express the earnest hope of Mississippi that North Carolina will cooperate with her, in the adoption of efficient measures for the common defense of the South." Thompson decided to discuss the matter with the President. Perhaps, the Secretary suggested, he could delay any concerted action toward secession until after Mr. Lincoln's inauguration on March fourth.

"Old Buck" wanted nothing more. Whatever qualms he may have felt—and they should have been severe—over sanctioning so irregular a mission could not overbalance the insatiate hunger growing in him for delay, delay, delay. He was anxious to have similar missions dispatched to South Carolina and Alabama. Advised that Senator Toombs of Georgia and Jefferson Davis were of a mind to go along with the Crittenden Compromise if the Republicans would, the time had come, the President decided, for Mr. Lincoln to arrive in Washington and put his shoulder to the wheel for peace. That ever-faithful Democratic work horse, Duff Green, accordingly was dispatched to fetch Mr. Lincoln or at least to obtain his endorsement of the Crittenden Compromise.

The Washington stew was thicker now, but had not yet boiled over. With Cass's resignation Jeremiah Black was named Secretary of State and for the new Attorney General Buchanan agreed to Black's old friend and neighbor from Franklin Square, Edwin McMasters Stanton. Both Buchanan and Black believed they knew what they were getting and neither ever had been more in error. On the surface no stancher supporter of Buchanan's proslavery wing of the Democratic Party seemed to exist than Stanton—eloquent spokesman for the Lecompton Constitution that would have made Kansas a slave state, loyal booster of the Dred Scott decision opening all territories to slavery, earnest campaigner for Breckinridge over Douglas. Stanton's recent record made it easy to forget that he once had been a rabid Free Soiler, or that as a child sitting on the knee of Benjamin Lundy he had vowed eternal hatred for slavery, or that occasionally in his home on Franklin Square he chatted through a pleasant evening with so ardent an abolitionist as Dr. Gamaliel Bailey, proprietor of the little journal that had given the world its first look into *Uncle*

Tom's Cabin. The Buchananites claimed Stanton, the abolitionists claimed Stanton, but only God and Stanton had the least idea of where he stood, or why, or for how long. Ultimately Black would discover the truth and among the kinder epithets he would apply to Stanton were "betrayer of his country" and "crawling sycophant." But that was later—much later than December, 1860.

On Monday, December seventeenth, Secretary of the Interior Thompson departed from Washington, with the President's consent, on his remarkable mission to persuade North Carolina to stand with Mississippi. On the same day in Columbia, South Carolina, delegates assembled in convention along with such interesting "observers" as Howell Cobb of Georgia. A smallpox scare hindered the labors of secession for a time while the delegates and their friends hastened on to Charleston—demonstrating, in the classic comment of Mrs. Chesnut, that men "insensible to fear" remained "very sensible in case of smallpox." Buchanan's ambassador of delay, Caleb Cushing, did not reach Charleston until the morning of the twentieth. Knowing what was coming, church bells already tolled—at noon the ordinance of secession was read, at one thirty o'clock unanimously adopted. In Washington the President was attending a wedding breakfast when a cry burst out:

"Thank God! Oh, thank God! South Carolina has seceded!"

As soon as a pale and shaken Buchanan could collect his wits, he asked his hostess, in little more than a whisper:

"Madam, might I beg of you to have my carriage called?"

So in Washington, divided capital of a divided country where the traditions and passions of the Deep South and Upper South encountered the ideals and prejudices of the West and New England, Christmas Day meant many things to many men.

To Buchanan, whose face surely reflected as "much unhappiness" as Mrs. Gwin mentioned in her letter to Mrs. Howell Cobb, it meant dealing with the three commissioners from South Carolina, en route to Washington as emissaries from a foreign power, on the ticklish question of what disposal to make of United States property within that state.

On Minnesota Row, where Douglas and Breckinridge resided, it meant a short respite for thinking through the next step in the knock-down fight they had transferred from the campaign to the Senate floor.

To Stanton, nodding the season's greetings across Franklin Square to his old friend Black, it meant plotting the dual game of titillating the risibilities of Buchanan by likening Lincoln to Paul Du Chaillu's ape while keeping Lincoln informed of the maneuverings within the Cabinet through confidential reports to Seward.

To John J. Crittenden it meant dreams of achieving a compromise that would have ennobled even dear old Henry Clay.

To Andrew Johnson it meant mailing hundreds of more copies of Unionist speeches and to Jefferson Davis it meant marking time while loyal Mississippians like Secretary Thompson conferred with the Governor of North Carolina and the other steps of the ultimate conspiracy were effected.

On I Street to General Scott it meant finding somewhere in Washington a ground-floor apartment so that all his strength could be conserved for pounding into the heads of Floyd and Buchanan the elemental responsibilities of a loyal army man.

To Seward it meant another letter to Lincoln, urging the consideration of John C. Frémont for Secretary of War, of Randall Hunt of Louisiana, and of John A. Gilmer or Kenneth Rayner of North Carolina "for other places," and, rather tipping his hand, Seward offered: "Should you think that any of these gentlemen would be likely to be desirable in the Administration, I should find no difficulty I think in ascertaining whether they would accept, without making the matter public."

To children Christmas Day meant presents; to the wives of many Southern members of Congress it meant packing to return home; to Galt, the jeweler, it meant marking down watches and silverware to "panic prices" . . .

And at Fort Moultrie in Charleston Harbor, Christmas Day to Major Robert Anderson meant pondering seriously the written orders from Buell that permitted him to defend his garrison in any reasonable manner upon "an act of hostility" or upon "tangible evidence of a design to proceed to a hostile act."

12

Tale of Two Cities

THE GROUP of officers around Major Robert Anderson seemed "silent and distrait." The first orange and rose hues of a setting sun streaked the sky above Fort Moultrie. The date was December 26, 1860. Captain Abner Doubleday spoke cheerfully to the assistant surgeon. "It's a fine evening, Crawford." The surgeon replied hesitantly; he appeared glum and embarrassed. Major Anderson spoke then, in a quiet voice:

"I have determined to evacuate this post immediately for the purpose of occupying Fort Sumter. I can only allow you twenty minutes to form your company and be in readiness to start."

But Doubleday had known since Anderson had inquired about the best method for spiking the guns that some such maneuver was in prospect. Forewarned had been forearmed to the extent that everything of personal value Doubleday owned had been sent to New York that morning. But Crawford's medical stores were unpacked. And the surprise would go heavily against Captain J. G. Foster, who recently had secured a house for his family outside the fort.

Yet Crawford and Foster might have guessed that something extraordinary was afoot when earlier that day Lieutenant Hall, the post quartermaster, had taken three chartered schooners and a number of barges across the harbor to old Fort Johnson. The pretext for Hall's mission was that Anderson intended to use some dilapidated buildings there to domicile wives and other noncombatants attached to Moultrie, but anyone who had examined those schooners and barges would have found them loaded with the supplies that troops would need for an extended stay in Sumter. Moreover, the ruse had worked perfectly—the Vigilance Committee had seen nothing unusual in Anderson's concern for noncombatants with a conflict threatening to break out at any moment. Now Hall was lying off Fort Johnson with his little fleet, awaiting the signal gun that would bring him back to Sumter to unload his cargo.

So Anderson, understanding the military importance of surprise, had employed that element effectively—both on the secessionists and his own garrison. Doubleday rushed to the barracks and formed and inspected his company, then rushed to his quarters and helped Mrs. Doubleday throw a few articles of personal wearing apparel into a trunk, then rushed her to a sand hill where she wouldn't be shot and where they could take "a sad and hasty leave," then strapping on his revolver and tying a blanket across his shoulders, rushed back to Anderson. Elapsed time: twenty minutes.

Anderson ordered Doubleday to advance without delay. About a quarter of a mile from the main gates of Moultrie stood a pile of rocks, once part of a sea wall, where the crossing boats had been sequestered. Doubleday marched his company to the rocks, marveling that "not a single human being" appeared; Lieutenants Snyder and Meade, two engineer officers, crouched behind the rocks and directed Doubleday to the boats he should use.

In the harbor—a grim omen—chugged the secessionist guard boat, *Nina*. The sun had set and the twilight deepened rapidly, so Doubleday crossed his fingers and gambled that he could row across undetected. Caps were pulled off, coats thrown open to conceal buttons and insignia, the muskets lying alongside the rowlocks covered. To an uncritical observer the appearance of the party was that of laborers returning to the fort.

The tide ran strong and Doubleday's oarsmen were unskilled. Suddenly the dusk was filled with an ominous silence as the paddle wheels of the *Nina* stopped. The shadowy walls of prisonlike Sumter humped their gloomy hulk against the horizon. Doubleday judged that not more than a hundred yards separated his party and the guard boat; but "a slight scrutiny" appeared to satisfy the secessionists and the paddle wheels of the *Nina* turned again. Putting their full backs into every pull, the oarsmen swept on.

Within moments the wharf of Sumter loomed in the twilight. Crowds of workmen, mostly wearing secession emblems, rushed forward. An angry shout rang out:

"What are these soldiers doing here?"

Doubleday was delighted to show them—with "charged bayonets"—driving "the tumultuous mass" within the fort and seizing the guardroom by the gate. A less rowdy welcome awaited Anderson, arriving with the engineers. Soon Captain Seymour's company appeared, thanking a merciful Providence for letting them pass undisturbed almost under the bow of the *Nina*. The signal gun was fired to bring Hall's schooners and barges.

Later the disunionist workmen were loaded aboard the barges and shipped off to the mainland. From them principally an unsuspecting Charleston learned that the best fort in its harbor now flew the Stars and Stripes. With daylight the city's cobbled streets clanged with the running footfalls of messengers, racing from house to house, ringing doorbells, shouting the doleful, infuriating news—in "some inexplicable manner" Sumter had been occupied!

Before Charleston suspected anything, Anderson addressed a letter to the Adjutant General of the Army, saying, "I have the honor to report that I have just completed, by the blessing of God, the removal to this fort of all my garrison, except the surgeon, four noncommissioned officers, and seven men." In two ways that Major Anderson could not then foresee, this letter was destined to have historic significance. For one, two days before Anderson's communication was officially received on December twenty-ninth in Washington, an effective secessionist underground already had flustered Secretary of War Floyd with the unpleasant intelligence that all hell had broken loose in Charleston—meaning, specifically, that with Anderson in Sumter the wearers of the blue cockade were certain to strike back before nightfall by seizing Castle Pinckney and Fort Moultrie. For another, Anderson had written an early entry for the millions of words that one day would fill the one hundred and twenty-eight volumes of *War of the Rebellion . . . Official Records of the Union and Confederate Armies.*

In Washington on the twenty-sixth of December the three commissioners from South Carolina who had come to deal with the United States concerning the disposal of Federal property within their borders were being warmly welcomed by secessionists in the capital. Brandy, wine, and bourbon flowed freely; Christmas cakes from Gautier's, saved for this rare occasion, added to the festive scene; oysters and lobster, wild turkey and partridge pleased the most exacting palates. A fine house had been rented on K Street, as befitted the ambassadorial position of the commissioners; and the fact that Colonel Drinkard, Floyd's chief clerk, lived next door could be reckoned a fortunate happenstance. James L. Orr, former Speaker of the House and an old pet of Buchanan's, knew the ins and outs of Washington like a glove on his hand; if Robert W. Barnwell and J. H. Adams, the other commissioners, followed Orr's lead, they showed their good sense. Conversations sparkled. For appearance's sake Buchanan might play hard to catch but at the right moment Trescott, the Assistant Secretary of State, would fix everything. And old Alf Iverson, Senator from Georgia, had come close to becoming everyone's darling with his cute speeches about how, now that Maryland and Virginia were warming up to secession, the logical capital for the forthcoming Southern Confederacy was right in Washington.

Then on the twenty-seventh the bombshell exploded. Anderson in Sumter! Floyd most of all couldn't believe the report—and *wouldn't* believe it since, as he telegraphed Anderson, "there is no order for any such movement." If Floyd ever had possessed any knowledge of Buell's written orders of December eleventh to Anderson, his overwrought mind no longer retained it. The courteous yet firm reply that soon came from Anderson in Charleston added no balm to the Secretary's bleeding spirit:

> The telegram is correct. I abandoned Fort Moultrie because I was certain that if attacked my men must have been sacrificed, and the command of the harbor lost. I spiked the guns and destroyed the carriages to keep the guns from being used against us.
>
> If attacked, the garrison would never have surrendered without a fight.

Actually the fascinations of that December day in Washington were just beginning—for no one more than Edwin McMasters Stanton, charily crossing Franklin Square on his way to his first Cabinet meeting. He entered a White House throbbing with tension and steeped in despair. An agitated Buchanan could not disguise his anger. "My first promptings," he admitted later, were to order Anderson back to Moultrie. Floyd certainly wouldn't stop him, yet Floyd had to reckon with his own precarious position in the Cabinet. The Virginian's prosecessionist sympathies in running the War Department were not the issue in dispute, but the recent disclosure of his involvement in the "purloining"* of eight hundred seventy thousand dollars of bonds held in trust for the nation's Indian wards by the Department of the Interior. Even so, Floyd filled the Cabinet meeting with noisy insults. The emotions of Floyd, declared Joseph Holt, were "absolutely uncontrollable," his fury that of "some baffled fiend" caught in the grip of "mingled mortification and anguish and rage and panic."

Secretary of the Interior Thompson, involved in the same "purloining" of Indian funds so that the Mississippian's day in the Cabinet were also briefly numbered, supported Floyd, and possibly another voice damning Anderson rested in the leathery throat of Isaac Toucey of Connecticut, Secretary of the Navy. Passions ran high and strained later recollections of this meeting which Stanton

* The word was Buchanan's.

felt impelled to describe to Christopher P. Wolcott, his brother-in-law, as a scene of "treason with bold and brazen front." The President's proposal that Anderson be ordered back to Moultrie—his "first promptings"—fell short in the end of appeasing the infuriated Floyd. Nothing less than ordering Anderson and his whole command out of Charleston Harbor would satisfy the Virginian now. Stanton declared afterward that, flabbergasted by such talk, he spoke sharply to Buchanan, declaring that to yield Sumter would be "a crime equal to the crime of Arnold and that all who participated in it ought to be hung like André"; and Postmaster General Holt insisted that the President replied, "Oh, no! Not so bad as that, my friend!—not so bad as that!" Defenders of Buchanan always have pronounced this story spurious. At eight o'clock the Cabinet meeting remained stalled in the same hotheaded impasse. Buchanan, dismissing his counselors, likewise remained hung over a fence. He hadn't ordered Anderson out of Sumter—yet.

The Washington tempest in no sense had reached full hurricane force. Over on K Street Messrs. Orr, Barnwell, and Adams, having lost the fattest lamb they had come to clip, reacted violently. In the scalding letter they addressed to Buchanan they reminded the President that they were in Washington as "representatives of an authority which could, at any time within the past sixty days, have taken possession of the forts in Charleston Harbor." The reason this had not happened was because they had trusted "your honor." But Anderson's occupation of Sumter had altered "to a most important extent, the condition of affairs under which we came." The difficulty in this diatribe was the fact that so useful a tool of treason as the magnetic telegraph could serve both parties. Washington knew now that the Palmetto flag flew over Castle Pinckney and Fort Moultrie, raising the delicate legal point of how even "alien" property rightfully could be seized without a declaration of war; and that a Federal revenue cutter also had been seized in Charleston Harbor, an act that approached outright piracy.

Indeed, circumstances had altered—for Buchanan, for Messrs. Orr, Barnwell, and Adams, but not for General Scott. Admitting that he had suffered "a bad night, and can scarcely hold his head up this morning," the old General lumbered over to the White House. Any thought of evacuating Sumter was outrageous, in Scott's opinion; rather, one hundred and fifty recruits should be sent at once from Governor's Island, along with "ample supplies of ammunition, subsistence, including fresh vegetables, as potatoes, onions, turnips," and, as a telling extra, "one or two armed vessels." All this, Scott could say, he had spelled out in a letter to Floyd; and he might have added one thing more. In late October by letter he had warned Floyd—a copy of which he had thoughtfully forwarded after the election to Mr. Lincoln in Springfield—that such an "act of rashness" as now had occurred at Castle Pinckney and Moultrie could only be avoided if all commanders along the Southern coast were placed on the alert. Scott had said then, as he maintained still, that "with a faithful Army and Navy and a moderate but firm Executive for the next twelve months, secession may be averted." The President never had the slightest cause to doubt what the old General believed should be the solemn duty of the Chief Executive.

That evening, December twenty-eighth, a wearied, distressed, confused President held another Cabinet meeting. Like a spent bullet, Floyd flung himself upon the sofa and remained there in sullen silence throughout the session. Thompson carried on the fight to oust Anderson from Sumter, and when all other arguments had been exhausted, fell upon the novel suggestion that Buchanan should order the evacuation as an act of "generosity" and as proof to South Carolina that "we mean you no harm." Stanton believed that he had heard everything now, and told Buchanan in a bristling voice: "Only the other day it was announced that a million of dollars had been stolen from Mr. Thompson's department. . . . All I can say is, that no administration, much less this one, can afford to lose a million of money and a fort in the same week."

Next morning Floyd emerged from his sulk long enough to resign, or, as one expressed it, to disassociate himself from Buchanan's "dishonored" Administration. At the Cabinet meeting that glum Saturday the President read the letter that he intended to send to the South Carolina commissioners. Toucey thought it good. But the others knew. The letter was an appalling document, even for Buchanan, since it conceded South Carolina's right to negotiate diplomatically for the forts and reaffirmed the weak doctrine that the government could not employ force to compel a state to remain in the Union. Neither Stanton nor Holt slept well that night, and Black apparently didn't sleep five winks. With daylight Black sought out Stanton and Holt. If Buchanan sent that letter, Black said, he would resign. Since commissioners were becoming quite the style in Washington, Black selected Toucey to carry his ultimatum to the President.

"Old Buck" approached the breaking point. A lifetime of cold loneliness, the empty heart that no woman could touch, an old bachelor in a crabbed world where there never had been the laughter of beloved children—all at once every meagerness of the past joined the present. Cass gone, Floyd gone, Thompson going, the disgrace of the Indian frauds—and now Black! Buchanan, feeling so terribly old, alone, deserted, awakened pity in Toucey, and he agreed to bring Black in person. "Old Buck" waited, filled with his turbulent emotions, bursting out in a tearful tone at the sight of Black: "Do you talk too of leaving me?" He would rewrite the letter. Black could help him.

Perhaps Sunday awakened Washington to a religious fellowship, for the day produced other concessions. Stanton assisted Black in redrafting the letter. A note, delivered to Buchanan, announced: "It is Sunday; the weather is bad, and General Scott is not well enough to go to church." In this third-person tone, which seemed to please the old warrior of Chippewa and Lundy's Lane, Scott appealed to the President to order two hundred and fifty recruits to Sumter on the morrow, together with extra muskets or rifles, ammunition, subsistence stores, and "a sloop-of-war and cutter," adding that despite his indisposition Scott would "wait upon the President at any moment he may be called." Buchanan also heard that Orr was in a much more amenable mood, and had declared that South Carolina, tired of being "sucked of so much of her blood," wasn't at all eager for a confederacy with the Gulf States. Trescott hurried to the Executive Mansion, presumably from conversations on K Street, with an idea for saving face on both sides. Suppose South Carolina withdrew its forces from Moultrie so that Anderson could move back? Even Floyd seemed overwhelmed with remorse and decided that Buchanan deserved an apology for the nasty tenor of his resignation. Amid all these overtures of friendship and conciliation, Black and Stanton labored stoically to stiffen the tone of Buchanan's letter.

The result, if not perfect, was better—much better—with Buchanan stating flatly he possessed "no authority to decide what shall be the relation between the Federal Government and South Carolina." That question, "in all its bearings," he must submit to Congress. Thus he, personally, could meet the commissioners "only as private gentlemen of the highest character." By setting aside Buell's orders of December eleventh he could concede that "Major Anderson acted upon his own responsibility, and without authority," although he insisted that for so "brave and honorable" an officer "justice required that he should not be condemned without a fair hearing." Nor could he ignore the Palmetto flag now flying over Castle Pinckney and Fort Moultrie:

> It is under these circumstances that I am urged immediately to withdraw the troops from the harbor of Charleston, and I am informed that without this negotiation is impossible. This I cannot do; this I will not do. Such an idea was never thought of by me in any possible contingency. . . .

With a day of the old year left, the President at last had put up his back. Multiple dangers still surrounded him—one, Scott warned next morning, was that because of Anderson's isolation "a system of forged telegrams from this place may be played off so successfully as to betray him into some false movement"—yet at least he had one moment of speaking out as President and Commander in Chief.

Charleston's feeling toward Buchanan turned coldly bitter; he was "double-faced," "treacherous," and hardly deserved "the poor credit of being called a well-intentioned imbecile." In contrast, J. W. DeForest, visiting the city in early January, heard Mr. Lincoln described as "not personally" a bad or dangerous man, and one Charlestonian even conceded that Mr. Lincoln was "a man of excellent private character" whose misfortune was to become "simply a sign . . . that we are in danger." Mrs. Chesnut, glad that Anderson had moved into Sumter while the Governor "slept serenely," gave "the condensed essence" of the table talk she heard: "Anderson has united the Cotton States. Now for Virginia! Anderson has opened the ball." And Mrs. Chesnut added: "Those who want a row are in high glee. Those who dread it are glum and thoughtful enough."

A phenomenon occurred that Major Anderson had neither anticipated nor courted. Overnight he became "Our Bob," a nation's folk hero. To the New Work *World* he must be compared to Leonidas at Thermopylae; "Jaspar" chased Mrs. Anderson down Charleston's King Street so that readers of the New York *Times* could know what went into her shopping bag; three exuberant New Yorkers offered to pay the expense of sending four hundred trained artillerists to Sumter and Anderson himself was surprised to "receive, nearly by every mail, letters of sympathy, and many of them from strangers"; citizens of Allentown, Pennsylvania, fired thirty-three guns (one for each state remaining in the Union) and citizens of Burlington, Vermont, rang thirty-three bells in honor of Anderson.

No soldier or officer inside Sumter knew the fort in any more intimate detail than the average resident of Philadelphia and Boston, Cleveland and Buffalo, Chicago and St. Louis. Soon at almost any dinner table one could learn that the gloomy brick walls of Sumter were "sixty feet high, and from eight to twelve feet in thickness"; or that the fort was "amply supplied with water from artificial wells, which are supplied by the frequent showers of rain"; or that a twelve-inch columbiad at an elevation of thirty-nine degrees had a range of three and a third miles. Artists sketched "the gallant officers" reading their newspapers in comfortable rockers before grated fires, the gunners on duty in the sally ports, and that memorable moment when the Stars and Stripes first waved over Sumter and the chaplain offered his solemn prayer that made all realize "Man's extremity is God's opportunity."

A controversy that had hinged on the question of slavery at the beginning of Christmas week rested more solidly on the question of Union as the New Year approached. An old army man in Louisiana, who remembered youthful years stationed at Moultrie when he had adored the "horse-racing, picnicing, boating, fishing, swimming, and God knows what not" of Southern life, knew now that once Louisiana seceded he would resign the best job he ever had held and risk life and fortune to save the Union. His name was William Tecumseh Sherman. Nor was he an exception. Anderson, moving quietly and unexpectedly into Sumter, touched an emotion that never had responded to a Garrison burning the Constitution on Boston Common. Boys who had been raised on Parson Weems' *Life of Washington*—and Lincoln was one of them—were grown into men who understood what Thomas Nast meant when he drew a sketch of the Father of the Country gazing with grim face at the author of an act of secession. Nast titled his drawing: "The Dream of a Secessionist—Washington and Valley Forge."

The South had been dealt a staggering blow, for abolitionist and patriot, Northern extremist and moderate had been led to a common rallying ground. Hereafter there would be less of New England, less of the West, less of the Eastern city dweller and more of the American in the hearts of those who pondered Mr.

Lincoln and the possible ordeal awaiting him. Love of Union was the impulse that could send the Twentieth Regiment from rock-bound Maine to die beside the Iron Brigade, those "damned black-hatted" fellows from the free soil of Wisconsin, upon the bloody slopes of Gettysburg. The mind of the North in one week had gained dimension, definition, purpose. Even the hesitant Border States henceforth would grow more hesitant, and a Galusha Anderson in St. Louis, characterized by Carl Schurz as "a free city on slave soil," would sense the change. The flood of crank letters reaching Lincoln in Springfield dwindled sharply.

Still, Washington remained edgy as the old year ended. Frayed secessionist nerves and sharp secessionist tongues were having an impact on this city that Southern politicians had so long domi-nated. The conviction, stemming no doubt from the house on K Street, persisted that under pressure "Old Buck" would capitulate, knowing full well that Southern hands had buttered his political bread. With the proslavery tide running strong in Virginia and Maryland, what was Washington but an isolated island? Where was the army that could defend it against any swift, determined push?

As far north as Baltimore an ugly, militant, secessionist pug-nacity gathered strength, and on the last day of December Thomas Cadwallerder, writing to the "Hon. Abe. Lincoln" from inside Baltimore, warned "it will be madness, for you to attempt to reach Washington . . . I have had my head shaved twice merely for making the remark that I consider you a gentleman." In Washington that same day the Chicago *Tribune*'s Joseph Medill grew fretful over the rising disunionist spirit in Maryland. "With only a carpet sack," Medill urged Mr. Lincoln, "get on the cars, and drop down on this city some day next week or very soon" and "knock over and disarrange all the plans of the traitors, and show them they [have] a second Jackson to deal with." Lincoln's presence in Washington, the journalist believed, would be "worth an army of 10,000 men," and he reminded the President-elect that "secrecy and dis-patch, Napoleon the great, said, were the talsmen of success."

Yet if disaffection in Maryland threatened the Union, loyalty in other Border States mobilized in a determined effort to save the Crittenden Compromise. Congress had adjourned for the holidays, but Democrats remaining in Washington caucused to find a new and more workable strategy for avoiding national disruption. Saulsbury from Delaware and Sebastian from Arkansas were Senators joining with such influential Congressmen as McClernand from Illinois, Barret from Missouri, and Harris from Virginia to swing Border State sentiment behind the compromise. A vote on secession was imminent in Georgia and on the twenty-ninth Douglas and Crittenden employed the magnetic telegraph to make a strong appeal to its voters: "We have hopes that the rights of the South and of every state and section may be protected within the Union. Don't give up the ship. Don't despair of the Republic."

The major stress in the Washington tug of war at the year's end, however, was between the House on K Street and the Executive Mansion. K Street reasoned that after Floyd's note of apology Buchanan would not accept the Virginian's resignation and this link between Secessia and the War Department would be mended. But "Old Buck" kept his back up; he was glad to dump Floyd, naming Joseph Holt, a Kentuckian of intense Union loyalty, as Secretary of War and putting Horatio King, a New Yorker of similar steadfastness to the central government, into the Cabinet as the new Postmaster General.

If this evidence of Buchanan's change of heart wasn't stunner enough on K Street, other shocks followed quickly. The price Holt exacted for filling Floyd's place in the Cabinet was the immediate reinforcement of Sumter and the last day of 1860 found Holt and Scott working over the details for dispatching two hundred and fifty recruits from Norfolk aboard the *Brooklyn*. That evening Buchanan sent his secretary to K Street with the clincher. The President had decided that no Federal property could be surrendered. The blow Buchanan had dealt the South was clearly re-

flected at the traditional New Year's Day reception at the White
House. Southerners appeared, boldly displaying their secession
emblems. Some refused to offer the President their hand as they
passed through the receiving line. The old bachelor held his head
high, but he must have known how deep was the wound that made
the Southerner forget his good manners. To add to the tension,
loyal Union men arrived wearing red, white, and blue ribbons.
Conversations often were coldly polite, the exchange of glances as
often hotly hostile.

Doubtless it was no surprise to Buchanan, this chore scarcely
behind him, when he received an explosive communication from
Messrs. Orr, Barnwell, and Adams. "You have probably rendered
civil war inevitable," sneered the commissioners from South Carolina. "Be it so." If Buchanan chose "to force the issue," then "relying upon Him who is the God of Justice, as well as the God of
Hosts" South Carolina would "endeavor to perform the great duty
which lies before her, hopefully, bravely, and thoroughly." Buchanan ordered the letter endorsed: "This paper, just presented
to the President, is of such a character that he declines to receive
it." Soon the key was turned on the door of the fine "ambassadorial" dwelling on K Street. Washington's more boisterous citizens thought the departing commissioners deserved at least a
serenade of tin pans and other reliable noisemakers, but the
metropolitan police wisely intervened.

Among the busier conspirators at the year's end was Stanton.
He "squat like a toad," said Holt, describing Stanton at one
o'clock in the morning pouring into the ear of Massachusetts'
Charles Sumner the undercurrents of treason that flowed through
the White House. Morning or evening or both, through a "certain Mr. Watson," Stanton kept in touch with Seward. In turn
Seward made himself the pipe line to Springfield, informing
Lincoln on the twenty-ninth that from what "I can see" of the
activities in "the councils of the President" he was pained to
report that "things are even worse there than we understood."
Next day Seward relayed gloomier information to Springfield:

"The President has decided to stand on his loyalty. Floyd resigned and the other seceders will. But we are trembling today, lest he may be overborne by seceding influences and recall all. The White House is abandoned to the seceders. They eat, drink and sleep with him." What both Seward and Stanton failed to realize was that timidity did not necessarily constitute treachery. In this respect Buchanan was himself a national symbol. As the country transformed "Our Bob" Anderson into a folk hero, the impulse that had been released even invaded the White House.

And what Lincoln realized, or thought, or intended to do was difficult to say, for he could be, as Billy Herndon once observed, "the most secretive, reticent, shut-mouthed man that ever lived." At rock bottom all Buchanan had achieved was what he had craved—delay. But the ordeal remained—Lincoln's ordeal. The Southern character and the Southern conscience either must smash the Union or the links must be forged to produce a national character and a national conscience. For a month in Springfield Lincoln had seen this problem in terms of forming a Cabinet and taking a stand on the Crittenden Compromise. He was a man who always had lived candidly with himself. In his mind, but more in his heart, rested the final force that Christmas week of 1860 on which the nation's destiny depended.

13

Lincoln as
A. Lincoln Knew Him

A. LINCOLN in May may have seemed a mere "prairie politician" to Seward but A. Lincoln in December displayed masterful gifts of political leadership and no one owed more to that ability than Seward. For a moralistic fellow, with a supersensitive conscience honed on the whetstone of a legal background, it was difficult to find the equal of Senator Lyman Trumbull of Illinois. En route to Washington after the election, Trumbull heard from reliable Republican sources in New York that while Seward was personally honest he was committed to a faction of the party notoriously corrupt. Did Mr. Lincoln dare risk appointing Seward to the Cabinet, fretted the scrupulous Trumbull, when he probably would dispense patronage to his followers to the great detriment of the party? Good humor, political judgment, the measure of Lincoln was in his reply to Trumbull: "I will myself take care of the question of 'corrupt jobs' and see that justice is done to all, our friends, of whom you write, as well as others." The date of this letter was December 8, 1860; that same day he wrote to Seward offering him the post in the Cabinet as Secretary of State.

Lincoln's principal trait, the practice that made him a "shut-mouthed man" to Herndon, was to live with a decision until he knew it was right, and then to make it in good conscience and with a loyal heart. The ability to think for himself and to trust his own judgment made him a man who rarely could be rushed to a conclusion or swayed by another's passion and ambition; moreover, when the issue seemed vital, he was as unwilling as Grant to be "hectored." Seward, wishing to fill the Cabinet with good ex-Whigs he could manage, came head-on against this hard side of Lincoln's character. Each of Seward's suggestions, Lincoln replied, he had "thought of" before "but not very definitely" with the exception of Senator John A. Gilmer of North Carolina. He had asked Gilmer to come to Springfield, with a view to offering him a place in the Cabinet, but had received no reply. He gave Seward some comfort: "If you ascertain his feelings, and write me, I shall be obliged. Our german friends might not be quite satisfied with his appointment, but I think we could appease them."

To some it seemed an evidence of weakness in Mr. Lincoln that so many of the candidates who had challenged his nomination at the Convention—Seward, Salmon P. Chase of Ohio, Edward Bates of Missouri, in a backhanded way even the very dubious Simon Cameron of Pennsylvania—should find places in his Cabinet. The man in Springfield had to be honest with himself, to the extent that it was possible after his managers at the Convention had "gambled, bought and sold me a hundred times," and if this were weakness then so it must be. But the Republican Party contained many divergent elements. What chance had his Administration unless all the major factions were represented in the Cabinet? Either he possessed the skill and leadership to make them work in harmony, for the good of the Union, or the wrong man had been elected President. And so Mr. Lincoln found the courage to match the astute, vain Seward with the equally ambitious, unswerving Chase, gaining a compromiser with a darling of the antislavery radicals. In heavy-browed, stolid-thinking Bates he gained a hero of loyalists in the Border States and in Montgomery Blair he gained an intimate contact with balky, secession-riddled Maryland. Connecticut's Gideon Welles gave him a New England conscience along with New England testiness and an utter lack of humor; and in Caleb Smith, to whom he was committed by a Convention pledge, he had at least a plodder and a spokesman for divided Indiana.

The appointment of Simon Cameron brought Lincoln face to face with his own self-image. Not without reason had Andrew Jackson called Cameron a man "not to be trusted by anyone in any way," or James K. Polk labeled him "a managing tricky man," or James Buchanan seen him as "an unprincipled rascal." "All that I am," Lincoln told a friend, "the Presidency and all else, I owe to the opinion of me which people express when they call me 'honest old Abe.' Now what would they think of 'honest old Abe' if he should make such an appointment as the one proposed?" Cameron, the child of poverty, who as manufacturer, mine owner, and railroad operator had become a millionaire, lived by the political credo so often ascribed to him—an honest politician was one who "when bought, stays bought." From Jacksonian Democrat Cameron had turned Know Nothing for the soundest of reasons—he understood the dominant antiforeign and anti-Catholic feelings in Pennsylvania—and he had turned Republican for the same reason that he would have announced himself an African Hottentot if he had believed therein rested future victory. A very weak favorite son candidate at the Chicago Convention, Cameron had promised Seward his support on the second ballot, then sensed the swing to Lincoln. He had understood also that David Davis and Leonard Swett, two of Lincoln's managers, were underplaying their own man. Repeatedly Lincoln warned his managers to bind him to no deals at the Convention, but as Davis had said, sitting down at the Tremont House to discuss with two of Cameron's henchmen whither Pennsylvania's vote was going on the second ballot, "Lincoln ain't here." Said Swett afterward, a masterpiece of understatement in the history of politics, "Our arguments prevailed."

And Lincoln was stuck with the arguments. Bluntly the President-elect asked Pennsylvania's Thad Stevens: "Is Cameron an honest man?" Bluntly Stevens answered: "I don't think he would steal a red hot stove." From Springfield on the twenty-ninth of December Henry Villard informed readers of the New York *Herald*: "The noon train from the East landed among us no less a personage than the greatest of Pennsylvania wirepullers, the renowned General Simon Cameron. The unexpected arrival of the General was somewhat of a stunner, not only to your correspondent but to the political schemers and intriguants in Springfield." One not so stunned was Leonard Swett, who had extended the invitation making it seem as though he spoke for Mr. Lincoln; nor was Swett surprised to find in Cameron's entourage John P. Sanderson, since that gentleman had been present at the Tremont House when the arguments of Mr. Lincoln's managers had prevailed. In the possession of the President-elect was a "Memorandum on the Charges against Simon Cameron," including such interesting items as "In 1849, in a Democratic Convention, he attempted to bribe a *convention*." A second memorandum listed fifty-eight Republicans, principally Pennsylvanians, who attested to the belief that the appointment of Cameron to the Cabinet "would be hailed by joy by the citizens of this state." On December thirty-first Cameron departed from Springfield, carrying a letter from Lincoln that he would nominate the Pennsylvanian as Secretary of War or Secretary of the Treasury, "which of the two I have not yet definitely decided."

Lincoln knew that "honest old Abe" had been blackmailed; Swett knew it and Cameron and Sanderson. Within a few days the President-elect withdrew his offer; but Cameron allowed Lincoln's letter to reach the press. Perhaps Thad Stevens knew his man when, asked to retract his statement about Cameron, he replied:

"Oh, well, I apologize. I said Cameron would not steal a red hot stove. I withdraw that statement."

For Lincoln the concession to Cameron provided a troubled conscience as the old year ended; if he would make good decisions, they deserved the ballast of his own dogged conviction. On the question of the Crittenden Compromise he never hesitated. On December fifteenth John D. Defrees, chairman of the Indiana State Republican Committee, wrote Lincoln confidentially from Washington that the threat of secession was greater than the West realized, and added: "The fartherest any of our Republicans are willing to go is to secure genuine popular sovereignty to the people of our Territories—not the Douglas sham." With no little spirit Lincoln replied:

> ... I am sorry any republican inclines to dally with Pop. Sov. of any sort. It acknowledges that slavery has equal rights with liberty, and surrenders all we have contended for. Once fastened on us as a settled policy, filibustering for all South of us, and making slave states of it, follows in spite of it, with an early Supreme court decision, holding our free-state constitutions to be unconstitutional.

William Cullen Bryant, editor of the New York *Herald,* grew greatly excited when he learned that Mr. Lincoln had "been visited by a well known politician of New York who has a great deal to do with the stock market"—probably meaning Thurlow Weed, who, at the behest of Seward, had spent nearly all of December twentieth in Springfield. Bryant feared "a plan of compromise manufactured in Wall Street" and warned that "the restoration of the Missouri Compromise would disband the Republican party." Lincoln assured the editor that there had not been pressed upon him "any such compromise as you seem to suppose, or, in fact, actually any compromise at all."

Not only had Weed not tried to exert the influence of his own or Seward's opinions, but also had carried back to Washington three resolutions that the President-elect had drafted and which, Lincoln took care to warn the scrupulous Trumbull, Seward was to present to the Committee of Thirteen in such a way as not to "let my name be known in the matter." The first, which was accepted, provided that the Constitution should never be altered by Congress to abolish or interfere with slavery in the state. The second suggested that the Fugitive Slave Law be amended to provide a trial by jury to the fugitive, but when changed in Committee to provide that the jury be selected from the state whence the fugitive had fled the Republicans rejected it. The third—asking Congress to recommend to the states revision of legislation concerning persons recently resident in the states and the repeal of all laws in conflict with the Constitution—never found any area of Republican agreement. Yet one result was obtained. Seward demonstrated at least a moderate amenability to Lincoln's leadership.

The visit to Springfield of Buchanan's personal emissary, Duff Green, was so closely guarded that there was no immediate notice of it in the press. Again Mr. Lincoln called on Trumbull to guard his interest, enclosing a copy of a letter to Green. "If, on consultation with our discreet friends," Trumbull decided the letter could do no harm, it could be delivered to Green. "I do not desire any amendment of the Constitution," Lincoln told Green frankly; if the American people wanted such amendments as the Crittenden Compromise proposed, he "should not feel justified, nor inclined, to withhold from them, if I could, a fair opportunity of expressing their will thereon." He declared "inviolate" the right of every state "to order and control its own domestic institutions," adding "and I denounce the lawless invasion, by armed force, of the soil of any State or Territory, no matter under what pretext, as the gravest of crimes." Although averse to a public statement "at this time," if six of the twelve Senators from Georgia, Alabama, Mississippi, Louisiana, Florida, and Texas would affix their signatures beneath his, he would authorize publication of the following:

> We recommend to the people of the States we represent respectively, to suspend all action for dismemberment of the Union, at least, until some act, deemed to be violative of our rights, shall be done by the incoming administration.

That Trumbull handed the letter to Green was not surprising; it was a statesmanlike document. Nor could anyone who knew

Lincoln, averse to "Pop. Sov." in any form, much mistake where he stood on the Crittenden proposals—if recent history had taught anything, then compromise in anyone's name or by any formula led invariably to filibustering and new demands for the extension of slavery. On that question he would not give ground. "Hold firm, as with a chain of steel," he advised Congressman Washburne of Galena, Illinois. Slavery, in Mr. Lincoln's view, had reached its limit. On this point he stood inflexible, unwilling to yield another inch of free soil. The game of compromise that still would be played out in grim drama in Congress already had been blocked and lost—in Springfield.

Soon Lincoln's mind would turn to drafting his First Inaugural and he would ask Herndon to fetch for him four references—the Constitution of the United States, Andrew Jackson's Proclamation of 1832 against Nullification, Webster's "Reply to Hayne," and Henry Clay's speech on the Compromise of 1850. But the greatest reference that he used might well have been entitled "Lincoln as A. Lincoln Knew Him."

Lincoln's speeches and writings at the time of his death exceeded one million words so that the record he left of himself would be longer than the Bible, including the Apocrypha, and longer than the complete works of Shakespeare. Yet the reading of Lincoln's own writings is a richly rewarding experience, revealing why the great humanity of the man became a national inspiration. By Christmas week, 1860, the whole Lincoln had jelled—then, as later, he was thin, bony, graceless, six feet four inches in his old carpet slippers, and his energy and endurance probably suffered from insufficient fat, sugar, and vitamins; then, as later, he was quick to tell a joke about himself in the midst of a knotty problem, for he had grown up with laughter and tears and understood how universal was the language of both. From early maturity to death he clung to the same principles and much the same ideas; in his writings those principles and ideas become living organisms, growing with the man, changing not in substance but in beauty of form, and his neighbors in New Salem and Springfield and later throughout America came to see him as a man of a fundamental creed whose scratchy pen and high-pitched voice spelled out his own Book of Proverbs. He belonged to that age in America distinguished for the rise of the common man, an impulse that no school or cult produced, but which came out of experience and the searching of the heart—that quality called individualism which linked Lincoln in an intellectual bond with Melville and Whitman. His method was that of the self-taught lawyer who looked closely at a proposition, then stood back and looked at it with detachment, testing it by syllogism, by the patterns of human behavior, and coming at last to a choice that put God at one extreme and the devil at another. For the moral Lincoln was a man of extremes. Right was an extreme and wrong was its opposite. Integrity was an extreme and expediency and compromise could be its undoing.

This was the man of Christmas week, 1860, forming a Cabinet, going to the nub of the weakness in the Crittenden proposals, and beginning to turn over in his mind the substance of his First Inaugural. Twenty-two years ago a mob in St. Louis had murdered a harmless mulatto on mere suspicion of wrongdoing and in Alton, Illinois, proslavery fanatics had killed Elijah P. Lovejoy for publishing an abolitionist newspaper. Greatly disturbed, Lincoln had spoken in Springfield on "The Perpetuation of our Political Institutions" and turning to the question of how Americans could protect themselves from "the caprice of the mob" had said:

> . . . Let reverence for the laws, be breathed by every American mother, to the lisping babe, that prattles on her lap—let it be taught in schools, in seminaries, and in colleges;—let it be written in primers, spelling books, and in almanacs;—let it be preached from the pulpit, proclaimed in legislative halls, and enforced in courts of justice. And, in short, let it become the *political religion* of the nation; and let the old and the young, the rich and the poor, the grave and the gay, of all sexes and tongues, and colors and conditions, sacrifice unceasingly upon its altars. . . .

In his First Inaugural he would say: ". . . to the extent of my ability, I shall take care, as the Constitution itself expressly enjoins upon me, that the laws of the Union be faithfully executed in all the states."

In 1850, writing notes for a lecture on the responsibilities of a young lawyer, he counseled:

> Don't stir up litigation. A worse man can scarcely be found than one who does. Point out to them how the nominal winner is often the real loser—in fees, expenses, and waste of time. As a peace-maker the lawyer has an opportunity of being a good man. There will still be business enough.

In his First Inaugural he would say: "Can aliens make treaties easier than friends can make laws? Can treaties be more faithfully enforced between aliens, than laws among friends? Suppose you go to war, you cannot fight always; and when, after much loss on both sides, and no gain on either, you cease fighting, the identical old questions, as to terms of intercourse, are again upon you."

A habit of Lincoln's lifetime was to write on scraps of paper ideas as they occurred to him. In 1854 he set down these beliefs:

> The ant, who has toiled and dragged a crumb to his nest, will furiously defend the fruit of his labor, against whatever robber assails him. So plain, that the most dumb and stupid slave that ever toiled for a master, does constantly *know* that he is wronged. So plain, that no one, high or low, ever does mistake it, except in a plainly *selfish* way; for although volume upon volume is written to prove slavery a very good thing, we never hear of a man who wishes to take the good of it, *by being a slave himself.*

In his First Inaugural he would say: "One section of our country believes slavery is *right,* and ought to be extended, while the other believes it is *wrong,* and ought not to be extended. This is the only substantial dispute."

And so thought by thought, argument by argument, Lincoln really needed no references as his First Inaugural took shape; in one form or another, it always had been there in his mind, the image he held of himself and his country. Prairie boyhood, storekeeper and postmaster and self-instructed surveyor, lawyer and politician and husband and father, all these experiences were in him: the mud of spring, the crack of the ax splitting rails, the love of people who struggled and survived. A note to the station-master in Springfield said: "The lady bearer of this, says she has freight at the depot, which she cannot get without four dollars. If this be correct, let her have the freight, and I will pay you any amount not exceeding four dollars on presentation of this note." Five days later Lincoln paid the amount; that side of him, the kindness, the sympathy, the understanding of how big the little tragedies could be always prevailed. To George P. Floyd, who sent him twenty-five dollars for some legal work, he wrote: "Fifteen dollars is enough for the job. I send you a receipt for fifteen dollars, and return to you a ten dollar bill." Half of the fifteen went to Herndon, of course; they divided fees as they came in, and avoided the nuisance of keeping books. An honest man, Lincoln—*that* always, in big and little ways, with himself and others.

The bells rang out the old year and welcomed in the new—and Lee heard them in Texas and Grant heard them in Galena, Illinois; the tones sounded through Charleston, and young men in long gray overcoats and French military caps marched along the cobbled streets, mingling their shouts with the other echoes that drifted across the harbor but faded before they reached old Sumter; in Washington, as the bells sounded, a tired President prayed, and secessionists in the bar at Willard's raised their glasses in salute to the rebel's dream; in Baltimore other glasses were raised and a toast drunk to the pledge that Lincoln would not live to be inaugurated; in New York Greeley heard them, glancing over a proof that told him the "Stock Market today has exhibited great buoyancy," and the Wood brothers winked across a table and down in Mackerelville there was a good fight over whether Bob had acted right in occupying that ——— fort; in

Boston Melville heard them too, and Emerson in near-by Concord.

An hour later Galusha Anderson heard the bells in St. Louis; in Chicago, the eighty "ballrooms" rocked in noisy welcome; and in Springfield, the President-elect looked up at the stars and wondered.

1861—a New Year—and in his First Inaugural he would say: "We are not enemies, but friends. Though passions may have strained, it must not break our bonds of affection. The mystic chords of memory, stretching from every battlefield, and patriot grave, to every living heart and hearthstone, all over this broad land, will yet swell the chorus of the Union, when again touched, as surely they will be, by the better angels of our nature."

PART II

Sumter Day, 1861

14

Where Yellowhammers Sang

SPRING crept along rivers with fine old Indian names—the Mobile and the Tombigbee, the Alabama and the Coosa, the Tallapoosa and the Black Warrior. Under a warming sun wild flowers spread brilliant carpets across the great rolling prairie of Alabama and slaves shouted at mules and plows turned over the sticky black clay that grew some of the finest cotton in the world. From deep in the thick growths of canebrake rose the trills of yellowhammers and their wings filled the air with golden glints.

Listening to the shouts of the plowboys, the songs of the birds, travelers jammed the decks of paddle-wheelers on the long journey from the Gulf of Mexico up the Mobile and Alabama to where Montgomery stood on its seven hills. Once the capital of Alabama had been in the western part of the state at Tuscaloosa, and Frederick Law Olmsted had wondered why the original site had been abandoned. Was Montgomery more centrally located or healthier or had the southern districts gained greater political influence? "The people here are not like you Northern people," an Alabamian told him. "They don't have to reason out everything so. They are fond of change, and they got tired of Tuscaloosa; the Montgomery folks wanted it there and offered to pay for moving it, so they let 'em have it. 'Twas just for the change."

Now as capital of the new Southern Confederacy old Montgomery teemed with visitors from the seven states that by February had broken away from the Union. Like Thomas

Cooper DeLeon of South Carolina, they climbed the steep hill
from the Alabama—"here scarce more than a biscuit-toss across"
—and reached wide, sandy Main Street, the city's chief artery. A
mile away, perched on other bluffs, stood the Capitol, to DeLeon
no "peculiarly stately pile," though the edifice dominated the
street "with quite a Roman vigor." Side streets, "uncertain in
direction and impractical as to pavement," ran into Main, but
clustered along them were fine old houses with pretty gardens and
spacious grounds. DeLeon surveyed these dwellings longingly,
and hoped for the best in finding accommodations in a city with
only two hotels. Montgomery Hall was the sort of place that
announced its character to the nose—country merchants, horsemen, and cattlemen had made it their headquarters for years.
The Exchange had more elegance—at least President Davis,
Cabinet members, and important persons stayed here.

Within a month after Mississippi had seceded on the ninth of
January, Alabama and Florida, Louisiana and Texas had joined
the parade; and by the fourth of February Montgomery had
begun bursting at the seams as delegates poured in to organize
a Provisional Government, frame a Constitution, and inaugurate
a President. A fortnight later the whole job had been finished,
and Mr. Lincoln, journeying to Washington for his own inauguration, might philosophize cheerily that "behind the cloud the sun
is shining still," but overcrowded Montgomery laughed heartily.
Except for Sumter in Charleston Harbor, Pickens in Pensacola
Bay, and two small forts off the Florida coast, all Federal forts
in these states had been seized along with every arsenal, customhouse, and lighthouse. The Post Office Department still func-
tioned, but then, observed Edward Pollard, transferring his base
to Montgomery, this service "the insurgents . . . arrogantly kept
for their own convenience." The Richmond journalist could not
conceal his astonishment at the "supreme ease" with which a
government had been swept "from the face of so large a territory
. . . without a drop of blood being shed, or even an arm per-
sistently raised to oppose the progress of the rebellion."

Poor Mr. Lincoln, a kinder spirit might have sighed—he could do nothing until after his inauguration on March fourth and then what more than to bolt the barn door and admit that seven of his best horses had been stolen? Gay, happy, carefree appeared Montgomery in its new role as a nation's capital, but when one scratched the surface the uneasiness, the jealousies, the animosities were quickly revealed. DeLeon thought that Montgomery was Washington "on a smaller scale," where "every knot of men had its grievances" and "state secrets were openly discussed in this Curbstone Congress."

The chatty Mrs. Chesnut, arriving with a husband who now represented South Carolina in the Provisional Congress, not only found "political intrigue . . . as rife as in Washington," but also the gossip as delightfully slanderous. To one observer Stephen R. Mallory of Florida, Secretary of the Navy, might seem a ridiculous figure with his "leaden eye," his clothes that fit a short, fat frame too tightly, and his commonplace talk that after five minutes made many forget why they had come to see him, but Mrs. Chesnut heard "he was so notoriously dissolute that a woman was compromised to be much seen with him." As for Governor Moore, everyone knew that "the old sinner had been making himself ridiculous with that little actress Maggie Mitchell"; and the middle-aged woman who babbled that it was a pity she wasn't a widow with all the eligible males now in Montgomery probably never forgot the comment of Mrs. Jefferson Davis: "If your husband is the best you could do when you were fresh and young, what better chance could you hope for now?"

Mrs. Chesnut had always loved Washington, and it was a joy to find the spirit, the spice, the bite of the old place recaptured here in Montgomery; then, turning a corner, she encountered one difference:

> I have seen a Negro woman sold on auction. I was walking. The woman on the block overtopped the crowd. I felt faint, seasick. The creature looked so much like my good little Nancy. She was a bright mulatto, with a pleasant face. She was magnificently gotten

up in silks and satins. She seemed delighted with it all, sometimes
ogling the bidders, sometimes looking quite coy and modest; but
her mouth never relaxed from its expanded grin of excitement.
I dare say the poor thing knew who would buy her. My very
soul sickened. It was too dreadful. I tried to reason. "You know
how women sell themselves and are sold in marriage, from queens
downward, eh? You know what the Bible says about slavery, and
marriage. Poor women, poor slaves."

Almost two weeks later Mrs. Chesnut was still boiling: "Any
lady is ready to tell you who is the father of all the mulatto
children in everybody's household but her own. Those, she seems
to think, drop from the clouds." Suddenly she was glad to be
leaving Montgomery; nor did Secretary Mallory fail to divert
her, telling of an affair of one of Buchanan's Cabinet members—
"like an old pelican slightly ill from eating too much fish."

The dominant figure in Montgomery was Jefferson Davis. No
dinner was complete without some gossip about the President.
Old Judge Thomas J. Withers growled that the Constitution had
been trampled underfoot when Congress provided the President
with a house; the Judge was disgusted, anyhow, to see Mr. Davis
paraded up to the inauguration in a coach drawn by six white
horses. Montgomery heard that Mrs. Davis hadn't wanted her
husband to be President, believing, or so Mrs. Chesnut quoted her
as saying, that "General of all the Armies would have suited his
temperament better." Edward Pollard, who respected Mr. Davis
no more than Mr. Buchanan, admitted Davis's social and cultural
virtues only to damn him the more heartily as one who "descended
to competition with his lieutenants, instead of exciting among
them a generous rivalry to serve his own central and crowning
fame."

Yet even those who served Mr. Davis with devotion sometimes
came to similar criticism; Robert Garlick Hill Kean, head of
the Confederate Bureau of War, would pass from the original
judgment of the President as "a *mule,* but a good *mule*" to that

of "a jackass," and words like "peevish," "fickle," "hairsplitting" would creep into Kean's opinions of Mr. Davis. The very ease with which the Confederacy had achieved the bloodless rebellion of February worked against the President; afterward came the heavy infighting of a government beleagured both from within and without, when the opportunities would be abundant to decide, as Kean declared, that the President was the "worst judge of men in the world."

Mr. Davis, as a man of intense likes and bitter hatreds, possessed a weakness that likely did him more harm than the inflammation of a facial nerve which regularly afflicted him with such spasms he was prostrated in almost blinding agony. Pollard, publishing his *Secret History* four years after the war, when passion hardly had cooled, characterized as a "remarkable presentiment" Mr. Davis's statement at his inaugural that "You will see many errors to forgive, many deficiencies to tolerate"; yet, Pollard conceded, "his worst enemies could never question his zeal or devotion."

So competent and affectionate a historian of the Confederacy as Douglas Southall Freeman combines something of Kean and Pollard in his judgment of President Davis:

> . . . His political life had been an endless struggle for a strict and rigid interpretation of legal right, and he was to prove himself too much of a constitutionalist to be a daring revolutionary. He hesitated to exceed the admitted limits of his authority as President, and when he did so he was as unconvincing as he was irritating; but he was instant to claim his full constitutional prerogatives, and in doing so he was often abrupt and sometimes unreasonable. Two things were certain to make him hostile; one was to accuse him of unfairness; the other was to impinge upon his authority as President. . . . With a political antagonist he would dispute to the last line of a long correspondence, in as high regard for logical victories in the theoretical points at issue as if he were speaking for *The Congressional Globe*. . . . His stubborn loyalty to friends of mediocre mind was to cost the Confederacy dearly. . . .

When Judge Withers snorted at the sight of the President riding to his inauguration in a coach and six, Jefferson Davis was fifty-two. Born in Kentucky on June 3, 1808, he was still an infant when Samuel Davis moved his family to a place near Woodville, in Wilkinson County, Mississippi. Since Jefferson was his tenth child, Samuel Davis could not resist hopefully giving the boy the middle name of Finis. The elder Davis has been described as a man of scant schooling, but of "good blood"; and young Jeff absorbed the bearing and habits of the aristocrat that were attributed to his father. A deep affection existed between the two, and in a letter in 1823, when economic misfortunes had overwhelmed Samuel Davis, the man counseled his youngest son:

> ... Remember the short lessons of instruction offered you before our parting. Use every possible means to acquire useful knowledge as knowledge is power, the want of which has brought misery and mischief on your father in old age—That you may be happy & shine in society when your father is beyond the reach of harm is the most ardent wish of his heart—

At the time Jeff attended Transylvania College in Lexington, Kentucky, the "Athens of the West," during the years when Horace Holley was liberalizing that institution to the scandalized discomfiture of Presbyterian supporters who heard themselves ridiculed for theological hairsplitting by a card-playing, horse-race loving college president. Holley was an intellectual pioneer; he fostered education in American literature, law, and medicine, breathing a vitality into Transylvania that transformed it from an obscure backwoods college into a flourishing and important institution of higher learning. Young Davis had no wish to leave Lexington where life was gay, books plentiful, conversations lively; almost grudgingly, he accepted an appointment to West Point and in hot August of 1824 had his first glimpse of the drab stone and stucco of the Academy's buildings. But in time he discovered that "public house or place where spiritous liquors are sold kept by one Benjamin Havens at or near Buttermilk Falls and distant about two miles from West Point" and came within a whisker of expulsion for being caught there drinking something stronger than the buttermilk for which the Falls were named. Young Robert E. Lee, who followed Davis to the Academy by a year, never was found off-bounds enjoying the consolations of Benny Havens'—Lee had one demerit in four years whereas Davis acquired 120 his first year, 70 his second, 137 his third—yet the Virginian was warmly welcomed into the Southern "set" that Albert Sidney Johnston dominated. So, too, were Joseph E. Johnston and Leonidas Polk, men destined to other leading roles in the Confederacy. When in 1828 Cadet Davis graduated from West Point no academic wreaths were pressed upon his brow; he stood twenty-third in a class of thirty-three.

Assigned to the First Infantry, Davis served at various posts in the wild Northwest, and during "the winter of the deep snow" (1831), alone except for his Negro servant on the Yellow River, suffered the pneumonia that affected his health for the remainder of his life. Later he fought in the Black Hawk War, then abruptly on June 30, 1835, resigned from the army. For two years Jeff had courted Sarah Knox Taylor, daughter of Colonel Zachary Taylor, who steadfastly refused to give his consent to their marriage. But a stubborn suitor and a persistent girl at last prevailed—"Some day," Sarah Knox told the hardheaded colonel, "you will see his rare qualities as I do"—and Jeff took his bride to Mississippi, where his brother Joseph had given him eighteen hundred acres to start life anew as a cotton planter. Tragedy struck quickly. Jefferson Davis, near death with the same dreadful malaria to which his bride of three months succumbed, insisted that the funeral be held in his sickroom. His grief was deep. Friends saw him, when his health returned, walking to the cemetery where he could gaze in melancholic silence at the brick-covered grave:

SARAH KNOX TAYLOR
WIFE OF JEFFERSON DAVIS
DIED SEPT. 15, 1835
AGE 21.

For the next eight years Jefferson Davis, cotton planter, lived a quiet life of retirement and study. Books, which he always had loved, became warm friends, and works like Adam Smith's *Wealth of Nations,* the writings of John Locke, and any volume that touched upon the history and interpretation of the Constitution absorbed his interest. A gentleness developed in this sensitive man that no one recognized more keenly than the slaves on the plantation. He knew every Negro child by name. No locks were placed on his corncribs so that any slave might feed his chickens. If a Negro fell "out of sorts" with the master, Jefferson Davis rested uneasily until he and the servant were back on friendly terms. He insisted that no slave could be punished for any offense unless he had been tried and found guilty by a court of fellow slaves. He provided regular dental care for his Negroes and built a nursery for children of mothers who worked in the fields.

Drawn into politics by Mississippi's exciting gubernatorial race of 1843, Jefferson Davis served as an elector for the Polk and Dallas ticket the following year. But by far the more important event occurred when en route to a political caucus in Vicksburg in 1842 he met briefly a tall, high-spirited girl whom brother Joseph had invited to the plantation for the Christmas festivities. Varina Anne Howell then was seventeen, and the mind that never failed in forming positive opinions of whomever she met retained impressions of this first encounter that could not have lasted more than half an hour. "He is the kind of person," Varina wrote her mother, "I should expect to rescue one from a mad dog at any risk, but to insist upon a stoical indifference to the fright afterward." Varina doubted if she would ever like him as much as she did his brother Joe. And she added: "Would you believe it, he is refined and cultivated, and yet he is a Democrat!" He was as well a persistent suitor for in late February, 1845 they were married. That fall Mississippi Democrats sent Davis to Washington as a member of Congress. The evenings he spent with his political idol, John C. Calhoun, were the bright moments to Davis in his brief time in Congress; speaking on the Oregon question, the Mississippian extolled "the love of Union in our hearts"; then, after less than six months in Washington, the outbreak of the War with Mexico brought Davis home to serve as a colonel with the First Mississippi Volunteers. Varina brought back vivid opinions of what it meant to be "a politician's wife," describing the experience as "everything which darkens the sunlight and contracts the happy sphere of home."

Jefferson Davis's record as a soldier and officer in Mexico earned him deserved distinction. Through a storm of shot he led a charge without bayonets against Fort Leneria at Monterey; and at Buena Vista, attacked by a superior force of Mexican lancers, he formed his men in the shape of the letter V, opened toward the enemy, and utterly routed the Mexicans by exposing them to a cruel covering fire. Wounded, he remained in the saddle until the battle ended, as stoically indifferent to personal danger as Varina had believed him to be on first meeting; and for his coolness and gallantry he was raised in rank to brigadier general. Offered the portfolio as Secretary of War in the Cabinet of President Pierce, Davis handled his post with vigor and imagination. He proposed the use of camels on the Western plains, introduced improvements in infantry tactics, iron gun carriages, muskets and pistols, approved the use of the Minié ball, ordered large guns cast hollow, adopted a larger grain of powder, and added four regiments to the army. A faith in his judgment in military affairs became almost an obsession.

In the Senate during the years of the Buchanan Administration, Davis clashed violently with Douglas on the question of "popular sovereignty." The Democratic Party, he believed, was the only national party, dedicated to the rigid enforcement of States Rights under the compact of the Constitution; and, he warned Douglas, should the party ever become "recreant to its principles . . . I for one shall be ready to leave it." Again the Mississippian told Douglas: ". . . he is a poor student of the world's history who does not understand that communities at last must yield to the dictates of their interests." Neither Davis nor Douglas would give ground; the Democratic Party fell apart, assuring the election of Mr. Lincoln; and after the New Year, when Congress reconvened, it became quickly evident that Republican opposition and secessionist fever had doomed the Crittenden proposals or any alternative compromise. On January twenty-first, after Mississippi had seceded, Davis delivered his farewell address to the Senate, declaring: "I am sure I feel no hostility to you, Senators from the North. I am sure there is not one of you, whatever sharp discussion there may have been between us, to whom I cannot now say, in the presence of my God, I wish you well." On parting, he offered his apology "for any pain which, in heat of discussion, I have inflicted"; and added: "I go hence unencumbered of the remembrance of any injury received, and having discharged the duty of making the only reparation in my power for any injury offered."

Washington buzzed with angry threats to arrest members of Congress from seceding states, and Greeley's *Tribune*, infuriated by the roles Davis and Albert G. Brown, his fellow Senator from Mississippi, had played in hastening the break between North and South, snarled: "Jefferson, if he were now President, would arrest them for treason, as he did Aaron Burr, on much slighter grounds. In the hands of Old Hickory, they would have fared still worse." Unmolested, Davis journeyed to Mississippi, delighted to learn he had been put in command of the state army with the rank of major general. He had only one wish now that he was home, he said, and that was "to repair my fences." He could not then believe of the Northern states that "the lust of empire" would impel them "to wage against their weaker neighbors a war of subjugation."

Meanwhile a fiasco in Charleston Harbor had strengthened the hands of secessionists who, unlike Jefferson Davis, both accepted the possibility of war and acted as though it already had been declared. On January second General Scott sent explicit instructions to Colonel Lorenzo Thomas, Assistant Adjutant General, to write Major Anderson he could return any fire upon Fort Sumter or upon any relief boat sent to provision the garrison.

But this letter was delayed in reaching Anderson and still had not been received on the ninth when the *Star of the West* arrived off Charleston Harbor with men, arms, and supplies for Sumter. Privately chartered, the vessel had left New York's Governor's Island after dark on the fourth; the secrecy was complete as far as Major Anderson was concerned, for he knew nothing about its departure or probable arrival; and whether secessionist agents in New York were as well mystified remains an interesting conjecture. Thomas did not write Anderson that he could protect the vessel, if attacked, until the fifth; Thomas might as well have handed the letter to Captain McGowan of the *Star of the West* to deliver in person if he managed to run by secessionist shore batteries and guard boats.

At one thirty in the morning, McGowan's steamship arrived and could find no guiding marks for Charleston bar. The *Star of the West* proceeded slowly, and at four o'clock, with the sounding giving four and a half fathoms of water, "discovered a light through the haze, which at that time crossed the horizon." Deciding the light was on Sumter, McGowan steered southwest for the main ship channel and "hove to to await daylight." There was a manly terseness in the Captain's account of subsequent events:

> ... As the day began to break, discovered a steamer just in shore of us, which, as soon as she saw us, burned one blue light and two red lights, as signals, and shortly after steamed over the bar and into the ship channel. The soldiers now were all put below, and no one allowed on deck but our own crew. As soon as there was light enough to see, we crossed the bar and proceeded on up the channel (the outer bar buoy having been taken away). The steamer ahead of us, sending off rockets and burning lights after broad daylight, continu[ed] on her course now near two miles ahead of us. When we arrived about two miles from Fort Moultrie —Fort Sumter being about the same distance—a masked battery on Morris [Island] opened fire upon us—distance about five-eighths of a mile. We had the American flag flying at our flagstaff

at the time, and, soon after the first shot, hoisted a large American ensign at the fore.

We continued on under the fire of the battery for over ten minutes; several of the shots going clean over us. One passed just clear of the pilot-house. Another passed between the smoke-stack and the walking-beams of the engine. Another struck the ship just abaft the fore-rigging, and stove in the planking, and another came within an ace of carrying away the rudder. At the same time there was a movement of two steamers from near Fort Moultrie—one of them towing a schooner—(I presume an armed schooner) with the intention of cutting us off.

Our position now became rather critical, as we had to approach Fort Moultrie to within three-fourths of a mile before we could keep away for Fort Sumter. A steamer approaching us with an armed schooner in tow, and the battery on the island firing at us all the time, and, having no cannon to defend ourselves from the attacks of the vessels, we concluded that to avoid certain capture or destruction, we would endeavor to get to sea. . . .

A reporter for the New York *Evening Post,* aboard the *Star of the West,* captured the bitter humiliation of those moments: "Why does not Major Anderson open fire upon that battery and save us? We look in vain for help; the American flag flies from Fort Sumter, and the American flag at our stern and bow is fired upon, and yet there is not the slightest recognition of our presence from the fort from which we look for protection. . . . Is it possible that Fort Sumter has been taken by the South Carolinians?" Inside Sumter the morning was no less galling. Men stood at their guns, ready for action, and yet Anderson, without specific orders, believed that he could not give the command to fire. The Morris Island battery was beyond the reach of Sumter's gun— even Captain Abner Doubleday, chafing at the indignity of the scene, admitted that—but Fort Moultrie was within range, and, insisted Doubleday, "we could have kept down the fire there long enough to enable the steamer to come in." For the remainder of his life Doubleday was plagued by one question. What if the *Star of the West* had "gone down before our eyes?"

15

The South Girds for War

SO THE secessionists, throwing their hats into the air, deciding (as Doubleday observed sourly) that Northerners were "harmless people," seizing Federal forts, customhouses, and lighthouses, descended on Montgomery in early February to elect a President for their new Confederacy. No one really wanted Jefferson Davis —least of all the Mississippi delegation, who saw him as the logical commander for their state army. Robert Barnwell Rhett coveted the office, but even then most secessionists understood that Rhett had pretty well exhausted his usefulness. Howell Cobb or Robert Toombs were strong candidates, since Georgia exerted a powerful influence in the Convention, yet if either Cobb or Toombs refused to yield supporters, a serious deadlock could result, depriving the Confederacy of the sweet smile of harmony it was turning to the world.

To South Carolina's James Chesnut the perfect compromise candidate was another Georgian, for all that Alexander Stephens arrived in Montgomery under the stigma of remaining "a Union man at heart." But Stephens would not accept the Presidency unless he could form a Cabinet of men with views similar to his own, which was more than even Chesnut could manage, good diplomat though he was. Almost everyone distrusted Cobb and wanted Toombs, and in the passion to stop Cobb no one apparently troubled to ascertain Georgia's own choice, which was Toombs. So Davis—a "safe" but "mean" man, grumbled one delegate—

won the Presidency, and despite the fact that the radical secessionists found Stephens a "bitter pill," the sickly, testy, disapproving
Georgian was named Vice-President. To South Carolina's Laurence
Keitt it became "a foregone conclusion" that Davis would be a
"failure" and his Cabinet "a farce"; but then Keitt, in the minority
as a Cobb man, only demonstrated to Mrs. Chesnut a habit with
South Carolinians where politics were involved: "We wrangled,
as we always do." Nor was anyone more surprised at the choice
than Jefferson Davis, who declared that "I had not believed myself as well suited to the office as others," but was "better adapted
to command in the field." Davis had no illusions as to the ordeal
before him. En route to Montgomery, he met his old friend,
Judge William L. Sharkey. What did the future portend? Davis
answered grimly: "A war, long and bloody."

If the Charleston *Mercury* could be trusted, Mr. Davis, greeting
the people of Alabama, reached Montgomery in hardly a peace-
loving mood: "The time for compromise, he said, had passed, and
our only hope was in a determined maintenance of our position,
and to make all who opposed us smell Southern powder and feel
Southern steel." It was talk like this that sickened the heart of another traveler in the South. On February first Texas voted 166 to 7
to secede from the Union. Colonel Robert E. Lee would have no
part in the schemes of the Texas fire-eaters. Homeward bound, he
stopped by a spring for lunch one day, and spoke his feelings to
Captain George B. Cosby, a fellow officer. Lee refused to surrender
his "confidence that Virginia would not act on impulse." Yet
what if Virginia did secede? "He had been ever taught," Lee said,
"that his first allegiance was due his mother State," and "under
no circumstances could he ever bare his sword against Virginia's
sons." As Lee spoke, Cosby remembered, "his emotions brought
tears to his eyes, and he turned away to avoid showing his
emotions."

The great difficulty that confronted Jefferson Davis in Montgomery was in forging a government that must contest with old

neighbors between rival *concepts* of what constituted right. The Confederate Constitution, in large measure the creation of Alexander Stephens, dramatized this subtle distinction, for the Confederate document was in most respects a copy of the Federal Constitution. Yet one important difference remained and that was in the frank use of the words "slave" and "slavery." The right of property in "slaves" was affirmed; the right to protect "slavery" in any new or acquired territory stipulated.

Both Davis and Stephens carried on to the end of their lives in the tedious and often carping books they would write the argument that the war between the Confederacy and the Union rested wholly upon points of Constitutional interpretation and that to call it "a slaveowner's war" insulted the South. "I have not attempted and shall not permit myself to be drawn into any discussion of the merits or demerits of slavery as an ethical or even as a political question," Davis wrote in *The Rise and Fall of the Confederate Government,* sounding like the cold, unapproachable man his enemies declared him to be whenever his motives were questioned; and yet his reminiscences belie his statement. Repeatedly he is confounded, stung, bitter because the world insisted on seeing the conflict in terms of freedom vs. slavery, antislavery vs. proslavery, free soil vs. slave soil. He keeps returning to these charges, plucking at them, as though they were nettles embedded in his spirit. He cannot see man's aspirations through any eyes but his own; never does the illusion of individuality seem more complete. One feels keenly his emotions as he writes— that he believes himself to be a good man and a kind man, that his was not a mean or narrow choice, that the world has been tricked by the ingenious propaganda of the Black Republicans. He cannot concede that history will sustain such libels upon the South; all of the issues that have turned other sections of the country against the South are untrue. Who save a Southerner ever used the ignorant African with such gentleness and understanding? He will not lose the Cause; he will not be defeated; posterity must judge him right.

Such was the conviction of the man who reached Montgomery in February to become President for the next six years of the Confederacy (the Constitution forbade re-election). And he asked even then, with a militant wave sweeping the young Confederacy, if the vast majority of Southerners now ready to die for their homeland were not persons who never had owned a slave or at most one or two. In rural areas where the yellowhammers sang— and elsewhere throughout the seceding states—knives were being honed down to a needle-point sharpness and blacksmiths repaired old hunting guns. A hundred military companies were forming— the Tallapoosa Thrashers, the Bartow Yankee Killers, the Southern Rejectors of Old Abe, the Cherokee Lincoln Killers—and poor whites and plantation owners drilled side by side as soon they would march shoulder to shoulder singing:

> We are a band of brothers,
>   And native to the soil,
> Fighting for the property,
>   We gained by honest toil;
> And when our rights were threatened,
>   The cry rose near and far,
> Hurrah for the Bonnie Blue Flag,
>   That bears a Single Star!

Yet is that the whole of the matter? Or is it possible that in a South mobilizing for war, as the spring of 1861 wore on, emotions were far more complicated than politicians admitted, if indeed they grasped all the forces involved? Johnny Reb, poor white, plowing his scrubby acres that spring, looked at the horizon and realized how little he knew about the country. Adventure called to his heart, and even its martial tone sounded sweet. At evening he walked up to the house to eat supper with Pa and Ma in the small, poorly furnished farmhouse he called home. There were no books to read beside smudgy oil lamps; the speech of the family was crude and phonetical, and in words like "cos" for "cause" and "redy" and "pore" and "specerlators" for "speculators" an almost total lack of education was reflected; in the barn were the spin-

ning wheels and looms of an even more primitive existence not
too long agone.

Johnny, finishing his supper, heard a galloping horse along the
road, and Johnny reflected bitterly that here rode the son of
the plantation owner who often tried to buy out the little farms of
the poor whites because he believed their shiftless habits were a
bad example for the slaves. The horse stopped, a voice shouted:
"Come, Johnny—join the Chickasaw Desperados! Come, Johnny,
we need you in the Hornets' Nest Riflemen!" Even in Johnny's
dreams such social acceptance had not seemed possible, and later
when well-bred girls made every young defender of Southern
liberty a hero with whom to flirt, or to kiss good-by, Johnny would
have been glandularly inadequate to a woeful degree not to have
responded.

In Johnny's mind existed another image that exerted a powerful
influence—the evil face of old Nat Turner! Almost thirty years
had passed since that muggy day when in Southampton County,
Virginia, old Nat, as trusted as ever a slave could be, rallied other
slaves around him to deliver his people from bondage. In two
bloody August days Turner and his mob killed nearly sixty white
people. Thereafter no year could pass in the South without someone mentioning, in sick, inward trembling, the name of Nat
Turner; mere rumors of slave insurrection could set in motion
an hysteria that might not be satisfied until at least one slave was
hanging from a tree; and it would have been an unimaginative
Southern editor or politician or preacher who did not see Nat
Turner's sinister face behind Black Republicanism.

Johnny responded instantly to such talk—the more so since
the only family Nat Turner and his killers spared had been poor
whites "because they thought no better of themselves than they
did of Negroes"; the more so when Frederick Douglass declared
that "to be a slave, was thought to be bad enough; but to be a
poor man's slave was deemed a disgrace"; the more so when slaves,
knowing their owners would protect them, were openly con-
temptuous of "white trash." No recruiting propaganda worked

better on Johnny than to ask, "You there—you want some big nigger bumping your womenfolks in the road or making eyes at your girl?" Johnny feared nothing more.

Deep-rooted resentments and hatreds and feelings of insecurity faded as Johnny became merged into the image of Southern Chivalry. So Johnny fetched his gun, oiled it, balanced it in his hand, and since in Johnny's speech there remained a rich frontier idiom he didn't care "how big those nigger-lovin' Yankees came," a gun made all men equal and if that failed—

"Why then," boasted Johnny to his Pa or Ma or his girl, "I'll just out with my knife and whittle him down to my size!"

Millions of slaves in the seceding states saw Johnny and the plantation owner's son drilling and parading and flirting with the girls; but slaves remained docile, almost amused, by all the war talk and speculation over what Mr. Lincoln and Black Republicanism might mean to them.

"Ain' you neber been see two dogs fightin' ober bone 'fo now?" one slave is on record as asking another.

"Cose I is," said the other, "but I dunno what dat dar got to do wid dis here."

"Well, you ain't neber been see de bone fight none, is yo'?"

For all that keeping the Negro in his place was used as an argument to incite Johnny to hone down his knife blade and repair his rifle, every outward appearance of the typical slave suggested indifference to this white man's quarrel. The slave knew what had happened to old Nat Turner once his avengers had caught up with him. And an underground existing between slave quarters quickly solidified the general slave attitude. If Mr. Lincoln meant to bring deliverance from bondage, well and good. They'd just wait till it came down the road, supported by Mr. Lincoln's soldiers. Meanwhile Old Massa could feed and clothe and house them—let him worry 'bout dat. A kind of secret, deep, tantalizing humor was in the situation; and out of Chicago in 1862 came one of the great songs of the war that captured the moment for which many a docile, good-humored slave waited:

Say, darkeys, hab you seen de massa,
    Wid de muffstash on his face,
Go long de road some time dis mornin'
    Like he gwine to leab de place?
He seen a smoke, way up de ribber,
    Whar de Linkum gumboats lay;
He took his hat, an' lef berry sudden,
    An' I spec he's run away!

        De massa run? ha, ha!
        De darkey stay? ho, ho!
        It mus' be now de kingdom comin'
        An' de year ob Jubilo!

As the spring days dropped from the calendar, the militant
spirit swept over Louisiana, Texas, Florida, Georgia, Mississippi,
and Alabama, calling to Johnny Reb on plantation or backwoods
farm to become a "Lincoln Killer" or "Southern Defender." In
Charleston, according to Horace Greeley's spies within the city,
centered the eye of the gathering hurricane. From an article entitled "The War Spirit in Charleston," readers of the *Tribune*
learned that although Mrs. Anderson had been permitted to visit
the Major in Sumter, "the crowd of idlers who are now assembled
here from all parts of the state," spoke of seizing her as a hostage.
Citizens of Taunton, Massachusetts, wishing to present Anderson
with a sword, aroused a new wave of antagonism.

"The city," reported Mr. Greeley's correspondent, "is full of
soldiery, and belligerent citizens," all of whom, in the idiom of
New York's Mackerelville, were "spilin' for a muss." Again:
"The more daring of the leaders ... are praying for some shedding
of Southern blood, in order to arouse the border states." A thousand volunteers stood ready in Georgia—"this play at war is fine
fun." Sour and sweet notes blended in the Charleston cacophony:
"Great dissatisfaction is expressed here at the lack of 'patriotism'
in North Carolina; while on the other hand, travelers from Virginia report the utmost of secession fury in the pot-houses of

Petersburg and other places." And the ladies—God bless them!—"fully share in the war spirit, and promise themselves, if blood should be spilt, to play the part at least of Florence Nightingale, if some do not that of Joan of Arc."

No one felt more keenly the martial pressure from Charleston than Jefferson Davis in Montgomery. Fortunately the President knew exactly where to place his hand on the man for this emergency, and so onto the stage of Secessia walked the short, brisk, buoyant figure of Pierre Gustave Toutant Beauregard.

Contreras, the plantation home of the Toutant-Beauregards, stood in the rich corn and cane country below New Orleans where cypress and live-oak forests cast dark shadows over sluggish swamps. Here on May 28, 1818, little Pierre arrived—doubtless howling lustily for attention even then. A heated family furore arose when, not yet sixteen, Pierre decided to enter West Point; as Beauregard's biographer, T. Harry Williams, points out, "even his father, who went further than most Creoles in associating with Americans, thought this was carrying collaboration too far"; but the lad had his stubborn streak to which he added the impudence of chopping the hyphen out of Toutant-Beauregard so that he would be placed higher on the class lists at the Academy. Everyone predicted a bright future for the young Creole, ranking second in a class of forty-five at graduation in 1838; and none praised him more highly than his artillery instructor, Robert Anderson, now sitting in uneasy anticipation inside Fort Sumter. How small the country really was in those years came out in the manner in which the paths of its sons so often crisscrossed, and the same Bob Anderson who taught Beauregard had, as a lieutenant, mustered Lincoln in and out of service in the Black Hawk War.

Commissioned a second lieutenant with the engineers, Beauregard served at Fort Adams in Rhode Island, at Pensacola, Florida, where he helped to construct coastal defenses, in Louisiana conducting a topographical and hydrographical survey of the islands of Barataria Bay where once Lafitte and his pirates had hidden, at

Fort McHenry in Baltimore, and in the forts at the mouth of the Mississippi before the War with Mexico came along to give him the chance for glory for which he yearned. He was a fine engineer and a brave soldier, and receiving two brevets he complained that he deserved three. The Creole touchiness and suspicion were never buried very far below the surface with Beauregard; and both his vanity and ambition stretched out like his name. He was bright in a bookish way about military matters, and old Scott recognized that ability; still, another young engineer, Robert E. Lee, could think more on his own and he received a third brevet.

After the war a second marriage brought Beauregard a powerful political ally in his new brother-in-law, Senator John Slidell. The influence of this mighty Louisiana boss helped in no small measure in 1853 to bring Beauregard his appointment as superintendent of the customhouse in New Orleans, and later still, even as Louisiana grew warmer day by day with secession fever, appointment as superintendent at West Point. The assignment was ridiculous any-where except in the United States in late 1860, where loyalty or disloyalty suspended on the thinnest hair of conscience, and so the highly prosecessionist Beauregard set off for his duties at West Point, naturally stopping en route in New York City to chat about the national situation with secessionists there. He was advising young cadets from Louisiana, "Watch me; and when I jump, you jump," when the War Department, taking a cold look at this in-credible appointment, revoked Beauregard's orders.

Peeved—after all, Louisiana had not yet seceded—Beauregard returned to New Orleans, demanding one hundred and sixty-five dollars for traveling expenses to return home to fight the national government and he never quite forgave the niggardliness of the Washington authorities in refusing to pay this amount. Other disillusionments awaited him in Louisiana. He returned to find Braxton Bragg in charge of the state army, an office Beauregard believed he deserved and with a none too well concealed huffiness he turned down a colonelcy and then made the grand gesture— he enlisted as a private in the Orleans Guards. But brother-in-law

Slidell was nudged behind the scenes, the proper letters went off to Jefferson Davis, and in mid-February the summons came to report to Montgomery.

Beauregard left New Orleans in high fettle, knowing that Braxton Bragg was chewing a jealous heart, and nothing in his interview with President Davis and Secretary of War Leroy Pope Walker (who insisted on making "Peter" out of "Pierre") spoiled the pleasant mood. Beauregard was offered a brigadier-generalship, which he was delighted to accept. He was offered the critical command in Charleston, and agreed that his background as a skilled engineer officer made him an excellent man for this delicate assignment. At long last he was fighting for a government that would honor his expense account. He reached Charleston on March third—the "Grand Creole"—and, confessed Mrs. Chesnut, "a hero worshipper was struck dumb because I said that so far he has only been a Captain of artillery or engineers or something."

Beauregard in Charleston, Davis in Montgomery . . . the stage of national drama six weeks hence was being set. Lee, journeying home from Texas, had reached Arlington Heights. Across the Potomac on March fourth President Lincoln was inaugurated and that day the new Confederate flag of seven stars was raised on the Capitol in Montgomery. In Charleston Rhett's *Mercury* said: "Let the argument proceed to the next logical and necessary step—an appeal to arms . . . We are ready." But the country wasn't ready—not quite yet.

16

"Everything Will
Come Out All Right"

EARLY in February Mr. Lincoln slipped away from Springfield to visit his stepmother in Coles County, Illinois. An old friend, who accompanied the President-elect on part of this tedious journey, remembered that Mr. Lincoln called Sarah Bush Lincoln "his best friend in this world" and declared that "no man could love a mother more than he loved her." Along the way a former acquaintance taunted the President-elect for "putting on style with his stove pipe hat." Mr. Lincoln grinned. The village school was dismissed so that the children could welcome the distinguished visitor; drums and fifes were "borrowed" from Oliver Harris's store, since the proprietor could not be found; and "while martial music was being played they picked up Mr. Lincoln and carried him about the front yard." Old friends, crowding in to greet the President-elect, recognized the pride in the eyes of Sara Bush Lincoln, seated in a rocking chair near her famous stepson; on the bed they saw the fur cape he had brought as a gift. Then, at parting, the woman spoke her secret dread:

"Abe, I'll never see you alive again. They will kill you."

"Don't worry," Lincoln said consolingly. "Everything will come out all right."

But would it? On the afternoon of the President-elect's last day in Springfield, he asked his partner not to remove the sign reading "Lincoln & Herndon."

"If I live," he said, "I'm coming back some time, and then we'll go right on practicing law as if nothing had ever happened."

They shook hands, old and trusting friends. "I am sick of office-holding already," Mr. Lincoln grumbled. The twelve-day journey from Springfield to Washington surely was among the ordeals that made him add, grumpily, "I shudder to think of the tasks that are still ahead."

A depressing fortnight followed. With events moving rapidly in Montgomery, Mr. Lincoln was reluctant to make any precipitate comment, and so impressed many as evasive, uncertain, a bungler like Buchanan. Almost illogically he assured the Ohio Legislature that although North and South held "different views . . . nobody is suffering." His special train approached Albany when the news came that Jefferson Davis had been inaugurated as President of the Confederacy and the charmer and actress, Maggie Mitchell, had danced upon the Stars and Stripes. With the Union breaking in two, Lincoln's fatigue, his awkwardness, his homespun manners and speech added to the growing disappointment. What kind of leader was this? A last straw to many was to find him appearing at the New York Opera House in black kid gloves. Then reports of a plot against the President-elect's life from the celebrated sleuth, Allan Pinkerton, and from Scott and Seward persuaded Mr. Lincoln to pass through a sleeping Baltimore and the outrageous story of a reporter that he reached Washington disguised in a Scotch-plaid cap and long military cloak increased the ridicule heaped upon him. "A noble entrance into the government of a free people!" sneered Mrs. Chesnut, but often Northern contempt was equally biting.

Washington had not changed greatly in the twelve years since Mr. Lincoln had lived here as the solitary Whig Congressman from Illinois. Tadpoles, malaria, and mosquitoes still bred in Rock Creek; the poorly laid cobbles along Pennsylvania Avenue gave the town its one paved street; every house had its open drain and Congressman Albert G. Riddle declared that "the Capital of the Republic had more malodors than the poet Coleridge ascribed to ancient Cologne." The two wings of the Capitol remained unfinished so that "the little old jug-like dome of the old central structure still occupied its place, utterly lost in the expanse of the acres of roof that it could not dominate." The Executive Mansion, "the little State Department, set squat on the ground," the edifices of War and Navy, the Post Office Department and of the Interior were the only completed public buildings; and Congressman Riddle described the Washington Monument, the Capitol, and the Treasury building as "melancholy specimens of arrested development."

Mr. Lincoln may have upset New York sophisticates by wearing the wrong gloves to the opera, but he knew that his first duty as President-elect was to call at the Executive Mansion. Buchanan was conducting a Cabinet meeting when the doorman presented Mr. Lincoln's card.

"Uncle Abe is downstairs!" exclaimed the astonished President.

So began Mr. Lincoln's first day in Washington. Before the day ended, surrounded by the clamor of appointment-seekers and official callers in the suite he occupied at Willard's, the man from Springfield revealed his tough fiber. Meeting in the Federal capital at the time was a Peace Conference attended by delegates from twenty-two states, who requested an audience that evening with the President-elect. Courteously Mr. Lincoln received the group in Parlor Number 6 at Willard's, and Lucius E. Chittenden, a member of the Vermont delegation, recalled how "his words arrested the attention; his wonderful vivacity surprised every spectator."

Speaking for Virginia, William C. Rives said that he had retired from public life, yet had believed it his duty to come to the conference in an effort to save the Union. "But the clouds that hang over it are very dark," Rives added. "I have no longer the courage of my younger days. I can do little—you can do much. Everything now depends on you."

Mr. Lincoln couldn't agree. "My course," he declared, "is as plain as a turnpike road. It is marked out by the Constitution. I am in no doubt which way to go. Suppose now we all stop discussing and try the experiment of obedience to the Constitution and the laws. Don't you think it would work?"

"Permit me to answer that suggestion," interposed George W. Summers from western Virginia. "Yes, it will work. If the Constitution is your light, I will follow it with you, and the people of the South will go with us."

What Chittenden described as the "sepulchral voice" of Virginia's James A. Seddon "sharply struck in":

"It is not of your professions we complain. It is your sins of omission—of your failure to enforce the laws—to suppress your John Browns and your Garrisons, who preach insurrection and make war upon our property!"

"I believe John Brown was hung and Mr. Garrison imprisoned," the President-elect replied dryly. "You cannot justly charge the North with disobedience to statutes or with failing to enforce them. You have made some which were very offensive, but they have been enforced, notwithstanding."

Seddon, destined in future months to serve in the Confederate Cabinet as Secretary of War, was a difficult man to sway. "You do not enforce the laws," he persisted. "You refuse to execute the statute for the return of fugitive slaves. Your leading men openly declare that they will not assist the marshals to capture or return slaves."

"Wrong in your facts again," said Mr. Lincoln. "Your slaves have been returned—yes, from the shadow of Faneuil Hall in the heart of Boston. Our people do not like the work, I know. They will do what the law commands, but they will not volunteer to act as tip-staves or bum-bailiffs. The instinct is not natural to the race. Would you join in the pursuit of a fugitive slave if you could avoid it? Is such the work of gentlemen?"

Seddon, cornered in these arguments, changed his base of attack. "Your press is incendiary!" he cried. "It advocates servile insurrection, and advises our slaves to cut their masters' throats. You do not suppress your newspapers. You encourage their violence!"

The prairie lawyer always had known how to handle a jury. He asked Mr. Seddon's pardon, but again he must disagree. No Northern newspaper, "not the most ultra," ever had advocated slave insurrection or throat-cutting. "A gentleman of your intelligence should not make such assertions," the President-elect said. "We do maintain the freedom of the press—we deem it necessary to a free government. Are we peculiar in that respect? Is not the same doctrine held in the South?"

William E. Dodge spoke then for the New York delegation. Referring to the "great anxiety" with which the country awaited Mr. Lincoln's inaugural address, Dodge declared: "It is for you, sir, to say whether the whole nation shall be plunged into bankruptcy; whether the grass shall grow in the streets of our commercial cities." Chittenden detected "a merry twinkle" in Mr. Lincoln's eyes. "If it depends upon me," he replied, "the grass will not grow anywhere except in the fields and the meadows." Dodge pressed the point. Did the President-elect mean that he would "yield to the just demands of the South?" His meaning, Mr. Lincoln explained, was that the Constitution must be "respected, obeyed, enforced, and defended, let the grass grow where it may." Chittenden observed, unable to conceal his own high spirit:

> . . . The faces of the Republicans wore an expression of surprised satisfaction. Some of the more ardent Southerners silently left the room. They were unable to comprehend the situation. The ignorant countryman they had come to ridicule threatened no crime but obedience to the Constitution. This was not the entertainment to which they were invited, and it was uninteresting. For the more conservative Southern delegates, the statesmen, Mr. Lincoln seemed to offer an attraction. They remained until he finally retired.

No one in Parlor Number 6 at Willard's that evening had need to question Mr. Lincoln's political sophistication. Almost every delegate he greeted by name and achievement; frequently he recalled their middle initials. Nor did he ignore the fact that this Peace Conference had been convened at the request of the Legislature of Virginia. The Old Dominion still stood firm against the secessionists. Virginia was a powerful ally in holding the Upper South loyal to the Union, and, to Mr. Lincoln, that victory must be won first if the Union was to be restored. Upon this faith during the next six stormy weeks many of his principal actions would be based—his inaugural address, the crisis within the Cabinet, his attitude toward Sumter. Some would call him vacillating, powerless, even two-faced; but he knew whither he was going—in his own time, in his own way.

Montgomery made its move in the game of Disunion against Union. Through Senator Hunter of Virginia intelligence reached Jefferson Davis that President Buchanan would be "happy" to receive "a Commissioner or Commissioners from the Confederate States" to consult toward "effecting equitable settlement of all questions relating to the common property of the States and the public debt," and in late February Judge Martin J. Crawford of Georgia arrived in Washington. Although the hour was half past four in the morning, Judge Crawford was "surprised to see Pennsylvania Avenue, from the old National to Willard's Hotel," crowded with men hastening to arrange a meeting with Mr. Lincoln, "the great political almoner." Affairs at the Federal capital, in Judge Crawford's opinion, had become "feverish and emotional"; members of the House and Senate he found occupying their seats with "manifestation of anxious care or gloomy forebodings." But to Judge Crawford the greatest shock was the near-hysteria that reigned in the Executive Mansion with

> Mr. Buchanan . . . in a state of most thorough alarm, not only for his home at Wheatland, but for his personal safety.* In the very few days which had elapsed between the time of his promise to receive a Commissioner from the Confederate States and the actual

---

* To corroborate Judge Crawford's recollections, President Davis recalled an earlier conversation when Buchanan had "thought it not impossible that his homeward route would be lighted by burning effigies of himself," and that "on reaching his home he would find it a heap of ashes."

arrival of the Commissioner, he had become so fearfully panic-stricken, that he declined to receive him or to send any message to the Senate touching the subject-matter of the mission.

The Commissioner had been for several years in Congress before the Administration of Mr. Buchanan, as well as during his official term, and had always been in close political and social relations with him; yet he was afraid of a public visit from him. He said that he had only three days of official life left, and could incur no further dangers or reproaches than those he had already borne from the press and public speakers of the North.

The intensity of prevalent feeling increased as the vast crowds, arriving by every train, added fresh material; and hatred and hostility toward our new Government were manifested in almost every conceivable manner.

Buchanan's weary ordeal ended at noon on March fourth when he called at Willard's to escort Mr. Lincoln to the inaugural ceremonies. Not quite so certain as Judge Crawford of the crowd's anti-Southern sentiments in this city where for years secessionists had flourished as comfortably as in Richmond or Baltimore, General Scott lined Pennsylvania Avenue, rooftops, street intersections, and the Capitol grounds with soldiers, cavalry, and artillery. If Mr. Lincoln knew that two riflemen lurked behind each window where the wings of the Capitol flanked the inaugural stand, he appeared as unruffled as the new black suit he had donned for the occasion. His address was spoken simply, in keeping with his temperate argument against the right of secession; his government, he said in the same calm voice, would "hold, occupy and possess" its forts and property, but there was no mention of any intention to "repossess" the forts or property already seized by the insurgents; and in passages of quiet eloquence he contended that "nothing valuable can be lost by taking time" until the Union was again touched "by the better angels of our spirit." Old Chief Justice Taney, looking to Mrs. Clay of Alabama like "a galvanized corpse," administered the oath of office; across the slopes guns boomed a salute to A. Lincoln, sixteenth President of the United

States; and Henry Watterson, reporting for a Louisville news-paper, thought: "He delivered that inaugural as if he had been delivering inaugural addresses all his life." This one he had.

North and South, men measured Lincoln's meaning. Greeley's *Tribune* found the address "marked by no useless words and no feeble expression"; in Greeley's judgment the address announced to twenty millions of people that "the Federal Government of the United States is still in existence, with a Man at the head of it"; and under a Charleston date line on March seventh the *Tribune*'s correspondent reported: "I heard Mr. Stephens say in Montgom-ery that the Inaugural is the most *adroit* State paper ever published on the Continent, and this is the general opinion of it also in Charleston." Mrs. Chesnut, reading the address, felt confused: "Comes he in Peace, or comes he in War? Or to tread but one measure as young Lochinvar?" The later recollection of Jefferson Davis was that he found in Mr. Lincoln's words hope "that the conservative and patriotic feeling still existing in the North would control the elements of sectional hatred and bloodthirsty fanati-cism." Depending on one's passions, the address could seem "coer-cive in the extreme" or "weak, rambling, and loose-jointed," or, as Grenville M. Dodge, builder of railroads, called it, "the greatest speech of the age" with "backbone all over"; but to Governor John Letcher of Virginia the Inaugural encouraged calm reflection. To this extent at least, Mr. Lincoln had hit his mark.

Young Henry Adams, still seeking his education, attended "the melancholy function called an Inaugural Ball," and confessed in later years "had young Adams been told that his life was to hang on the correctness of his estimate of the new President, he would have lost." Adams "looked anxiously for a sign of character" and

> . . . saw a long, awkward figure; a plain, ploughed face; a mind, absent in part, and in part evidently worried by white kid gloves; features that expressed neither self-satisfaction nor any other familiar Americanism, but rather the same painful sense of be-

coming educated and of needing education that tormented a private secretary, above all a lack of apparent force. Any private secretary in the least fit for his business would have thought, as Adams did, that no man living needed so much education as the new President but that all the education he could get would not be enough.

If at the Inaugural Ball the President's mind seemed "absent in part," there was good reason. Next morning his appointments to the Cabinet would go to the Senate for confirmation, and the case of Seward remained unsettled. Two days previously, convinced that Mr. Lincoln intended to permit Salmon P. Chase to become the dominant figure in the Cabinet, Seward had asked to have withdrawn his acceptance of a portfolio. The President, having no intention of being badgered by Seward's huffiness, had requested the countermanding of the withdrawal by not later than nine o'clock on the morning of the fifth, and had admitted frankly, in the privacy of his own rooms, "I can't afford to let Seward take the first trick." Nor the last, he might have added, since Seward, a high-strung player at politics, was bound to try again. Concession still convinced Seward as the only way—concession amounting to capitulation. Young Adams saw Mr. Lincoln, fretful over his white kid gloves; but Mr. Lincoln had the deeper worry over whether, when he went to his office in the Executive Mansion next morning, the letter from Seward would be there.

It was. So also was the letter that on the previous day Mr. Holt, still serving as Secretary of War, had received from Major Anderson. Grim facts were stated grimly. Sumter now held just enough bread for twenty-eight days, pork for a few days more, and beans, rice, coffee, and sugar for periods of from eight to forty days. In the next few days Sumter either must be re-enforced or abandoned; and, enclosing the reports and estimates of his nine officers, Major Anderson wrote: "I confess that I would not be willing to risk my reputation on an attempt to throw reenforcements into this harbor within the time for our relief rendered necessary by the limited supply of our provisions, and with a view of holding possession of the same, with a force of less than twenty thousand good and well-disciplined men."

Holt admitted his "surprise." Anderson's previous correspondence had "contained no such intimation." Scott, called into consultation, offered little comfort to the troubled President. He had discussed the matter thoroughly with Brigadier General Totten, the chief engineer, Scott said; not only did he believe that "evacuation seems almost inevitable," but also he would be very much surprised "if indeed the worn-out garrison be not assaulted and carried in the present week." No one understood more clearly than the President's secretaries, Nicolay and Hay, the shock in the situation that confronted Mr. Lincoln:

> This was a disheartening, almost a disastrous, beginning for the Administration. The Cabinet had only that day been appointed and confirmed. The presidential advisers had not yet taken their posts—all had not yet even signified their acceptance. There was an impatient multitude clamoring for an audience, and behind these swarmed an army of office-seekers. Everything was urgency and confusion, everywhere was ignorance of method and routine. Rancor and hatred filled the breasts of political opponents departing from power; suspicion and rivalry possessed partisan adherents seeking advantage and promotion. As yet, Lincoln virtually stood alone, face to face with the appalling problems of the present and the threatening responsibilities of the future. . . .

But Nicolay and Hay were not quite right. Lincoln was not alone in the nation's heart. Since Christmas week Sumter had become something more than a pile of brick in Charleston Harbor. It was a symbol, like the Cradle that was on the nation's mind when its meaning had become clear, like the Cross that would be in the nation's consciousness when its meaning at last was fulfilled. It was birth and death and resurrection for the nation, that fort— not in those words then, not in those thoughts then, except as a poet and a people have a sense of voices on the wind. Other forts had been lost in succeeding weeks. Since December twenty-seventh the Palmetto flag had flown over Moultrie and Castle Pinckney, within sight of Sumter; on January second Georgia had seized Forts Pulaski and Jackson; on January fourth Alabama had occupied Fort Morgan; on January eighth the militia in North Carolina had seized Forts Johnson and Caswell; on January tenth Louisiana had taken Forts Jackson and St. Philip on the Mississippi and Fort Pike on Lake Pontchartrain; on January twelfth Florida and Alabama troops had occupied Forts Barrancas and McRae and had held Fort Marion at St. Augustine since the seventh (although Fort Pickens in Pensacola Bay and the minor forts of Taylor and Jefferson off the Florida coast remained in Federal hands); on January twentieth Mississippi had seized the fort at Ship Island; and on February twentieth the Lone Star of Texas had flown over Forts Chadbourne and Belknap. To a nation faced with the dark threat of war these were severe military losses, and yet the whole of them didn't equal the emotional impact of Sumter. Sumter was personal. Sumter was everything in the living memory of national patriotism.

In his inaugural address Mr. Lincoln had not promised to "re-possess" any of the lost forts; but those that remained—Sumter most of all—he would "hold, occupy and possess," and the pledge reflected the national spirit. Yet Scott, Totten, Anderson each be-lieved Sumter could not be re-enforced. Mr. Lincoln took the problem to his Cabinet. Seward spoke passionately of South Caro-lina's responsibility for "revolution" but was against starting a war to "regain a useless and unnecessary position." To relieve the fort, in Cameron's opinion, would be "unwise"; and Welles, Smith, and Bates agreed. Chase wanted "firmness" without war, though he didn't elaborate on the art of eating his cake and having it too; alone of the seven Montgomery Blair didn't give a damn if hell froze over—he was for re-enforcing Sumter. The President thanked them all very kindly. Sometimes, faced with a decision that posed seemingly insurmountable obstacles, he remembered the children of Israel on the shore of the Red Sea. "Stand still and see the salvation of the Lord," Moses said. The President would wait.

The prayer that was in the President's heart was shared by the man who lived across the Potomac in the mansion on the hill. Soon Colonel Robert E. Lee would receive a letter from L. P. Walker, Confederate Secretary of War. "Sign before a magistrate the oath of office herewith and forward the same, together with your letter of acceptance to this office," urged Walker in offering Lee a brigadier-generalship, the highest rank he then could authorize. Perhaps Lee replied to Secretary Walker, but if so the answer never has been found. Lee had no sympathy for what was then happening in Montgomery; like Mr. Lincoln, his hope rested with the moderate tone of the Virginia Convention that had been meeting in Richmond since February thirteenth. Fire-eaters of various stripes had addressed the Convention—on the eighteenth Fulton Anderson from Mississippi and Henry L. Benning from Georgia, picturing the danger to Virginia of remaining with the Union; on the nineteenth John S. Preston of South Carolina, calling the Union unnatural and monstrous and declaring that North and South never could be reunited "unless the economy of God were changed." Yet as late as April fourth, taking a test vote on secession, a two-to-one majority in the Convention would rule against that step. Lincoln and Lee had good reason for playing the same game, although for different stakes. And meanwhile Seward played another game, rather close to his vest.

On March twelfth John Forsyth of Alabama reached Washington to join Judge Crawford in pressing upon the Lincoln Administration, "upon such terms of amity and good will as the respective interests, geographical contiguity, and general welfare of the two nations may render necessary," Confederate "overtures for the opening of negotiations." Seward's position was that he could not admit any of the seven states now comprising the Montgomery government "have, in law or in fact, withdrawn from the Federal

Union"; but through intermediaries—Supreme Court Justices John A. Campbell of Alabama and Samuel Nelson of New York— Seward negotiated unofficially with the Confederate Commissioners. Campbell remained in Washington even though his state had seceded, confessing that "I was willing to accept whatever peace might bring, whether union or disunion."

Nothing in the interview with Seward should have discouraged Campbell. True, the Secretary of State opened the conversation with the rather technical explanation of why he could not receive the Commissioners; but then, Seward said, "if Jefferson Davis had known the state of things here" he needn't have troubled to send them. After all, Seward added, and he must have known that he would be interpreted as speaking for Mr. Lincoln in the diplomatic bombshell he was about to explode, "The evacuation of Sumter is as much as the Administration can bear." It is difficult to judge what Seward's motivations were; that very day (March fifteenth) Mr. Lincoln had asked his Cabinet members for written opinions on what position should be taken toward Sumter, but these reports were not due until the following day and Seward played God if he thought he could divine what the President's disposition would be. Perhaps Seward was so sure there was no way to go except down the road to appeasement that he decided to become the zealous trail blazer; at any rate Campbell could only act upon what he heard. He intended to write Jefferson Davis; what should he say to him about Sumter?

"How far is it to Montgomery?" Seward asked.

"Three days."

"You may say to him," Seward decided, "that before that letter reaches him, the telegraph will have informed him that Sumter will have been evacuated."

Campbell, in high glee, dispatched his letter to Montgomery that evening. Next day, reading the written opinions of the members of the Cabinet concerning Sumter, the result was what Mr. Lincoln might have expected—five favoring evacuation, Chase with a leg over both sides of the fence, and Montgomery Blair insisting, as brother Frank believed, that a compromise on Sumter promised no gain since "the condition means war, and nothing but war, fierce and desperate war." There wasn't an ounce of appeasement in Montgomery, who had been the counsel for Dred Scott; and the suspicion that Mr. Lincoln might be hedging on Sumter brought out all of the explosive streak that resided beneath Blair's deceptively stolid, learned, dignified exterior. Apparently his dander was sufficiently aroused for him to stomp from the Executive Mansion to 1651 Pennsylvania Avenue to see his father, Francis P. Blair, Sr., now seventy and an old hand at Washington politics.

Did the senior Blair go to counsel Mr. Lincoln? Finding the President gloomily alone in the council room, did old Blair lay it on the line—telling Mr. Lincoln that if he wished to smash the Republican Party and have an aroused American people demand his impeachment he could evacuate Sumter? Did he come to stiffen the President's backbone, fearing a Lincoln who could tell John B. Baldwin, a Unionist member of the Virginia Convention, that if Baldwin would promise him Virginia he would evacuate Sumter, considering "A State for a fort is no bad business"?

Perhaps. In any event, Montgomery Blair remained in Mr. Lincoln's Cabinet. And if the President wished to speak in his own behalf, he could have replied that he already had sent Captain Gustavus Vasa Fox (afterward Assistant Secretary of the Navy) to make a personal inspection of Sumter. Later two old friends, S. A. Hurlbut and Ward H. Lamon, performed similar missions in Charleston as his eyes and ears. Mr. Lincoln knew what he was doing. He was on the shore of the Red Sea, heeding Moses: "Stand still and see the salvation of the Lord."

The critical question was how much patience authorities in Montgomery and Charleston possessed for standing still. In early February the little steamer *Marion* had carried away the wives and children of the defenders of Sumter, but there was no wet eye among Charlestonians for a scene that wrung Northern hearts— the men mounted on top the ramparts, a gun fired in a signal of farewell as the ship passed, those on deck responding with "weeping and 'wavering adieux' to husbands and fathers." A month later the ebullient Beauregard arrived, and the sense of urgency in getting the business settled at Sumter increased.

Beauregard virtually electrified Charleston; even his Negro servant, Frederick Maginnis, who strutted around as the intimate of those in the inner councils, was accepted in good humor. Beauregard's immediate decision was that Sumter must be exposed to a circle of fire and he began rearranging batteries accordingly. There was never any doubt in Beauregard's mind that he prepared for war—he was a soldier of purpose and glamor, attended by a Spanish barber and valet—and F. W. Pickens, who followed Gist as governor, clearly adored the bustling Creole. By March seventeenth Pickens was urging on Mr. Davis that Beauregard's command "be enlarged" to include the entire Charleston coastal area. "There is no man who could have been selected that could give such general confidence and satisfaction as he does," Pickens declared. "We are all delighted with him." Beauregard likewise sent happy news to Montgomery; he was "pleased with this place, & its people, who are so much like ours in La. that I see but little difference in them."

The Charleston that Mrs. Chesnut had found so depressing at Christmas she found in late March to be "a dear, delightful place." Montgomery with its "detestable hotels" could not compare with it. And for all that Mrs. Chesnut, never failing for malicious gossip, might repeat that Colonel Whiting "does the work" and Beauregard "reaps the glory," she could not deny that he had given Charleston vitality. Everything was exciting—the men going off to the island forts to practice target shooting, the conversations in French since "we know the black waiters are all ears now, and we want to keep what we have to say dark," the rush to the photography galleries to have one's visage immortalized. Charleston, alert to the intrigue with which South Carolinians themselves overflowed, was ready—eager, really.

That spirit certainly reached Montgomery. Jefferson Davis, who neither could read Mr. Lincoln's mind nor guess Seward's motives, waited five days after receiving Judge Campbell's exuberant letter promising the evacuation of Sumter. Impatient for results, the President dispatched a telegram to Beauregard, inquiring if Sumter had been evacuated or if there was even probability of such action. Major Anderson was still working on Sumter defenses, Beauregard replied. Davis forwarded this ominous message to Campbell in Washington.

Secretary Seward received Justices Nelson and Campbell twice again. "The Secretary," Campbell reported, "was buoyant and sanguine; he spoke of his ability to carry through his policy with confidence." The delay, Seward explained, had been "accidental," and did not involve "the integrity of his assurance that the evacuation would take place." A wise old diplomat in his own right, Campbell added: "I repeated this assurance in writing to Judge Crawford, and informed Governor Seward in writing what I had said."

With Mr. Lincoln and Secretary Seward each running the national government, according to his own ideas, the weeks ahead in Washington promised still other fascinations. But the critical question remained. How much patience existed in Montgomery and Charleston?

17

Fateful Weeks

THE opinion at Washington, Judge Campbell wrote a friend, was that "secession movements were short-lived" and the Confederate government "would wither under sunshine." Least of all would Mr. Lincoln deny that he considered time his most valuable ally—time for the moderates to beat down the fire-eaters in the Virginia Convention; for Fox, Hurlbut, and Lamon to probe beneath emotions and ascertain the true situation in Charleston and Sumter; and, a third of the way across the continent in Missouri, for the Unionists to gain the upper hand.

Surrounded on three sides by Free States offering asylum to fugitive slaves, Missouri looked upon the Confederacy with doubt, suspicion, and some resentment. When on February twenty-eighth Claib Jackson called a Convention at Jefferson City, the governor's ardent hope was to deliver Missouri to the Montgomery government. Jefferson City was a cheerless place of muddy streets, bare and skimpy hotel accommodations, and at night tallow candles and oil lamps accomplished little more than "to make darkness visible." Since the Legislature, largely prosecessionists, was still in session, the delegates to the Convention were crowded into "a small, repulsive court-house." Other factors depressed the loyal Union men of Missouri, and one remembered: "When I got to Jefferson City and heard nothing but the *Marseillaise* [the song was extremely popular with Southerners] and *Dixie* in place of *The*

Star-Spangled Banner I felt uneasy enough, and when I heard Governor Jackson speak I felt badly. . . . I recollect, with my colleague, Mr. Broadhead, hearing *Dixie* played on the streets, and we stepped up to the leader of the band and asked him to play *The Star-Spangled Banner*; he said, being a foreigner, 'Me 'fraid to play that.' We assured him that there was no danger, and he played one stanza of *The Star-Spangled Banner,* but immediately went off into *Dixie,* and of course we went off in disgust."

If Missouri was to be saved, Union men decided, the Convention had to be moved to St. Louis, where the secessionist spirit was less rampant. The point was won when a group of private citizens of St. Louis agreed to pay the railroad fares of the delegates. Still, in contesting with the wily Claib Jackson, the Union men had to face the hard reality that theirs was an uphill battle all the way. Four-fifths of the members of the Convention had been born and raised in Slave States. "By a secret prearrangement," Galusha Anderson reported, "in companies of from six to twelve, the members of the Convention were daily invited by Union men to dine with them; and . . . at the tables and in the parlors of the best and most intelligent men and women of the city . . . deep-rooted prejudice began gradually to give way, and new light, unobserved, penetrated the minds of the members of this sovereign Convention, and, as one by one the days passed, the hope of the disloyal that Missouri would secede was constantly on the wane."

After all, Union men argued, the climate of Missouri was better adapted to the white man than the black; in a decade the slave population had increased 25 per cent and the white population 100 per cent, and against a taxable value of forty-five millions in slave property must be placed a value in other property of more than three hundred fifteen millions. The hope for compromise appealed strongly to "timid men"; and many responded to the position that the seven states which had seceded had been carried out of the Union "by ambitious politicians." Had Missouri been consulted then by "the cotton lords of the South Atlantic and Gulf States"? Why should she lick their boots now? And so the Convention resolved "That at present there is no adequate cause to impel Missouri to dissolve her present connection with the Federal Union," and the Union men of St. Louis could reckon they had handed Mr. Lincoln a major victory in his cold war with Secessia. Nor was the impact of Missouri's action to be lightly measured in the ultimate course of Kentucky, West Virginia, Delaware, and Maryland, each of which also stayed in the Union.

For years the Arsenal in St. Louis had been commanded by Major William H. Bell, a North Carolinian whose extreme pro-slavery sympathies reputedly included promising that while he would defend the Arsenal against all mobs he would not oppose state troops. Then in early February St. Louis had its first glimpse of thin, angular Captain Nathaniel Lyon, Connecticut-born and itching "to stay the idiotic, fratricidal hands now at work to destroy our government." Lyon, a short, rough, rugged fellow, now forty-two years of age, whose clear blue eyes were piercing and whose stubby, reddish-brown beard hinted at latent belligerency, had served in various army posts in Florida, Mexico, northern California, and Kansas. A devoted Free Soiler, he preferred war rather than see expire "before the arrogance of secession" the "great rights and hopes of the human race." Lyon was saying nothing with which Missouri's Frank P. Blair, Montgomery's brother, did not wholeheartedly agree. Blair and Lyon made a spunky team.

Major Bell, removed from command at the Arsenal and ordered to New York, resigned. In command of the Department of the West was Brigadier General William Selby Harney, then past sixty and a native Louisianian; while outwardly loyal, St. Louis Unionists like Galusha Anderson understood Harney "was so interlinked with Southern families, both by blood and friendships of long standing, that he was unfitted to command where grave and delicate questions, involving old neighbors and intimate friends, were constantly arising." A tougher nut for Blair and Lyon to crack was Major Peter V. Hagner, who outranked Lyon, and who refused to fortify the Arsenal or to arm the Republican Wide-Awakes that Blair had converted into the Home Guard.

Toward mid-March, the growling, open hostility of the secessionist Minute Men so worried Harney that he decided to do something, and by giving Lyon command of the troops at the Arsenal and placing the ordnance stores under Hagner, succeeded in achieving a triumph of stupidity.

Old Claib Jackson moved deftly in aiding secessionists by appointing four commissioners (of his own sentiments) who, with the mayor of St. Louis, were to have "absolute control of the police, of the local voluntary militia, of the sheriff, and of all other conservators of the peace." Then on April first Daniel G. Taylor, "a plastic, conditional Union man, openly opposed to Lincoln," was elected mayor. The "battle within the Arsenal for the Arsenal" was being won by maneuver, except that Lyon wouldn't stand for it. He'd arm Blair's Home Guard, and to hell with the governor's commissioners. What if Hagner interfered?

"I'll pitch him into the river," Lyon said.

Harney capitulated and gave Lyon the supreme command. The Arsenal had been saved for the Union, and again time was winning for Mr. Lincoln.

On an evening in early March, learning that Mrs. Abner Doubleday was now in Washington, Mr. Lincoln called unexpectedly. Could he see the Captain's letters from Sumter and so acquaint himself with conditions within the fort? His particular interest, the President said, was in regard to the resources of the garrison. What precisely he learned that evening is not known. The Captain had passed troubled weeks inside Sumter. He had heard General D. F. Jamison, South Carolina's new Secretary of War, declare that his state "was determined to have Fort Sumter" and "they would pull it down with their fingernails, if they could get it no other way." He had a good story about the bloodthirsty Rhett, who had stormed into the governor's office demanding that Sumter be taken "without further procrastination."

"Certainly, Mr. Rhett," the governor answered. "I have no objection! I will furnish you with some men, and you can storm the work yourself."

"But, sir," exclaimed Rhett, "I am not a military man!"

"Nor I either," the governor said, "and therefore I take the advice of those who are!"

Doubleday's mind was uneasy about Major Anderson, who said he was opposed to coercion and that if Kentucky seceded "he should throw up his commission and go to Europe." In the first week of March the South Carolinians completed an ironclad floating battery, which they proposed to anchor off the gorge of Sumter where "it could beat down our main gates, and make wide breaches in the walls for an assaulting party to enter." Learning that the garrison had nothing but pork and hard biscuit, a wealthy New York gentleman "sent us several boxes of delicacies" and "the great tobacconist, John Anderson, of New York, also sent a large supply of the best quality of tobacco, having learned that the men felt the loss of their smoking more than any thing else."

The first of the six most fateful weeks in American history—the period between Mr. Lincoln's inauguration and the attack on Sumter—now had ended. The President was patiently seeking out the bits of the puzzle that, pieced together, must form peace or a sword. No one could tell which—least of all perhaps the politicians Mr. Lincoln once described as "a set of men who have interests aside from the interests of the people, and who, to say the most of them, are, taken as a mass, at least one long step removed from honest men." If Lincoln were willing to sacrifice Sumter to avoid war, then he stacked the deck against himself when at the close of his first week in office he selected Gustavus Vasa Fox to act as an emissary to Charleston. Fox, a brother-in-law of Montgomery Blair, was an experienced Navy officer who had already tried to convince the Buchanan Administration that by using tugs protected by cotton bales men and supplies could be put into Sumter. Fox had not surrendered this notion; like Blair, he was for holding

Sumter and Mr. Lincoln knew it when the President sent him to Charleston. Here, as should have been expected, the Confederates refused to permit him inside the fort without an escort and Captain H. J. Harstene, another Navy man who had resigned to serve the South, was given that assignment.

On March twenty-first Fox reached Sumter with Harstene constantly "within ear-shot," to make certain "he did no harm to the Confederacy." Harstene asked Doubleday if he thought Anderson would object to moving the floating battery to within a hundred yards of the main gates of Sumter, and could not understand Doubleday's surprise at the inquiry. "Anderson has allowed these batteries to be built around him," Harstene said, "and has permitted so many things to be done, that I don't see why he should not go a step further and allow this." Writing to the War Department from Sumter two days later, Captain J. G. Foster advised Chief Engineer Totten: "Of the Floating Battery, or 'Raft,' nothing further is known, except that Capt. Harstene, while here with Mr. Fox . . . made the remark that it was 'very formidable.' " In the exchange of remarks between Fox and Anderson something less than clarity resulted. Anderson wasn't at all certain that a relief expedition was in prospect; Fox came away, believing that the shortages of supplies had been exaggerated. Montgomery Blair's brother-in-law hurried back to Washington to tell the President— and doubtless the Postmaster General—that his scheme for relieving Sumter would work.

Mr. Lincoln's second pair of eyes within Charleston belonged to the redoubtable Virginia-born Ward H. Lamon, who had practiced law in Danville, Illinois. A robust fellow whose office was over a saloon in a building that likewise housed a bordello, Lamon had owned a good trotter and a trick monkey and since he bulged in all quarters was once called "Jumbo" by "a brazen woman at a race track." Devoted to Lincoln as a counselor and friend, he had been with the President's party since leaving Springfield. "Let your President attempt to reenforce Sumter," Lamon said the governor of South Carolina told him, "and the tocsin of war will be sounded from every hilltop and valley in the South." A crowd with a rope sought out poor "Jumbo" in his Charleston hotel, determined to hang "a damned Lincoln abolition hireling," but Laurence Keitt broke up the mob, roaring: "Stop, you insult Lamon, and you insult me!" A visit to Sumter convinced Lamon that the provisions there would not last beyond April fifteenth. Not surprisingly, he found Anderson "deeply despondent"; the garrison, he thought, was "spoiling for a fight." On instructions from Mr. Lincoln he went to discuss the situation with the postmaster, and discovered that individual no longer associated himself with the Federal government. In character, Lamon packed all these activities into one day in Charleston.

On the train returning to Washington Lamon met Stephen A. Hurlbut. A native of Charleston who had practiced law in Belvidere, Illinois, Hurlbut had visited his sister in Charleston and later had a long talk with that stanch Unionist, Judge James L. Petigru, under whom Hurlbut had studied four years. No policy that Lincoln could adopt, in Hurlbut's opinion, could "prevent the probability of armed collision"; Southerners, he said, "expect a golden era" in the expansion of trade "and material prosperity"; and he advised the President:

> If Sumpter is abandoned it is to a certain extent a concession of jurisdiction which cannot fail to have its effect at home and abroad. Undoubtedly this will be followed by a demand for Pickens and the Keys of the Gulf. To surrender these if Pickens has been or can be reinforced tarnishes the National honor and the U. States ceases to be a respectable Nation. At all hazards and under all circumstances during this stage of proceedings any Fortress accessible by the Sea, over which we still have dominion should be held. If war comes, let it come.

"If war comes" . . . at the end of the first of those six fateful weeks, Mr. Lincoln had posed three questions to General Scott. "To what point of time," Mr. Lincoln asked, "can Major Anderson maintain his position at Fort Sumpter, without fresh supplies or reinforcement?" Scott replied that he could not say "with absolute accuracy," and added:

> . . . Reckoning the [batteries] troops at 3,500 (now somewhat disciplined) the batteries at 4 powerful *land,* & at least one *floating* —all mounting guns & mortars of large calibre, & of the best patterns; & supposing those means to be skillfully & vigorously employed—Fort Sumter with its less than 100 men—including common laborers & musicians—ought to be taken by a single assault, & easily, if harassed perseveringly for several previous days & nights by threats & false attacks, with the ability, from the force of overwhelming numbers, of converting one out of every three or four of those, into a real attack.

Next the President asked: "Can you with all the means now in your control, supply or reinforce Fort Sumpter within that time [before supplies were exhausted]?" Scott answered: "No: Not within many months."

Finally the President asked: "If not, what amount of means, & of what description, in addition to that already at your control, would enable you to supply & reinforce that fortress within the time?" And Scott replied:

> A fleet of war vessels & transports, 5,000 additional regular troops & 20,000 volunteers, in order to take all the batteries in the Harbor of Charleston (including Ft. Moultrie) after the capture of all the batteries in the approach or outer Bay. And to raise, organize & discipline such an army, would require new acts of Congress & from six to eight months.

So did the documents and opinions pile up on Mr. Lincoln's desk. Another came from an old friend in Springfield:

"Dear Old Abe"

We hear with pain and regret that you are debating about Evacuating Sumter lowering our Glorious old Flag that Washington through so many trials and Privations unfurled and sustained to be trampled on by traitors and to be made the hiss and scoff of the World. Do you know that Genl Washington or Jackson never said *"I cant"* and do you know that your old crippled friend that has always stood by you for the last 20 years and fought by your side for & with you, has never yet uttered that word, except in derision. Say the word By the Eternal, Fort Sumter *shall* be reinforced and that glorious old Flag sustained and my word for it 100,000 good and true men with Jim Hill amongst them will at once respond to the call. . . . You are now head of this nation and of course know more and better than we the reasons that are leading to this result but for Gods sake for Humanity and for your own honor don't let that word *Cant* form any part of the reasons.

Yours Truly
James L Hill

Mr. Lincoln, not yet a month President, faced the decision. Scott, the Army man, looked upon the immediate provisioning of Sumter as an impossibility and Fox, the Navy man, believed it could be done. Why not sacrifice Sumter and re-enforce Pickens, where the risk seemed less? But Lamon and Hurlbut said bluntly that no compromise would work. The Cabinet, except for Blair and possibly Chase, favored evacuating Sumter. Nicolay and Hay picture Lincoln appearing on March twenty-ninth after a sleepless night. Had the letter from crippled Jim Hill been in his thoughts? Would the people sustain him if at Sumter he allowed the "traitors" to make the national flag "the hiss and scoff of the World?" Lincoln met his Cabinet that day. The steamer *Pocahontas* at Norfolk, the steamer *Pawnee* at Norfolk, and the revenue cutter *Harriet Lane* at New York were to be placed under sailing orders with one month's stores and three hundred seamen were to be kept ready for duty in New York with an additional two hundred men held ready in the garrison at Governor's Island.

"Say the word By the Eternal," advised Jim Hill, "Fort Sumter *shall* be reinforced . . ."

Lincoln did.

In Montgomery, to Thomas C. DeLeon, Jefferson Davis looked "worn thin to almost emaciation by mental and physical toil."

Davis's features had "sharpened," the lines in his face "deepened and hardened," DeLeon thought; his thin lips had "a firmer depression," the lower jaw "was closer pressed to its fellow"; he listened with eyes shaded by their lids, "suddenly shooting forth at the speaker a gleam from the stone-gray pupil [he had lost the sight of one eye months previously] which seemed to penetrate his innermost mind." A parlor at The Exchange served for his office and, DeLeon observed, "little ceremony, or form, hedged the incubating government." His manner was "quiet" and to the people he was "the grand embodiment . . . of their grand cause."

Reports from Charleston revealed the visits from Fox and Lamon. The governor of South Carolina insisted that Fox had been allowed inside Sumter only upon "the pledge of 'pacific purposes,'" and that Lamon had announced "he had come to try and arrange for the removal of the garrison, and, when he returned from the fort, asked if a war-vessel could not be allowed to remove them." The governor replied that a war vessel would not be permitted to enter the harbor and Lamon was represented as believing "Major Anderson preferred an ordinary steamer." Moreover, by the governor's account, Lamon "hoped to return in a very few days for that purpose." In the Senate, Douglas, "who was certainly not suspected of sympathy with secession," insisted "that whoever permanently holds Charleston and South Carolina is entitled to the possession of Fort Sumter." These portents, joined with the glib assurances Seward was giving Justices Nelson and Campbell that Sumter would be evacuated, should have given Mr. Davis great comfort.

But the Confederate President was in a peculiar predicament. To the extent that time favored Mr. Lincoln in strengthening Union sympathy in such widely separated states as Virginia and Missouri, time worked against the dream of a large Southern nation. The problems confronting the young Confederacy were of such deep complexity that the mere prospect of war should have chilled its President to the bone. Yet the South bristled with a belligerent spirit; it talked war and threatened war and whipped itself into a frenzy over slight and fancied provocations—such as rumors of an intended slave insurrection for which no shred of evidence had been produced or the wish of citizens in Taunton, Massachusetts, to present a cane to Major Anderson.

To the objective observer the Confederacy remained in every respect—and perhaps in the kindest language—an untested government. Its greatest weakness, of course, was financial and was based on what it called Cotton Diplomacy. The South believed, as W. H. Russell of the London *Times* wryly commented, "that the Lord Chancellor sits on a cotton bale"; and Mr. Davis boldly told his people: "It is alike our interest, and that of all those to whom we would sell and from whom we would buy, that there should be the fewest practicable restrictions upon the interchange of commodities." Certainly it was a captivating vision to think of John Bull poking Mr. Lincoln in the nose if he in any way interfered with the cotton trade. But need John Bull pull Confederate chestnuts out of this rebel's fire in the spring of 1861?

Quite the opposite, Britain was not too concerned with cotton that spring. Britain had bought heavily of the American crops of 1859 and 1860 and was overstocked momentarily with raw cotton; and her cotton-goods markets in India and China had for two years suffered "indigestion and loss of appetite." John Bull could afford to take even more time than Mr. Lincoln to see just where this quarrel between his American cousins was going. From the British viewpoint all the Confederacy truly had demonstrated to this date was the fact that it possessed a legal argument. As an "incubating government," to use DeLeon's apt phrase, it talked rough and big and posed before the world full of fight, but there was more to nationhood than that. Its Congress would have to raise taxes; its Congress would have to provide for the common welfare while maintaining States Rights, which could prove a delicate balance indeed. What the future might bring provided interesting speculation, and John Bull admitted it; but for the moment he had problems at home and in Europe of a far more pressing nature.

The tragic blunder toward which the Southern people were

rushing with cheeks aglow and eyes shining reflected nothing so much as the lack of intellectual inquiry that for the past several decades had been a Southern habit. The idea the South understood least of all, as Major General J. F. C. Fuller, a British authority, has shrewdly observed, was the tendency of civil wars to "find their nearest comparison in the wars of religion." The Southern people talked war while totally unprepared for the most passionate kind of war, and Mr. Davis seemed no more perceptive than Rhett in his eagerness to hurl his people blindly against the guns and bayonets.

Historians differ as to what happened during the six most fateful weeks in American history following the inauguration of Mr. Lincoln. Professor David M. Potter of Yale University takes the position that Mr. Lincoln began with the belief the Union could be held together without war, but when provisions ran low at Sumter, his hand was forced. An accomplished Southern scholar, Professor Charles W. Ramsdell of the University of Texas, contends otherwise; Mr. Lincoln, he insists, "maneuvered the Confederates into firing the first shot in order that they, rather than he, should take the blame of beginning bloodshed." The difficulty in this thesis is the fact that throughout all six weeks Mr. Davis thought in terms of war already existing. On March eighteenth—Mr. Lincoln had been in office just a fortnight—Mr. Davis wrote Governor Pickens that he was not "one of those who felt sanguine hope that the *enemy* would retire peaceably from your harbor"; to Mr. Davis the "enemy" must choose "how he will go" and in any event "his stay must soon be measured by our forebearance." Another British military authority, Brigadier General Colin R. Ballard, poses an interesting conjecture:

> . . . [Mr. Davis] might himself have sent a cargo of provisions to Anderson and invited him to remain in Sumter as the guest of the Confederacy—pending the settlement of certain diplomatic questions between two Governments which were not at war. This would have won sympathy from many pacifists in the North. It would have kept him right in the eyes of foreigners, who knew

nothing and cared less about the laws of the Constitution but assumed that he had some legal point. Most certainly it would have embarrassed Lincoln, who could neither withdraw his garrison nor leave it there under such conditions.

Why all the desperate urgency, this measuring of Confederate "forebearance," in settling the Sumter crisis? General Ballard suspects that the fear in Mr. Davis's heart concerned "the more sober Confederates," who, if granted the time for continued reflection, "might wobble back under the flag of the Union." Mr. Davis in his letter of March eighteenth to Governor Pickens in trigger-happy Charleston, said: "To have Fort Sumter uninjured is important to us, and for that reason if there were no other we should prefer that he ["the enemy"] should go peaceably." In *The Rise and Fall of the Confederate Government*, ignoring entirely how his own mind thought in these terms of undeclared war, Mr. Davis established his innocence by detailing Seward's tricky diplomacy with Justices Nelson and Campbell, ridiculing the "absurdity" of attempting "to disassociate the action of the President from that of his Secretary," and finding it "impossible to believe that, during this whole period of nearly a month, Mr. Lincoln was ignorant of the communications that were passing between the Confederate Commissioners and Mr. Seward." In short, Mr. Lincoln was a liar and Mr. Davis was a sucker.

Not that Seward didn't play his diplomatic game of hide-the-thimble with the Confederate Commissioners to the end. By late March, with Beauregard's circle of batteries making Major Anderson and his little garrison inside Sumter more than ever lame ducks in a hostile pond, Governor Pickens had to report that Lamon had not reappeared nor had the promised "ordinary steamer" arrived. Justice Campbell was urged to call again on the Secretary of State.

Seward was as cordial as ever. He admitted that Lamon had "no agency" from the President nor "title to speak." He provided a written statement for the Confederate Commissioners, promising "that the government will not undertake to supply Fort Sumter without giving notice to Governor Pickens."

Justice Campbell was no fool; this statement was not quite the unqualified guarantee to evacuate the fort that Seward had given earlier. Had there been a change of mind?

"None," Seward answered.

Appropriately this interview took place on April Fool's Day.

18

Fateful Days

SEWARD still wanted to be President. He watched Mr. Lincoln, besieged by patronage seekers—even during Cabinet meetings, Attorney General Bates declared, there was a constant squabble "about the distribution of loaves & fishes"—and Seward thought how thoroughly incompetent to hold the highest office in the land "the prairie politician" proved himself. Seward read the sharper editorial criticisms of Mr. Lincoln's policies and believed the nation was going to pot with this distracted backwoodsman at the head of it. And so on April first Seward delivered to Mr. Lincoln one of the most astonishing documents in American history. Entitled "Some Thoughts for the President's Consideration," Seward began bluntly by charging that "We are at the end of a month's administration without a policy either domestic or foreign." The need to meet patronage demands, he said, had "prevented attention to other and more grave problems"—a situation which, if continued, "would not only bring scandal on the Administration, but danger upon the country."

The Secretary of State told the President how he should run the country. *"Change the question before the Public from one upon slavery, or about slavery,"* Seward proposed, "for a question upon *Union or Disunion.* In other words, from what would be regarded as a Party question to one of *Patriotism or Union."* To achieve this remarkable distinction, Seward proposed evacuating

221

Fort Sumter but holding every other "fort and possession in the South"; and to unify the country, he would pick a war with Great Britain, Spain, or France. "It must be somebody's business," Seward declared, "to pursue and direct" such a policy "incessantly"; and either the President or "some member of his Cabinet" must get down to that business. "It is not my special province," Seward concluded. "But I neither seek to evade or assume responsibility."

To have fired Seward on the spot would have divided the Republican Party and have given the nation even uneasier feelings about the Administration now running its government. Mr. Lincoln drafted a patient reply to the Secretary of State. In his Inaugural, the President reminded Seward, he had declared that he intended "to hold, occupy and possess the property and places belonging to the government, and to collect the duties, and imposts"; Seward had given that policy his "distinct approval at the time." And, inquired Mr. Lincoln, almost suggesting a chuckle as he wrote, "I do not perceive how the re-enforcement of Fort Sumpter would be done on a slavery, or party issue, while that of Fort Pickens would be on a more national, and patriotic one." To Seward's proposal that directing the government must be "somebody's business," the President answered flatly: "*I* must do it." With these thoughts on paper, the evidence indicates that Mr. Lincoln decided against sending the letter. The likelihood is that he saw Seward in person, settled the dispute between them in a friendly interview, and told him to consider the matter closed. Not until thirty-three years later, when Nicolay and Hay published an edition of Mr. Lincoln's letters, was either document made public.

Seward's average was rather low that April Fool's Day; he fooled no one. From Washington, Confederate Commissioner Crawford telegraphed Pickens in Charleston: "I am authorized to say that this Government will not undertake to supply Sumter without notice to you. My opinion is that the President has not the courage to execute the order agreed upon in Cabinet for the

evacuation of the fort, but that he intends to shift the responsibility
upon Major Anderson by suffering him to be starved out. Would
it not be well to aid in this by cutting off all supplies?" Pickens,
in forwarding this dispatch that April Fool's Day to Montgomery,
appended a note from Beauregard: "Batteries here ready to open
Wednesday or Thursday. What instructions?"

Like everyone else in Charleston, the little Creole was growing
itchy to get the war started. The widowed Caroline Howard Gilman, driving along the Battery, saw Sumter "like a noble stag
at bay," and wondered: "When will it be surrendered?" The
men of the city, she admitted, were growing so impatient "it
requires all the wisdom of their superiors to keep them cool."
Since December they had labored "like journeymen" and "dra-
goons, who have been waited on all their lives, curry their own
horses."

From what Fox had "hinted" and Lamon had said, Major
Anderson had convinced himself that any day he would be
peaceably relieved, yet here it was the first of April, no official
action was taken, and "his position daily became more em-
barrassing." A request to move the laborers from the fort was
refused, on orders from Montgomery, and the long-suffering
Anderson reconciled himself to the disappointment of not being
able to stretch his rations another week. On April second, Captain
Doubleday wrote his wife a gloomy letter; dysentery had broken
out "and the Doctor is afraid it will spread"; grumbled the depressed Doubleday: "Every one is weary of the confinement here.
It is nothing but walking around the parapet, eating and sleeping." What little could be done to prepare Sumter against an
attack now had been completed, sometimes with considerable
ingenuity. Two five-gallon demijohns filled with powder had
been planted as mines under the wharf; along the esplanade extending the length of the gorge wall, piles of stones concealed
magazines of gunpowder that could be fired from within the fort;
and to hinder a hostile landing on the narrow strip of "riprapping"
between scarp wall and tidewater large stones were rolled into

the water. "The men," said Captain James Chester, "could count on their fingers the number of days between them and starvation"; yet there "developed no discontent," disproving "a favorite belief among secessionists that the pinchings of hunger would arouse a spirit of mutiny."

The little schooner *Rhoda B. Shannon,* out of Boston with a cargo of ice for Savannah, almost started a war on April third. Confused in bad weather, her captain entered the wrong harbor. A shot from a Confederate battery on Morris Island crossed her bow. The schooner ran up the United States flag and two more shots were fired, then the full batteries opened on the vessel. The firing was poor, but one shot "went through her mainsail above the boom," and prudently lowering her flag, the *Rhoda B. Shannon* went out to the bar.

Sumter exploded with excitement and Anderson, assembling his officers, asked what he should do. Five favored "an immediate reply," three wanted delay until officers could visit the island and schooner. Anderson, relying on orders from Washington on January tenth and February twenty-third that he should act only on the defensive, decided on delay. The Confederates, receiving a party from the fort, contended coolly that they were instructed to fire upon any ship under the United States flag after a warning shot across her bow; the captain of the schooner declared he had displayed the flag in order to obtain a pilot, a customary procedure. Before this "international incident" was concluded, a conference was held between officers from the fort and Pickens and Beauregard, and word relayed to Anderson that "no attempt would be made to reinforce Fort Sumter with men or provisions, and that the President intended to shift the responsibility upon Major Anderson by suffering him to be starved out."

Anderson felt stung by the report. "I cannot think," he wrote the War Department next day, "that the Government would abandon, without instructions and advice, a command which has tried to do all its duty to our country." He refused to believe the government would take any course that "will leave my motives and actions liable to misconception"; he should not be left without instructions, "even though they may be confidential"; and with a good soldier's pride he added: "After thirty odd years of service I do not wish it to be said that I have treasonably abandoned a post and turned over to unauthorized persons public property intrusted to my charge." On the sixth Anderson again wrote Washington, insisting that "the sooner we are out of this harbor the better." The national flag, he said, ran "an hourly risk of being insulted," his hands were "tied" by his orders, and in any case he had not the "power" to protect the fort.

Yet if Anderson felt depressed and abandoned that sixth of April, even more turbulent emotions could be found in Washington where an angry Secretary of the Navy and an excitable Secretary of State asked for a midnight meeting with the President. Of the three warships that Welles could assign to an expedition to relieve Sumter, the steam frigate *Powhatan* alone possessed the firepower to handle the Confederate shore batteries while the tugs were delivering supplies to the fort. On April fifth Captain Samuel Mercer was ordered to depart at once with the *Powhatan* and proceed to a point ten miles east of Charleston light. Before Mercer could leave the Brooklyn Navy Yard, however, young Lieutenant David D. Porter arrived with orders signed by Mr. Lincoln and bearing the surprising endorsement: "Recommended. Wm. H. Seward."

That Mercer should be relieved by an officer inferior in rank seemed enough irregularity for one order; but the document Porter brought also cautioned that the *Powhatan* was "bound on secret service" and "under no circumstances" should authorities at the Navy Yard "communicate to the Navy Department the fact that she is fitting out." Nor was this the strangest part of the change in plans; another order, again signed by Mr. Lincoln, sent the *Powhatan* to Pensacola Harbor where "at any cost" she was to prevent "any expedition from the mainland reaching Fort Pickens or Santa Rosa." Andrew H. Foote, commandant at the Navy Yard, was filled with justifiable suspicion.

"Porter," Foote growled, "these are ticklish times. How do I know that you are not going to run off with the ship? I must telegraph immediately to the Secretary."

Porter protested, pointing out that the orders specifically stipulated that *"secrecy"* must be maintained. Foote grumbled that the ship was "unfit to go"; Porter replied that he would "take her as she was." His luggage, when delivered, was addressed to "American Minister, Vera Cruz." From New York flashed a guarded inquiry to the Navy Department. What did it all mean? Was Welles running the Navy or Seward? Upon that point no one wanted a quicker answer than Welles. On the way to see Mr. Lincoln, a crestfallen Seward admitted that "old as he was, he had learned a lesson," and henceforth "he had better attend to his business and confine his labors to his own department," a sentiment to which Welles "cordially assented."

The President gave a straightforward account of the mix-up. Seward and Porter had prepared the orders and he had signed them, trusting that they were correct. "I ought to have been more careful and attentive," Mr. Lincoln said. The fault was all his. But in no case should the *Powhatan* be sent to Pickens when it was needed at Sumter. "On no account must the Sumter expedition fail or be interfered with," the President said sternly. The *Powhatan* must be returned to Captain Mercer.

Seward protested but, rather curtly, Mr. Lincoln told the Secretary of State to send the order at once. Porter had started down New York Harbor with the *Powhatan* when a swift steamer overhauled him and brought the new order: "Deliver up the *Powhatan* to Captain Mercer. W. H. Seward." Seward? Who was he to overrule sailing orders signed by the President? Porter continued on to Pensacola Bay.

Seward's answer was that, greatly excited, he mistakenly signed his rather than the President's name to the telegram. That explanation didn't satisfy Welles and no explanation could convince Montgomery Blair that Seward's motives didn't rest somewhere between delusions of grandeur and outright treason. To add to the deep distrust of Seward, two telegrams had been brought to Welles, both of which had been sent to Charleston.

"Positively determined not to withdraw Anderson," one message read. "Supplies go immediately, supported by naval force under Stringham if their landing be resisted. A Friend." To Seward's discomfiture the "Friend" turned out to be James E. Harvey, a well-known Washington correspondent and native Charlestonian whom Seward recently had named Minister to Portugal. Again the President gave Seward the benefit of the doubt; the Secretary, in "imprudently" imparting the secret of the mission to Harvey, had been guilty of "a gross error of judgment, and a breach of confidence, but not an act of treachery." With good reason could Seward remark in later weeks that "The President is the best of us."

Forewarned by Harvey's telegram, orders from Montgomery on April seventh cut off all communication between Sumter and the city and instructed Beauregard "to act as if he was in the presence of an enemy intending to surprise him." Thus ended for Anderson, the President, Seward, and Welles a trying week. Within Charleston the excitement mounted to the point of giddiness. "We fool on into the black cloud ahead of us," Mrs. Chesnut thought. "Old Pick," the governor, sported "a better wig." After the incident involving the *Rhoda B. Shannon*, Mrs. Chesnut confided to her diary: "One's heart is in one's mouth all the time." It would be more so after Monday, April eight, when a remarkable young man reached Charleston as an emissary from President Lincoln. His name was Robert S. Chew, he worked in Seward's Department of State, and he held very distinct ideas concerning protocol.

Mr. Chew presented himself at the governor's office that morning, accompanied by Captain Talbot, a soldier in Anderson's garrison. While "Old Pick" sat rigidly beneath his "better wig," Mr. Chew read stoically from the paper he had brought: "I am directed by the President of the United States to notify you to expect an attempt will be made to supply Fort Sumter with provisions only, and that if such attempt be not resisted no effort to throw in men, arms, or ammunition will be made without further notice, or in case of an attack upon the fort." Mr. Chew handed Pickens a copy of the paper—unsigned, unaddressed.

Beauregard was summoned but Mr. Chew would not repeat the message since that procedure varied from his instructions. Pickens read the paper to Beauregard, and in order to give the paper official status, Pickens and Beauregard signed a statement of the circumstances under which the document had been received. Would Mr. Chew carry an answer to Mr. Lincoln? Mr. Chew would not; he had not been so instructed. That Pickens and Beauregard were close to explosive anger was revealed in the later report by Samuel Crawford, surgeon at Sumter:

> . . . A request upon the part of Captain Talbot, that he might proceed to Fort Sumter for duty, was peremptorily refused by both Governor Pickens and General Beauregard, as well as permission to communicate with Major Anderson, even with the understanding that Captain Talbot should return at once to Charleston; and very significant hints were given that the immediate departure of these gentlemen would be prudent. At the hotel there were signs of excitement and disapprobation at the presence of Mr. Chew, the object of whose mission had become rumored about the city. They were conveyed quietly from the hotel in a carriage, and under the escort of an aide of the Governor and one from General Beauregard to the station near midnight. By direction of General Beauregard their journey was impeded and broken. At Florence they were detained for some hours, and all telegrams sent by them were, by the same authority, communicated to him at Charleston. They reached Washington on the fourth day [whereas the journey to Charleston had required two].

That was Incident Number One, April 8, 1861. In Washington Justice Campbell had called on Seward the day before, and had been assured that the "Faith as to Sumter [was] fully kept. Wait and see." But Confederate Commissioner Crawford waited less than twenty-four hours before telegraphing Beauregard that although accounts were "uncertain, because of the constant vacillation of this Government," the Confederate Commissioners "have no faith" in the reassurances given. "The war policy," Crawford reported, "prevails in the Cabinet at this time." The impact upon Beauregard of this dispatch, together with the interview with Chew, was reflected in orders telling all military reserves to proceed to their stations, and the Surgeon General was advised to prepare his ambulances and make other necessary provisions for caring for the wounded. And that was Incident Number Two, April 8, 1861.

That day, to Surgeon Crawford, Major Anderson "seemed nervous and anxious." On the seventh, in the last mail to reach Sumter, a letter from Secretary of War Cameron told him: "Hoping still that you will be able to sustain yourself till the 11th or 12th instant, the expedition [to relieve you] will go forward; and, finding your flag flying, will attempt to provision you, and, in case the effort is resisted, will endeavor also to reenforce you." Specifically Anderson was ordered to "hold out, if possible, till the arrival of the expedition," although Cameron added that it was not the intention of the President "to subject your command to any danger or hardship beyond what, in your judgment, would be usual in military life." If, as Surgeon Crawford commented, Anderson was "deeply affected" by this communication, his depression was increased on the morning of the eighth when on the upper end of Sullivan's Island the Confederates knocked down a house and revealed a battery of four heavy guns that would command the only anchorage near the fort.

Anderson poured out his troubled heart in a reply to the War Department; it was "now too late" for him to "give any advice in reference to the proposed scheme of Captain Fox," and the result, he feared, would "be disastrous to all concerned." A gallant man can still remain an honest man, and Anderson proposed to be precisely that: even if the expedition reached the fort, "the loss of life (as I think I mentioned to Mr. Fox) in unloading her will more than pay for the good to be accomplished"; without sufficient oil "to keep a light in the lantern for one night" the boats must "rely at night upon other marks"; and he concluded:

> We shall strive to do our duty, though I frankly say that my heart is not in this war, which I see is to be thus commenced. That God will avert it, and cause us to resort to pacific means to maintain our rights, is my ardent prayer!

The letter, intercepted in Charleston, was forwarded to Montgomery instead of Washington. And that was Incident Number Three.

United States vessels were reported standing off the bar of Charleston Harbor—the attack could come tonight! "I crept silently to my room where I sat down to a good cry," confessed Mrs. Chesnut. Later—"to make sure that we were unhappy enough"—Mrs. Wigfall, wife of the Texan ex-Senator, said, "The slave owners must expect a servile insurrection, of course." Bitterly Mrs. Chesnut thought: "Why did that green goose Anderson go into Fort Sumter?" The New York *Times* supplied a lively report of other events:

> At midnight Charleston was thrown into great excitement by the discharge of seven guns from Citadel square, the signal for all the reserves to assemble ten minutes afterward.
>
> Hundreds of men left their beds, hurrying to and fro towards their respective destinations. In the absence of sufficient armories, at the corners of the streets, public squares, and other convenient points, meetings were formed, and all night the long roll of the drum and the steady tramp of military, and the gallop of the cavalry resounding through the city, betokened the close proximity of the long-anticipated hostilities. The Home Guard corps of old gentlemen, who occupy the position of military exempts, rode through the city, arousing the soldiers, and doing other duty required by the moment.

Rhett labored on the editorial for the morrow's *Mercury*. "We have patiently submitted to the insolent military domination of a handful of men in our bay for over three months after the declaration of our independence of the United States," he asserted. The reward for this "discretion, forebearance, and preparation," Rhett declared, was the throwing down of the gage—"and we accept the challenge." Nor was Rhett the least bit sorry to see joined at last "the issue between the hostile hirelings of Abolition hate and Northern tyranny, and the people of South Carolina defending their freedom and their homes."

But war did not come that night. Nor on the next or the next or the next.

In Montgomery, informed of the details of Chew's conversation with Pickens and Beauregard, Jefferson Davis had to justify—at least to his own conscience—the war he was about to start. Like Secretary Seward, he was anxious to avoid slavery as a cause of his troubles; and unlike Mrs. Chesnut, when he turned a corner in Montgomery and saw a pretty mulatto girl on the auction block, something didn't die within his spirit. Concede the right of secession, his stubborn legalistic mind said, and the very ground on which Sumter stood had been "ceded by South Carolina to the United States *in trust* for the defense of her own soil and her own chief harbor." For Mr. Lincoln to claim it as "public property" was "utterly untenable and unmeaning"; indeed, by holding the fort Mr. Lincoln committed "an act of war." And rationalized Mr. Davis: "He who makes the assault is not necessarily he that strikes the first blow or fires the first gun." After almost four months of "remonstrances and patient, persistent, and reiterated attempts at negotiation," the time had come to break "this grip . . . on the throat of South Carolina." The Confederacy had suffered enough of the "fraud and prevarication practiced by Mr. Lincoln's Administration."

At least this was Mr. Davis's apologia in later years, and one could scarcely expect him to confess that in South Carolina he held a bear by the tail. The Rhett gospel of war-the-sooner-the-better was largely out of hand; Mr. Davis couldn't stop it now, if he wanted to. The Confederate government, comments T. Harry Williams, was "behind a big diplomatic eight ball." If Sumter were provisioned, how many months longer would it flaunt the flag of Federal power before the secessionists? The manner of the government in Montgomery, Rhett later sneered, cherishing no affection for Mr. Davis, was to work in "secret sessions" so that almost "all important business was transacted away from the knowledge and thus beyond the criticism of the people."

For a day, confronted with the difficult decision of whether to trigger a war, the sessions in Montgomery weighed the risks. As far as Sumter was concerned, even if the Federal sloops of war should get into the action, the situation would be a push-over. In a letter that Pickens sent Mr. Davis by special messenger on April ninth the governor reported that by the tenth he expected "to have about 6000 men then on the harbour, batteries and forts." Conceivably they should be a match for Major Anderson and his hungry little garrison. "I trust we are ready," Pickens wrote, "and if they come we will give them a cordial reception, such as will ring right through this country, I think." Pickens hoped that "we are not mistaken"; at any rate, he added, "we will try and do our duty."

But after Sumter—what? A fort for how many lives in how many future battles? It was as well, perhaps, if the question wasn't asked. South Carolina had been spoiling too long for this fight to be denied any longer; and on April tenth through the Secretary of War the Montgomery government gave its consent, informing Beauregard:

> If you have no doubt of the authorized character of the agent who communicated to you the intention of the Washington Government, to supply Fort Sumter by force, you will at once demand its evacuation, and if this is refused, proceed in such a manner as you may determine, to reduce it. Answer.

Gladly Beauregard responded: "The demand will be made to-morrow at 12 o'clock." Montgomery was confused. "Unless there are especial reasons . . . you should make the demand at an early hour," Secretary Walker wired back. "The reasons are special for 12 o'clock," Beauregard retorted—meaning specifically that he wanted to distribute to the batteries a shipment of powder that had arrived that morning from Augusta, Georgia. "The beginning of the end is coming to a final closing," reported the Charleston correspondent to the New York *Day Book*, swept away by his own cliché. "Fort Sumter will be attacked without waiting for the fleet. Everything is prepared against a land attack. The enthusiasm is intense, and the eagerness for the conflict, if it must come, intense."

The fleet for the relief of Sumter was now at sea. The *Harriet Lane*, transferred from the revenue service, sailed on the fifth; the tugs *Uncle Ben* and *Yankee* and the transport *Baltic* cleared Sandy Hook on the ninth; the sloop of war *Pawnee* also sailed on the ninth and the sloop of war *Pocahontas* followed on the tenth. A heavy northeast gale swept the coast all the way and the seas rolled high. The tug *Uncle Ben* was driven into Wilmington, North Carolina, and captured; the tug *Yankee* was swept by the gale to the entrance of Savannah before she could turn back; and the owners of the tug *Freeborn*, alarmed by the storm, refused to let her leave New York. The *Harriet Lane* was the first to reach the rendezvous point. There was no sign of the other vessels.

In Washington that tenth of April Mr. Lincoln had time for only two short notes—one to Secretary of War Cameron urging him to send "at once" a drill officer to Governor Curtin of Pennsylvania and requesting Secretary Chase to interview a representative of the American Bank Note Company about the engraving of Treasury notes. Postmaster Blair began talking to his father about who could lead the Union army should war come. A fine man, Montgomery Blair thought, lived right across the river in Arlington Heights—Colonel Robert E. Lee. While neither Blair could know that Lee had already turned down a generalship in the Confederate army, both could have known that later Lincoln had offered Lee a colonelcy and he had accepted. The elder Blair must have liked his son's suggestion for he would drop over to the War Department and discuss the proposal with Cameron and Scott.

On the morning of the eleventh the Confederate Commissioners decided to leave Washington and the story they gave the reporter for the New York *World* charged Mr. Lincoln's Administration "with gross perfidy." They were now forced "to return to an outraged people," the Commissioners announced; in their "firm" conviction war had become inevitable. With "diplomatic relations" between the Union and the Confederacy thus officially severed, Beauregard was free to deliver his demand upon Major Anderson to evacuate Sumter or take the consequences.

Shortly after noon a boat flying a white flag chugged across Charleston Harbor to Sumter. In her stern sat Colonel James Chesnut, Captain Stephen D. Lee, and Lieutenant Colonel Chisolm, all aides-de-camp to Beauregard. For an hour Anderson and his officers consulted with the group, and then in a courteous note, the Major stated that the demand was one "which I regret that my sense of honor, and of my obligations to my Government, prevent my compliance." Surgeon Crawford was a witness to the subsequent scene:

> The messengers at once, and without further conversation, took their leave. Anderson accompanied them as far as the main gate, where he remained; and as the messengers were about to enter their boat a few yards distant, he asked: "Will General Beauregard open his batteries without further notice to me?" This interrogatory caused a momentary hesitation and embarrassment, when Colonel Chesnut replied, "I think not," and finally said, "No, I can say to you that he will not, without giving you further notice." Anderson then remarked that he would await the first shot, but that he would be starved out anyway in a few days, if General Beauregard did not batter him to pieces with his guns.

The remark was but partially heard by the messengers, who had now entered their boat. The writer was present, when Colonel Chesnut asked him in regard to the remark of Anderson, when, upon a request to that effect, Major Anderson repeated it. Colonel Chesnut asked if he might report it to General Beauregard. Anderson declined to give it the character of a report, but stated that it was the fact of the case. The boat then left the work. . . .

So a wisp of hope remained! New instructions were sought from Montgomery. The government, Secretary Walker wired Beauregard, did "not desire needlessly to bombard Fort Sumter." If Anderson would state the time of evacuation, "and agree that in the meantime he will not use his guns against us unless ours should be employed against Fort Sumter," then Beauregard might "avoid the effusion of blood." Night closed in. The little garrison in Sumter went to bed. Charleston was still at peace.

At one o'clock on the morning of the twelfth Colonel Chesnut and Captain Lee returned to the fort. Anderson wrote another letter to Beauregard, "cordially uniting" in the desire "to avoid the useless effusion of blood"; he could not hold out later than noon of the fifteenth and would be ready to leave then; he would not fire upon Beauregard's forces "unless compelled to do so by some hostile act against this fort or the flag of my Government, by the forces under your command, or by some portion of them, or the perpetration of some act on your part against this fort or the flag it bears, should I not receive prior to that time controlling instructions from my Government or additional supplies."

Chesnut and Lee refused to receive these instructions. At three thirty o'clock they handed Anderson a note, announcing by authority of General Beauregard that "we have the honor to notify you that he will open the fire of his batteries in one hour from this time."

One hour! To Jefferson Davis, taking the trouble to italicize Anderson's stipulation that he included the flag of his government as a possible object of hostile attack, Beauregard's hand had been clearly forced. The little boat with a grim Chesnut and Lee sitting in her stern headed back for the Charleston wharf. One hour and war—a war that could end a legal argument in a single stroke, through all recorded history one of the oldest motives for war. And yet a human argument remained—an argument as old as war itself. Now for a moment a struggle of heart and spirit rested here—a struggle that had started in that barbarous jungle of unrecorded history when man had emerged to find a cool stream where he had experienced the joy of freedom amidst dark fear, and the water had felt good upon his feet. He would always remember. He would always yearn.

That spring at Gaeta the final blow was struck in the national unification of Italy under Victor Emmanuel and the House of Savoy; and Italy's great statesman Cavour, dying from a stroke, murmured happily that he had won "a free Church in a Free State." That February in an imperial ukase Czar Alexander II issued an Act of Emancipation affecting forty-seven million serfs.

Feudalistic barriers crumbled slowly, bitterly, inexorably—one in southern Europe, another to the north in the frozen steppes of Russia, a third here in Charleston Harbor. For without the institution of slavery the legal argument could not have existed; it was the base, the torment of the American conscience—of man's conscience wherever the sun shone and dreams endured. Once man had killed his enemies, next he had enslaved them, and now he groped toward a higher plateau of civilization. Once Mr. Lincoln had said: "Now I protest against that counterfeit logic which concludes that, because I do not want a black woman for a *slave* I must necessarily want her for a *wife*. I need not have her for either, I can just leave her alone. In some respects she certainly is not my equal; but in her natural right to eat the bread she earns with her own hands without asking leave of any one else, she is my equal, and the equal of all others."

One hour and war—between governments, between human attitudes, between interpretations of the same Holy Scripture.

Death at ebb tide, low water, the full of the flood . . . before daybreak that morning the sloop of war *Pawnee* reached her rendezvous point off the Charleston bar. When Gustavus Vasa Fox boarded the *Pawnee* he found Commander Rowan in a bad mood. He intended to remain ten miles east of Charleston light and wait for the *Powhatan*, Rowan insisted—and with the *Powhatan* steaming on to Pensacola Bay Rowan promised himself a considerable respite.

"I am not going in there to begin a civil war," Rowan declared. But the transport *Baltic* went in, followed by the *Harriet Lane*.

Within Sumter, Captain Doubleday, who was sleeping, felt a hand on his shoulder. It was Anderson. Beauregard had determined to open fire in an hour, the Major said. "I remained in bed," Doubleday recalled. But generally the men of the garrison were awake. At four thirty in the direction of Mount Pleasant came a flash of light and the dull roar of a mortar. "The eyes of the watchers," Captain James Chester remembered, "easily detected and followed the burning fuse which marked the course of the shell as it mounted among the stars, and then descended with ever-increasing velocity, until it landed inside the fort and burst. It was a capital shot."

19

"Freedom Is Saved"

WAR! WAR!! WAR!!!

Charleston, April 12—The fight has commenced.
This is all I can say at present.

FROM these terse words the Philadelphia *Inquirer* learned that Sumter had been fired upon. Reading the bulletin outside the *Inquirer's* office, Philadelphians forgot the desks awaiting them, the stores they should open. There was no clue yet that, in Captain Chester's description, "the batteries opened on all sides, and shot and shell went screaming over Sumter as if an army of devils were swooping around it"; no clue to the emotion of Mrs. Chesnut at the sound of that first shot: "I sprang out of bed and on my knees, prostrate, I prayed as I never prayed before."

An early report from Baltimore, swept by the swift excitement that gripped Philadelphia, stated ominously that "the telegraph line at Charleston is under the surveillance of the Secession party." Censored, fragmentary, the news raced across the country. Whatever people had set out to do that morning, they stopped. Startled, dismayed, they stared at the first bulletin—in New York's Printing House Square, in Boston, in Chicago, in St. Louis, in the little town of Keosauqua, Iowa, where General J. M. Tuttle, then county treasurer, remembered that "knots of men could be seen everywhere, excitedly speculating on what probably would be done." Once the shock wore off, once the sullen silence broke, then, the

238

New York *Times* observed, "nothing for years . . . brought the hearts of all the people so close together." In the industrial towns of Connecticut the first intelligence of the attack on Anderson's little garrison was phrased in spirited language: "The traitors are firing on Sumter. Anderson answers gun for gun!" Wherever men gathered above the Mason and Dixon line the same growlish threats were heard: "Avenge the insult! . . . Reinforce Sumter! . . . Vindicate the nation's honor!"

SECOND DESPATCH
Charleston, April 12—The ball has been opened at last and the war is inaugurated. . . .
Every available space facing the harbor is filled with anxious spectators.

Mrs. Chesnut dashed to the roof: "The women were wild, there on the house top. Prayers from the women and imprecations from the men; and then a shell would light up the scene." Emma E. Holmes wrote in her diary: "Though every shot is distinctly heard and shakes our house, I feel calm and composed." Not until daybreak lighted the fort, could Anderson's gunners respond; he fed them breakfast first—"fat pork, very rusty indeed" but "most of the men worried down a little of it."

Not for days—for years—would the full story be known. Yet impossible though it seemed, the excitement in Philadelphia mounted hour by hour. At Third and Chestnut Streets, waiting for the bulletins that told so little, thoroughfares became almost impassable. One young man, calling the "American flag only a rag," had "his nasal organ violently peeled in front of the *Bulletin* office, and found safety in making a sudden departure up Third Street." In Baltimore two men wearing Southern cockades were assaulted and mobbed, one on Baltimore Street, the other on South Street. At the Laura Keane Theater in New York the enterprising manager of that establishment's lively burlesque show was prouder than ever of the tableau in which Major Anderson waved an American flag surrounded by scantily attired chorines representing Liberty, Justice, Pocahontas, and the Spirit of '76. Commodore Vanderbilt told a reporter: "My steamships are at the disposal of the government." Connecticut proclaimed April fourteenth as "Battle Sunday."

Newspaper editors across the nation, gauging the emotions behind the tense faces awaiting the next bulletin, began to understand patterns of behavior. The stunned eyes belonged to those who had clung so long to some such straw as the Crittenden Compromise to avert war. Those who seemed awed into silence were men who by force of political habit had argued that the South should be allowed to go, and the actuality of war shattered them. But the many looked animated, and thanked God that if war had to come, it had been no longer delayed. The editor of the Philadelphia *Press* captured what those faces portrayed: "Henceforth each man, high and low, must take his position as a patriot or a traitor—as a foe or friend of his country—as a supporter of the Stars and Stripes or of the rebel banner."

THIRD DESPATCH

Charleston, April 12 (Received in Philadelphia at 9:30 P.M.)—The firing has continued all day without intermission.

Two of Fort Sumter's guns have been silenced.

Is is reported that a breach has been made in the southeast wall of Sumter. . . .

Anderson gave orders to man only the casemate guns, principally to save manpower. Along the barbette tier of Sumter the shell guns stood loaded but unmanned. The temptation was more than Sergeant John Carmody could endure. Captain Chester watched as Carmody "stole up on the ramparts and deliberately fired every barbette gun in position on the Moultrie side of the work. The guns were already . . . roughly aimed, and Carmody simply discharged them in succession . . . But Carmody's effort aroused the enemy to a sense of his danger. He supposed, no doubt, that Major Anderson had determined to open his barbette batteries, so he directed every gun to bear on the barbette tier . . . But the contest was merely Carmody against the Confederate States; and Carmody had to back down, not because he was beaten, but because he was unable, single-handed to reload the guns." Through the day Mrs. Chesnut watched and thought finally: "Do you know, after all that noise, and our tears and prayers, nobody has been hurt. Sound and fury signifying nothing! A delusion and a snare!"

But Mrs. Chesnut was wrong. All through the day Philadelphia police took into custody outspoken secessionists. With nightfall groups roamed the streets in the City of Brotherly Love, hunting well-known pro-Southerners, jeering outside their homes, demanding that they display the American flag. One group remembered that the secessionist *The Southern Monitor* was published in Philadelphia; and the discovery that the paper had suspended publication bitterly disappointed those who had brought a rope to hang its editor. In Baltimore brokers raised the rate of discount on Southern funds, and in Chicago after a shaky morning brokers decided that "the worst had happened and behold stocks only suffered a little over one per cent."

In silent contemplation that evening men wondered how they could help. In Saulisbury, Connecticut, George Coffin decided to offer the government one hundred tons of iron to be made into cannon balls. Citizens of North Branford, Connecticut, spoke of unfurling a handsome flag on the spot where in 1776, after Sabbath service, Parson Ells rallied the young men in his congregation and led them to war. In divided St. Louis the Union men were silent but Galusha Anderson knew that "their thoughts were hot within them."

New York City's Printing House Square had lived through a tumultuous day. Beyond doubt James Gordon Bennett remained shaken at the memory of the angry crowd that, recalling the *Herald*'s constant harping on concession, had stormed down Nassau and Ann Streets shouting:

"Come out, you yellow-bellied Secessionist!"

"Beauregard and Bennett, heroes of the South!"

Once Bennett had found the courage to appear, he had been jeered all the way down Fulton Street to Broadway. At home at last in Washington Heights, Bennett talked over the difficult day with his son. Henry Villard must be summoned from Washington so that he could carry to Mr. Lincoln in person the message that the *Herald* intended "energetically and wholeheartedly"—later Bennett changed the last word to "unconditionally"—to support the government "in putting down the Secessionists' rebellion by force of arms." Young Bennett mentioned his yacht *Rebecca*, a fine craft that would make a good cutter for the revenue service.

FOURTH DESPATCH

Charleston, April 12 (Received in Philadelphia at 10:30 P.M.)—The Bombardment of Fort Sumter still continues.

The floating battery and Stephen's battery are operating freely.

Fort Sumter continues to return fire.

It is reported that three war vessels are outside the bar.

"There are some few ladies who have been made perfectly miserable and nearly frantic by their fear of the safety of their loved ones," Emma Holmes wrote in her diary, "but the great body of the citizens seem so impressed with the justice of our Cause that they place entire confidence on the God of Battles." An angry gunner in Doubleday's command, seeing the crowds gathered in the city, gave the noncombatants a nasty scare. When no officer was near, he directed two forty-two-pounders at the onlookers. "The first shot," Captain Chester reported, "struck about fifty yards short, and, bounding over the heads of the astonished spectators, went crashing through the Moultrie House. The second followed an almost identical course, doing no damage except to the Moultrie House, and the spectators scampered off in a rather undignified manner." Outside the bar, the three ships still waited for the *Powhatan*. The sea rolled so heavily that the transport

Baltic, steaming toward the harbor, was caught in a ground swell and ran onto Rattlesnake Shoals.

In the North most people, including the President of the United States, read these later dispatches early next morning. Washington awakened Saturday to screaming newsboys; to late habitués of the bar at Willard's who, having kicked off their shoes not too long before to snatch a short nap, now groped to find their shoes; to government workers, waiting for the horsecars; to reedbirds in the marshes along the Potomac, the pink blossoming Judas trees along Rock Creek, the sweet scent of lilacs. Mr. Lincoln, listening to the newsboys hawking their extras that fateful day, impressed his two secretaries with his "steadiness of word and act." Both Nicolay and Hay had learned by now that "while others fretted at things that were," all of Mr. Lincoln's "inner consciousness was abroad in the wide realm of possibilities, busily searching out the dim and difficult path towards things to be. His easy and natural attention to ordinary occupations afford no indication of the double mental process which was habitual with him."

FIFTH DESPATCH

Charleston, April 12—The firing has ceased for the night, to be renewed at daylight . . .

The report was in error. With nightfall a new anxiety plagued the beleaguered garrison, and Captain Chester explained why: "The fleet might send reenforcements; the enemy might attempt an assault. Both would come in boats; both would answer in English. It would be horrible to fire upon friends; it would be fatal not to fire upon enemies. The night was dark and chilly. Shells were dropping into the fort at regular intervals, and the men were tired, hungry, and out of temper. Any party that approached that night would have been rated as enemies upon general principles. Fortunately nobody appeared; reveille sounded, and the men oiled their appetites with the fat pork at the usual hour by way of breakfast."

So through the night Anderson and his garrison waited as the President waited, all the North waited. With morning, Nicolay and Hay declared, the Cabinet "as by a common impulse, came together and deliberated." Its talk was "brief, sententious, informal." At the newspaper and telegraph offices, in the lobbies of the hotels, the crowds grew larger. But the news, filtering through, was hours old. From New York came the consoling intelligence that Wall Street was standing firm, that every dispatch read in the Stock Exchange brought a new burst of cheers for Major Anderson, that government bonds stiffened with the renewed determination to stand by the country. The "universal sentiment," reported the *Tribune,* was "no compromise now with the Rebellion." Mr. Lincoln, inquiring about the current dispatches, "said but little beyond . . . criticizing the probability or accuracy of their details." Otherwise he received visitors, listened to suggestions, and signed routine papers.

SIXTH DESPATCH

Charleston, April 12 (Received in Philadelphia, April 13th, 2 o'clock, A.M.)—The bombardment of Fort Sumter is still going on, every twenty minutes, from the mortars.

It is supposed that Major Anderson is resting his men for the night, as he has ceased firing.

The vessels of war are reported outside, but they cannot get in. The sea is rough.

Nobody on the Carolina side has been hurt by this day's engagement.

The floating battery works well.

Every inlet is well guarded.

There are lively times on the Palmetto coast.

Indeed, there were lively times. In Columbia, South Carolina, thirteen-year-old Emma Florence LeConte recalled: "The joy— the excitement—how well I remember it. For weeks we had been in a fever of excitement. On the day news came of the Fall of

Sumter we were all sitting in the library at Uncle John's. The bell commenced to ring. At the first tap we knew the joyful tidings had come. Father and Uncle John made a dash for their hats—Jule and Johnny followed. We women ran trembling to the veranda—to the front gate, eagerly asking the news of passers-by. The whole town was in a joyful tumult."

Long before the dispatches came announcing that with daylight the Confederates had begun pouring red-hot shot into Sumter, that fires were breaking out everywhere, enveloping even the powder magazine, any newspaperman worth his salt could guess the probable ending. And what did it all mean?

"Fort Sumter is lost, but freedom is saved," began Greeley's editorial. Then, as though jabbing his pen deliberately at Bennett, came typical Greeley sentences: "It seems but yesterday that at least two thirds of the journals of this city were the virtual allies of the Secessionists, their apologists, their champions. The roar of the great circle of batteries pouring their iron hail upon Sumter, has struck them all dumb." Bennett's *Herald* admitted, a bit prissily, that "there can be but two parties—a Northern and a Southern party; for all other parties will cease to exist." Raymond's *Times* declared that the curtain had fallen on act one of "the great tragedy of the age." Yet the people would respond . . . "They ask nothing better than to be allowed to fight for the Constitution which their fathers framed." Even the remarkable Fernando Wood, feeling the sweep of the city's emotions, toiled over a new proclamation. "Let us ignore the past," wrote the mayor, probably wishing that he could, "rising superior to partisan considerations, and rally to the restoration of the Constitution and the Union as they existed in the days and in the spirit of our fathers."

THE LATEST
SEVENTH DESPATCH

Charleston, April 13—12:30 A.M.—It will be utterly impossible to reinforce Fort Sumter tonight, as a storm is raging, and the sea is very rough. . . .

About seven o'clock in the evening surrender terms were reached between Beauregard and Anderson. The men would leave the fort the following day. They would salute their flag with fifty guns. Understanding the type of news that moved the hearts of readers, the *Tribune* reported: "Three men, apparently laborers, reading the despatches, wept when they learned the flag had been hauled down."

On the fourteenth, Connecticut observed its "Battle Sunday" and in fine old Colonial churches fronting town squares where the forsythia was coming into bloom, "ministers prayed that the foes of the nation might be smitten down." Churches everywhere were reported filled to overflowing. In Newark, New Jersey, a schooner in the bay displayed a Palmetto flag; a party of "glass-house boys" rowed to the vessel, threatening to pitch the captain overboard and sink the vessel; soon the Stars and Stripes spread out to the breeze from the schooner's mast and onlookers cheered lustily. In Baltimore the *Fanny Crenshaw,* lying at Chase's wharf, had its Palmetto flag ripped down by an angry mob, but succeeded in raising it again under police protection. Reports indicated that this was no "day of rest" in Baltimore; immense crowds congregated before newspaper offices to obtain extras and read the latest bulletins from the South; and American flags were "numerously displayed" in the harbor, on the shipping, and throughout the city. Yet an ominous note was sounded: "The rumored intention of the Northern military to march through Maryland, in order to coerce the South, has created a feverish excitement."

Sunday brought to Chicago one of those brilliant, cloudless days that often steal across the prairies in April. Church attendance fell off as streets were crowded with men and women anxious to learn if "anything new" had been reported. "The Germans," said the *Tribune,* "congregated in their saloons and beir-halls [sic] and brimful of patriotism and zeal for the country and the Government, gave their valor full expression in words, not to say that they are men who allow sentiments of that sort to rest with words alone." The Tremont House seemed to draw the biggest throng, and, confused by events in Charleston, Chicagoans asked: "Will Quincy granite burn? Are bricks combustible?" Thinking over the day, the *Tribune*'s reporter concluded: "Everybody was up to war point."

Washington awoke that Sunday to a sense of anxiety bordering on despair. George Ashmun, stanch Republican from Massachusetts numbered among his personal friends Stephen A. Douglas. Knowing Douglas was still idolized by the large majority of the Northern wing of the Democratic Party, Ashmun debated through the day the wisdom of appealing to Douglas to issue a statement in support of the national government. Late that afternoon Ashmun called his carriage and drove to Minnesota Row. His interview with Douglas did not start on a happy note.

Once Douglas said snappishly: "Mr. Lincoln [has] dealt hardly with me in removing some of my friends from office, and I don't know as he wants my advice or aid."

But Ashmun persisted. The question had risen to "a higher dignity" than party politics. Douglas put aside his pique. He would go with Ashmun to see the President and offer his "cordial and earnest support." It was almost dark when Ashmun and Douglas drove to the White House. Mr. Lincoln was alone, and in a friendly manner "prepared the way" for the interview by reading the proclamation he intended issuing next morning.

Douglas rose from the chair. "Mr. President," he said, "I cordially concur in every word of that document, except that instead of a call for seventy-five thousand men I would make it two hundred thousand. You do not know the dishonest purposes of those men (the Rebels) as well as I do—" He walked to the wall map, pointing out the strategic points that should be instantly strengthened—Fortress Monroe, Washington, Harper's Ferry, Cairo in southern Illinois. The country must achieve a firm, warlike footing—and, Ashmun recalled, he "found in Mr. Lincoln an earnest and gratified listener."

Driving home, Ashmun praised Douglas warmly. He had "done

justice" to his own reputation, to the President, to the country. When the President's proclamation was telegraphed to the country, a statement from Douglas should go with it.

"Drive to your room at Willard's and I will give it shape," Douglas said.

Ashmun copied the statement for the Associated Press, and the original he preserved as "cherished evidence of the highest character, that whoever else may have fallen by the wayside from 'false brethren,' Mr. Douglas was not one of them." On Monday, along with Mr. Lincoln's call for seventy-five thousand volunteers, America read:

DISPATCH TO THE PRESS BY MR. DOUGLAS
SUNDAY EVENING, APRIL 14, 1861

Mr. Douglas called on the President this evening and had an interesting conversation on the present condition of the country. The substance of the conversation was that while Mr. Douglas was unalterably opposed to the administration on all its political issues, he was prepared to sustain the President in the exercise of all his constitutional functions to preserve the Union, and maintain the government and defend the Federal capital. A firm policy and prompt action was necessary. The capital of our country was in danger and must be defended at all hazards, and at any expense of men and money. He spoke of the present and the future without reference to the past.

Before Christmas Mr. Lincoln had written from Springfield: "The people, under Providence, will set all right." To that faith he still clung.

20

"We Are Coming, Father Abraham!"

THE PEOPLE! In New York City Simeon Draper told his wealthy friends from the Union League Club: "Damn the swallow-tails; let's go for the ground tier!" To give New York the kind of demonstration needed to support the President's call for troops, bring him fifty or sixty stevedores, laborers, "and such people from around the docks," and Draper believed the right result would follow. With a flag and a drum and fife corps, Draper started his workingmen up Broadway. At Wall Street —by careful prearrangement—forty or fifty "gentlemen" joined the procession, among them LeGrand B. Cannon, who remembered: "The effect was electrical. All Wall Street emptied out and cheered for the flag. . . . Within twenty-four hours the flag was flying from every churchsteeple in the city, and the whole place was ablaze with patriotic enthusiasm."

The people! Before the week ended Stephen A. Douglas rode the Baltimore & Ohio to rally the Democratic majorities in the counties of southern Illinois behind Lincoln's call for troops. At Bellaire, Ohio, close to Wheeling, thousands who had ridden special trains from all parts of western Virginia, cheered the Little Giant. "This great valley," shouted Douglas, the man of inexhaustible passion, "depends upon maintaining inviolate and forever that great right secured by the Constitution, of freedom of trade, of transit, and of commerce, from the center of the continent to the oceans that surround it." The fire in the Senator's voice lighted his call to these valley people: "Unite as a band of brothers!" And the finger that in the old days so often in derision or reproach had sought out Lincoln's gawky figure, now pointed to the Ohio River. The audience cheered and he thundered on: "The Almighty has so arranged the mountains and the plain, and the water-courses as to show that this valley in all time shall remain one and indissoluble. Let no man attempt to sunder what Divine Providence has rendered indivisible!"

The people! In St. Louis the Reverend Galusha Anderson walked to evening service under a clear sky. No clergyman for months had dared to take a stand for or against the Union, and Anderson, mounting the pulpit, noticed that large numbers of secessionists had come to church this fine balmy evening. One deacon knew his intention and said: "Well, if you must preach on secession, give them a 12-inch columbiad." For the Scripture lesson Anderson read from the thirteenth chapter of Romans, wherein Paul teaches the duty of obedience to established government. Then he began the sermon—conscious of the hush that fell over the congregation, of the flicker of the gas in the pauses between sentences, of hostile eyes, and of one bronze-faced stranger who began crying out "*A*-men." Anderson said: "I wish to bear my own individual testimony, to express the feelings of my heart. I love my country—I love the government of my country—I love the freedom of my country. It was purchased by the blood of our fathers, and when I become so base, so cowardly, so be-sotted that I dare not speak out in behalf of that for which they fought so bravely, I pray that my tongue may cleave to the roof of my mouth!" For the concluding hymn he selected "My Country, 'Tis of Thee," and the secessionists in the congregation refused to open their hymnbooks. Yet others sang; and a group of pro-Union Methodists, homeward bound from their own serv-ice, stood under an open window and joined in the hymn. Ander-son believed that a burden had been lifted from his soul: "My mistake was that I had not spoken sooner. With a light heart I went back to my home and slept."

The people! The New York *Herald* for April sixteenth carried a unique advertisement:

WANTED: A Captain of Cavalry

The Cavalry department of the Northern army is, without a doubt, the one most lacking in efficiency. To supply this flagrant need is the desire of several gentlemen of this city, two of whom have in their handsomest manner offered to supply horses and equipments for the first fifty volunteers who shall be unable to mount and equip themselves. All that is needed now to effect an organization is a competent leader, and to anyone sufficiently well versed in tactics to command such a troop, a superb horse, half brother of the celebrated Patchem, and a full suit of regimentals will be guaranteed. Those desirous of joining will please call upon G. W. Richardson, 21 Maiden Lane.

One hundred and fifty volunteers responded to the advertisement and the proprietor of Palace Garden offered the use of his hall without charge.

The people! In Norwich, Connecticut, a donor to the local militia sent his check, "Payable to Stars and Stripes, or bearer." In less than three days more men in Chicago responded than could be taken into the city's militia organizations; a headline writer for the *Tribune* spoke for Chicago if not for the President in declaring "Old Abe's Blood is Up"; and on the Sunday following Lincoln's proclamation the first troops departed on the Illinois Central "amid the tears and shouts of the thousands who thronged the lake shore to bid them farewell." Editorialized Bennett's *Herald*: ". . . there is no desire among the merchants or capitalists of New York to shirk the issue, or to evade the responsibilities of the contest. Upon New York will devolve the chief burden of providing ways and means for the war; our financial community accepts the duty, and will perform it." The Philadelphia *Inquirer* prodded its readers: "Take your place in line. The American flag trails in the dust." And in Louisville the *Journal,* warning the secession leaders that "the sympathies of honest and sensible men are not likely to go with the wrong-doers," asked: "Who that loves his country would see it humiliated and its honor trampled on?" In West Roxbury, Massachusetts, plans were made to convert historic Brook Farm into Camp Andrew, and in this Utopia of the Unitarian apostle George Ripley where once the men had strolled in tasseled caps and the ladies in gay muslin dresses, workmen began clearing away a parade ground where a thousand men could drill and buildings in which aesthetic New Englanders once had studied Latin and Greek became "the protecting hospital" and "the instructive guard-house." Old soldiers in almost every Northern town searched through bookcases and trunks for dog-eared copies of Hardee's *Tactics* and were surprised at how much they had forgotten.

The people! Posters on store fronts along the length of Main Street in Galena, Illinois, announced a meeting of citizens in the Court House on April eighteenth. Captain Sam Grant, though still considering himself "a comparative stranger" in the community, as the town's one professional soldier was asked to preside. It was warm and uncomfortable on the crowded second floor of the Court House, and Grant, with characteristic dry humor, remembered: "With much embarrassment and some prompting I made out to announce the object of the meeting. Speeches were in order, but it is doubtful whether it would have been safe just then to make other than patriotic ones. There was probably no one in the house, however, who felt like making any other." Postmaster B. B. Howard, a Breckinridge Democrat, gave one speech, but another Democrat, John A. Rawlins, was the evening's star. At the entrance to the Court House a friend stopped Rawlins and pleaded: "John, you don't want to go up there and talk to that crowd; it's a God-damned Black Republican meeting!" But Rawlins was fed up with Democrats who couldn't see "it is simply country or no country" now and he cared nothing about Democrats still carping about the November elections when they had come within fifty-seven votes of carrying Galena. Rawlins wanted to speak as a man who had "favored every honorable compro- mise," and he brought his audience to its feet shouting: "We will stand by the flag of our country, and appeal to the God of battles."

Walking away from the meeting, Grant told his brother Orvil: "I think I ought to go into the service."

Orvil agreed. "I'll stay home and attend to the store," said Orvil, who at Christmas time had sneered that the "Chivs" would never fight.

The people! Two days after the President issued his call for volunteers, Governor Andrew told the Fourth Massachusetts Volunteers: "You have come from the shores of the sounding sea, where lie the ashes of the Pilgrims, and you are bound on a high and noble pilgrimage for liberty, for the Union and Constitution of your country." By railroad the Fourth Massachusetts traveled from Boston to Fall River, where, unexpectedly, they boarded the steamer *State of Maine*. Three days later the Fourth Massa- chusetts lay off Fortress Monroe in the gray morning light, "waiting for the sunrise gun to see what flag would be raised"; when the Stars and Stripes was hoisted, the Bay State boys sailed in and announced themselves. "Thank God!" cried a voice within the old fort; for two nights the little garrison of two hundred men "had lain on their arms on the parapets" of this "most important of all the defences along our coast." Next morning disgusted secessionists, indignant at the swift reinforcement of Fortress Monroe, were "full of threats and curses." Yet the week's ending was not so happy for the Sixth Massachusetts, and especially for Addison O. Whitney and Luther C. Ladd, mechanics, of Lowell, and for Charles A. Taylor, decorative painter, and Sumner H. Needham, plasterer, both of Boston. Their names by Sunday would be known to millions.

The people! On the afternoon of April eighteenth—the day when the posters in Galena called its citizens to a meeting in the Court House—Colonel Robert E. Lee hitched his horse to the post at 1651 Pennsylvania Avenue. The name plate on the door read Francis Blair, Sr. Lee knew something about old Blair—he was the former editor of the *Congressional Globe* and his son Montgomery was in Mr. Lincoln's Cabinet—but he couldn't know the background of this meeting to which he had been summoned. Montgomery Blair had seen Mr. Lincoln, then Francis Blair had seen Mr. Lincoln, then both Blairs had talked to Secretary of War Cameron, who had talked to General Scott, who had talked to John Lee, a cousin who had arranged the present meeting. So much smoke must indicate a little fire—and since it certainly did, Francis Blair, Sr. came straight to the point. Giving the clear impression that he spoke for the President, Blair asked: "Will you take command of the Union armies in the field?" In 1868 Lee wrote to Maryland's Senator Reverdy Johnson:

> . . . After listening to his remarks, I declined the offer he made me, to take command of the army that was to be brought into the field; stating, as candidly and as courteously as I could, that, though opposed to secession, and deprecating war, I could take no part in the invasion of the Southern states.

The more difficult interview came later with old Scott—himself Virginia-born, a father-mentor who had taught Lee more about war than he had learned studying Napoleon, Hannibal, and Caesar at West Point. Attack on the flank, prepare the battle plan through careful reconnaissance, hit the enemy by surprise—thus Scott had taught them all in Mexico, Lee and Grant and Beauregard and a score of others now scampering to join with North or South. Scott spoke with distress, learning of Lee's decision: "You have made the greatest mistake of your life." If Lee intended to resign, then "do so at once—your present attitude is equivocal." Lee had no wish to resign unless Virginia seceded. As the two men talked, the Washington *Star* appeared with stories—as yet unverified—that the Virginia Convention in Richmond had passed an ordinance of secession and that three ships had been sunk in the mouth of the Elizabeth River.

Next morning Lee was in Alexandria, shopping in John Mosby's drug store, when he read the news that Virginia had left the Union. "I am one of those dull creatures that cannot see the good of secession," he told Mosby, and the druggist made note of the remark beside his ledger entry of the amount Lee had just paid him. Sadly, Lee mounted his horse and rode home to Arlington Heights. Only yesterday he had said to Francis Blair: "If I owned 4,000,000 slaves, I would cheerfully sacrifice them for the preservation of the Union." But that was yesterday—and today—and tomorrow and tomorrow . . .

At home the older Lee boys, Custis and Rooney, stormed that the people of Virginia had lost their heads. The father prayed and knew, as a Virginian, what he must do. "If I have done wrong, let him do better," he told his wife, not wishing to influence Custis. On the twenty-second Lee caught the train for Richmond; in Galena, Grant was packing for the journey to join the Eleventh Illinois voluntary infantry in Springfield. For both men all doubt had ended.

In Bangor, addressing itself to "Democrats of Maine," the misnamed *Union* advised: "When the government in Washington calls for volunteers or recruits to carry on the work of subjugation and tyranny under the specious phrases of 'enforcing the law,' 'retaking and protecting of public property' and 'collecting the revenue,' let every Democrat fold his arms and bid the minions of tory despotism do a tory despot's work." In Paterson, New Jersey, the *Reporter* believed that "in ten days Lincoln will probably have 200,000 volunteers . . . to prosecute the John Brown schemes of his party," and in Utica, New York, the *Observer* observed: "Of all the wars which have disgraced the human race, it has been reserved for our own enlightened nation to be involved in the most useless and foolish one." These protests, scattered, almost certain in April, 1861, to arouse anger and result in what one witness described as "personal collisions," were the first murmurings of that political dissent which would unite "Peace Democrats" and Copperheads in an unsuccessful effort in 1864 to thwart the re-election of Mr. Lincoln. The Baltimore riots—despite Mr. Greeley's insistence on calling them "The Rattlesnake's Fangs"—belonged in another category.

Perhaps, as Henry Adams suggested, the military nature of the Republican Wide-Awakes during the Presidential canvass had conditioned the North to accept war in a single weekend—to accept it with an intensity amounting almost to the fervor of a holy crusade. The reports from Baltimore during the bombardment of Fort Sumter indicate that the emotion of Philadelphia and New York and Boston and Chicago aroused similar strong reflexes here. Then on the fifteenth the President issued his proclamation, and within four days Baltimore became the first battleground of the war. Why? "Plug uglies," snorted Greeley's *Tribune,* missing the point that advanced Southern sympathizers and extremists were only one element in the crowds who rioted at the sight of Northern troops passing over Maryland soil en route to the South. Another element—perhaps the smallest of the three involved—were youths attracted by the noise and excitement. Some of these youngsters may have been roughs, but others came from respectable Baltimore families. And again, among the rioters, were "sober, intelligent men, many of them Union sympathizers," and these, one of their own members admitted, "were knocked clear off their balance by the announcement that Northern troops were marching on the city."

The North had gone to war swiftly, vigorously. On Monday the President had called for troops and on Thursday troops from Pennsylvania and the West were scheduled to change from one railroad station to another in Baltimore. On the eighteenth of April a large, excited crowd assembled at Camden Station, awaiting the arrival of the troops. The civilians sang "Dixie." They cheered for the Confederacy. Disembarking from the trains, the soldiers were "pushed and hustled" but none was hurt seriously and the march started for Mount Clare Station, where the troops were to retrain for Washington. The crowd "guyed and hissed," cheered for Jeff Davis, groaned at the mention of Abe Lincoln, but with protection from the city police the troops reached Mount Clare Station. Suddenly the crowd grew more aggressive, and Frederic Emory remembered:

> . . . The troops were subjected to numberless indignities, such as being spit upon, taunted, hustled . . . the mob all the while indulging in wild curses, groans and yells, with threats such as these: "Let the police go and we'll lick you!" "Wait till you see Jeff Davis!" "We'll see you before long!" "You'll never get back to Pennsylvania!" . . . Several of the more adventuresome rioters caught some of the soldiers by the coat tails and jerked them about . . .

Still, with police protection, the troops boarded and the cars began to move. A stone was thrown. With a rush the rioters started after the slowly receding train. Once more the police checked the angry swarm.

Frustration heightened the excitement, and, Emory testified, "the staidest and soberest citizens were infected by it." Baltimore became a city where business was forgotten. By afternoon in the center of town the crowd was estimated at two thousand. Meanwhile, without notifying the Baltimore authorities, the government ordered another rail convoy to leave Philadelphia. Early next morning thirty-five cars left with twelve hundred troops from Boston, Lowell, and Acton—the Sixth Massachusetts under command of Colonel Edward F. Jones—and a regiment of one thousand Pennsylvanians under command of Colonel William F. Small.

Unruly Baltimore rubbed sleepy, angry eyes and began that Friday in an ugly mood. At about eleven o'clock "it came noised abroad" that the troops had arrived at the President Street depot. Mayor George W. Brown, gaining word of the expected arrival an hour earlier, rushed his police by mistake to the Camden Street Station. The crowd, gathering in numbers, selected narrow Pratt Street to make its stand. About eleven thirty the first horse-drawn car appeared. Jeers rose shrilly, but the car was permitted to pass. The next eight cars also went through, suffering only verbal indignity. Near Commerce Street the brake of the tenth car failed. It stopped. Now, said Emory, the rioters

> . . . began to attack the occupants with stones. Windows were broken, and a few of the soldiers were hurt, but not seriously. Finally the driver of the car became frightened, lost his head, and, having attached his team to the other end of the car, started to haul it back to the depot. The mob followed the car, stoning it all the while, but the driver having urged the horses to a run, succeeded in distancing them. . . .

This taste of an enemy in retreat whetted the mob's temper. Across the bridge on Pratt Street, rioters—aided by Negroes summoned from work on the near-by wharves—threw up a barricade, "Paris fashion." A car filled with sand was dumped on the barricade. Others tore up pavement and car tracks for a distance of perhaps fifty yards. Colonel Jones formed the Sixth Massachusetts in double file outside the depot and gave the order to force a passage on foot.

Meanwhile a rioter appeared, amid wild cheers, carrying a Confederate flag. Northern sympathizers jeered, shook fists, rushed, and broke the flagstaff. The melee had now a new character—the flag-bearer and a companion throttled one of the attacking Unionists almost to the point of death, "the shreds of the flag were caught up and tied to the flagstaff"—and in triumph the cheering, taunting defenders of the South shouted that if the Massachusetts troops marched to the Camden Street Station, they would do so behind the Confederate flag. Colonel Jones cried, "Forward march!" Spread across his path were the rioters, refusing to yield ground. Luckily the Baltimore police had found the trouble spot; night sticks ended a series of scuffles and the soldiers at last moved—but "the Confederate flag was borne to the front, and they were compelled to march for several squares behind this flag."

That flag remained a goad to exasperated Northern sympathizers. Again fists flew, again the Unionists fell back, mingling with the troops to find refuge. The mob, almost out of hand now, attacked the troops "with stones and other missiles." Private William Patch, struck in the back with a paving stone, sprawled on the ground. His musket was wrenched from his hands. Badly beaten and bleeding, he was rescued by the police. Colonel Jones roared, "Forward—double quick!" The soldiers broke into a run, "ducking and dipping to avoid the stones." The rioters pursued at "full tilt." Two Massachusetts soldiers, knocked down, scrambled up and escaped. Ahead stretched the barricade at the Pratt Street bridge. A shower of paving stones filled the air. Said Emory:

> . . . The troops faltered, and finally, in the face of a second shower of stones, came to a dead halt. The patience of the commander was at last exhausted. He cried out in a voice, which was heard even above the yells of the crowd, "Fire!" The soldiers leveled their pieces, and the crowd seemed to pause, as if to take breath. The soldiers fired. A young man . . . fell pierced by the ball.
>
> A hoarse yell of fear and rage went up from the mob, but it did not give way. The troops fired again and again, and the crowd wavering, they rushed upon them with fixed bayonets and forced a passage over the barricade. A scene of bloody confusion followed. As the troops retreated, firing, the rioters rushed upon them, only to be repulsed by the line of bayonets.
>
> Some of the rioters fought like madmen. Finally the mob, exasperated by their failure to prevent the passage of troops, made a desperate rush upon them, and one young man, who was in the front rank of the rioters, was forced close upon the soldiery. One of the soldiers raised his gun, took deliberate aim at the rioter and fired. The cap exploded, but the gun failed to go off. The rioters rushed forward, seized the gun, wrested it by an almost superhuman effort from the soldier's grasp, and plunged the bayonet through the man's shoulder. . . .
>
> At the intersection of Charles and Andrew Streets, Andrew Robbins, a soldier from Stoneham, Mass., was shot in the neck by a rioter. He was carried into a drug store near by, and was protected from the mob. At Howard Street a strong force of rioters from Camden Station met the troops and refused to

yield. The soldiers fired again and the mob gave way. The soldiers again started at the double quick and reached Camden Station without further trouble. Thirteen cars were drawn out, and the soldiers left the depot amid the hisses and groans of the multitude. . . .

Behind, dead, they left Whitney and Ladd, mechanics, of Lowell; Taylor, decorative painter, and Needham, plasterer, both of Boston. Twelve civilians were dead. The Great Rebellion had produced its first casualties.

What did it all mean? Certainly the British couldn't understand. "Nature, or something that stands in its stead," grumbled the London *Times*, "is still strong with Americans. They fight 'willing, but with unwilling minds.'" Clearly confused, the *Times* asked: "Are they in earnest, or are they playing at war, or dreaming that they strike, and still strike not? It sounds more like a dangerous game than a sad reality." And the London *Economist* believed that "if it be war" a "premature" recognition of the Confederacy would depart from British policy and "express a political *bias* in favor of the seceders." That ever-faithful diarist at the American legation in London, Benjamin Moran, admitted grimly: "The full reports of the fight at Fort Sumter are now here & we cut a sorry enough figure. Every body is laughing at us." But after the Baltimore riots no one need question where Moran's loyalty rested: "The southern slave tyrants must now be treated without mercy."

From across the ocean, Moran had spoken perceptively. If this was a war over a point of Constitutional legality, then the Cabinet might dispute it, Commons debate it, the press ridicule it, but the people of England, and of Europe, could not comprehend it. But if it were a war against slavery, if it represented something so deep in the tide of human aspiration that it would sweep over and inundate a South that blocked a deep inward craving of all men in all climes, then the people knew why the North fought. Americans could understand the political factors involved in Union vs. Disunion; abroad, the issue was more simply defined for the workingman. It was an old and useless and wicked culture, this Southern slave culture. Mr. Lincoln always would have wise and patient friends in England—John Bright and Richard Cobden, among others—but the workingman had been reached by *Uncle Tom's Cabin*. Human slavery was indefensible. In British homes, pubs, railroad stations, barber shops—where, in the end, the fate of monarchs and prime ministers rested—it took just one act, the Emancipation Proclamation, to send a Cockney woman shouting through the streets of London, "Lincoln's been and gone and done it!"

England, too, stirred with a brave, new fervent democracy, rooted in the working class, and the British government's sympathy with the South could not reach the Britisher in pub and railroad car once he became convinced that the Northerner truly believed what he sang marching to battle:

> In the beauty of the lilies Christ was born across the sea,
> With a glory in His bosom that transfigures you and me . . .

On April 19, 1861—the day of the Baltimore riots—Lincoln declared a blockade of the Southern coast, severely threatening British towns in Lancashire, whose economic happiness depended on Southern cotton. "Would any sane nation make war on cotton?" South Carolina's Senator James H. Hammond once asked. Mr. Lincoln would and did—on paper in April of 1861, since the Union navy consisted of twenty-nine steam-propelled ships of war, with which to patrol and blockade some 9,164 miles of enemy waterways—but what of Lancashire? Year by year, as the Union navy grew and the blockade tightened, cotton could pile up on Southern wharves for all Lancashire cared, just so long as the North fought against slavery and honestly held to the faith of Julia Ward Howe:

> As He died to make men holy, let us die to make men free,
> While God is marching on!

For that, the workingman of Lancashire would pull in his belt and grit his teeth, as would the working class in Manchester, and across the Channel in Paris.

Yet during Sumter week, and for two years afterward, Mr. Lincoln had good reason for hesitating. Baltimore rioted, Stephen Douglas traveled to his spirited speech in Bellaire, Ohio, and as a son of the Border States Mr. Lincoln knew how delicate was the balance that, if prematurely upset, could extend the war. The seemingly inexhaustible Douglas, alert to these same high stakes, drove himself to speeches before other cheering audiences in Columbus, in Indianapolis. By April twenty-fifth, he reached Mr. Lincoln's Springfield. John A. Logan, a downstate political power, accused Douglas of selling out the party. "By God, you can't deliver it!" Logan declared. But in large measure Douglas did—and Logan with it to fight with Grant at Vicksburg and to march with Sherman to the sea. Now Douglas substituted the valley of the Mississippi for the valley of the Ohio, speaking of "a war of self-defense on our part . . . of those great rights of freedom of trade, commerce, transit and intercourse from the center to the circumference of our great country." His fervor led him across the prairies to Chicago, where on June third high fever began to sap the last strength from his exhausted body. Had he any message for his mother, his sister, his sons? "Tell them," Douglas murmured, "to obey the laws and support the Constitution of the United States." Death came to him then, in victory, for the Border States whither he had journeyed remained loyal.

Lee bound for Richmond, Grant for Springfield . . . from Minnesota, Wisconsin, Iowa, from Maine, Massachusetts, Connecticut, from Chicago, Columbus, Detroit, they came, boys in blue with tin canteens to oppose the boys in gray with cedar canteens . . . this was whither it had led, all the mixture of regional interests and emotions and traditions. The war they fought had many names—Civil War, War Between the States,

War for Southern Independence. The government called it the War of the Rebellion, and published one hundred and twenty-eight volumes of official records to tell how men died, but not why.

After a time a war just seems to go on and on. But there was purpose here. And design. And ideal. And a duty:

> It mus' be now de kingdom comin'
> An' de year ob Jubilo!

For he was always there, the Negro—had been there through all the years before—waiting, waiting. Nothing in the Bible said that only a man with a black skin could be enslaved. So, too, could be the man with a white skin.

And therein rested the issue at rock bottom. In the minds of men the war could have many reasons. In the heart of mankind it could have but one ending:

> Mine eyes have seen the glory of the coming of the Lord,
> He is trampling out the vintage where the grapes of wrath
>   are stored;
> He hath loosed the fateful lightning of His terrible,
>   swift sword,
> His truth is marching on.

History is emotion also—and in song a nation can document its purpose. In Christmas week, North and South, the shape of the conflict was defined. On a Sunday the full story of Sumter became known, and a nation resolved to suffer its bloody ordeal.

Then came another April, another Sunday.

PART III

Palm Sunday, 1865

21

At City Point

ONE GRAY, misty morning in late March, 1865, a carriage brought Mr. Lincoln to the Sixth Street wharf. The President, worn out and breaking in health, boarded the steamer *River Queen* en route to City Point, Virginia. That indefatigable diarist, Secretary Welles, still unflinching in his self-appointed role as a chronicler of the war and Mr. Lincoln, noted: "He wishes the war terminated, and to this end, that severe terms should not be exacted of the Rebels."

The nation worried about Mr. Lincoln. What one Washington correspondent wrote, others echoed: The President had been "carried further toward his grave by four years in the White House than he could have been by ten years of constant labor in the courts or on the farm." Nothing must happen to Mr. Lincoln now, the nation prayed. With the buds swelling on the trees and the forsythia bursting into yellow flame, the air tingled with expectancy; in front of Petersburg, Lee could not stand off Grant much longer; any day, any hour the death of the Confederacy could come.

In principle, old Jeff Davis had been strung to a sour-apple tree in January, when the House had at last passed the Thirteenth Amendment. Slavery was finished, a weight lifted forever from the American conscience. And when the issue had wavered, who but Mr. Lincoln had come forward, once more the man of magic,

267

to turn the tide? Congressman James M. Ashley of Ohio had done Mr. Lincoln's logrolling on that occasion, and it had taken quite some doing. But the promise of a Federal appointment to the brother of one doubtful Democratic Congressman had worked; an attorney for a railroad had found irresistible the assurance of friendly votes against the threat of certain unfriendly legislation.

To Frederick Law Olmsted it was "the wholesome, patriotic devotion of the solid, industrious, home-keeping people" who carried Mr. Lincoln through gloomy nights and dark days; but the astute Charles A. Dana found all the true strength within this man who "understood politics because he understood human nature":

> The great quality of his appearance [declared Dana] was benevolence and benignity: the wish to do somebody some good if he could; and yet there was no flabby philanthropy about Abraham Lincoln. He was all solid, hard, keen intelligence combined with goodness. Indeed, the expression of his bearing which impressed one most, after his benevolence and benignity, was his intelligent understanding. You felt that here was a man who saw through things, who understood, and you respected him accordingly.

Dana worked for Secretary of War Stanton so that his perceptions had to be alert, and in analyzing the essence of Mr. Lincoln's genius he observed shrewdly: "He never stepped too soon, and he never stepped too late." Others might push, but the President, believing in the people, always waited until they caught up to his beliefs; then he issued the Emancipation Proclamation or threw his strength behind the Thirteenth Amendment. A man without illusions, thought the admiring Dana; a man who could face hard facts, who never tried to "foretell things."

Lincoln was not only representative of the frontier tradition in the age in which he lived, but was representative as well of a coming type of American who would build the nation into a world power. The war divided almost evenly into two cycles. In the first two years vast armies were trained and equipped, a blockade on paper became a blockade in reality, and enormous strides forward were made in perfecting the instruments of human destruction. By 1863 Lincoln had the business of war organized; and how spectacular this achievement must be called was illustrated by what it meant for the Army of the Potomac to move into battle at Gettysburg. Those blue-clad columns, wending their way northward to find Lee, stood for a phenomenon in organization that only could be equaled if one morning a city like Albany or Columbus or Indianapolis arose and walked away with all its clothing, food, medicine, ammunition, horses, wagons, people.

Yet even in the midst of war Lincoln did not lose the vision of the whole nation that would emerge ultimately. During these four tragic years—and despite the constant harassment of Indian attacks—the population of the territories trebled, vast mineral resources were discovered and developed, railroad surveys were pushed ahead, mercy and justice became the basis of new Indian policies, and a program of immigration was urged in which labor was clearly the master of capital. In his message to Congress on December 1, 1862, the President asserted:

> A nation may be said to consist of its territory, its people, and its laws. The territory is the only part which is of certain durability. "One generation passeth away, and another generation cometh, but the earth abideth forever." . . . That portion of the earth's surface which is owned and inhabited by the people of the United States, is well adapted to be the home of one national family; and it is not well adapted for two, or more. Its vast extent, and its variety of climate and productions, are of advantage, in this age, for one people, whatever they might have been in former ages. . . .

So spoke the President who in another month would sign the Emancipation Proclamation; who believed that the nation's strife "pertains to ourselves" rather than to any geographical factor; and who would create the Department of Agriculture, calling it "the people's department." So spoke the President who negotiated treaties with England and Russia for a telegraph system that would link the United States into a network of world-wide com-

munication and who thought in terms of an international postal
union. So also spoke the President who wondered what would
happen to people as they grew older, and what was the responsibility of a government in insuring those years to come, and in 1864
he proposed that Congress provide "a limited amount of some
future issue of public securities . . . exempt from taxation" to
"enable every prudent person to set aside a small annuity against
a possible day of want."

In 1864 Lincoln repeated to Congress what he said in 1863—that
if slaves, once emancipated, were to live ever again in bondage,
the nation would have to elect another President. And he spoke
of foreign slave traders as "enemies of the human race" who must
be forever denied asylum in the United States. Some historians
contend that as Lincoln drew upon the manpower and resources
of the North to achieve victory, he also borrowed morals to crush
the Great Rebellion, and they argue that this debt remains substantially unpaid almost a century later. Yet such assertions do
not alter the fact that as there had been an age of Washington and
Jackson, now there was an age of Lincoln when a new moral force,
whether borrowed or given freely, had triumphed. The cost in
human life, as far as anyone could estimate, would be staggering
—for the North, including those dying from wounds, 360,222
dead and another 275,175 with one leg or no legs, with one arm
or no arms, with one eye or sightless; and for the South 258,000
dead and the total wounded never counted. Yet a nation's conscience justified this sacrifice, and speaking for that conscience
Mr. Lincoln said in his Second Inaugural:

> . . . If we shall suppose that African Slavery is one of those
> offenses which, in the providence of God, must needs come,
> but which, having continued through his appointed time, He
> now wills to remove, and that He gives to both North and
> South, this terrible war, as the woe to those by whom the offence
> came, shall we discern therein any divine departure from those
> divine attributes which the believers in a Living God always
> ascribe to him? Fondly do we hope—fervently do we pray—

that this scourge of war may speedily pass away. Yet, if God wills that it continues, until all wealth piled by the bondman's two hundred and fifty years of unrequited toil shall be sunk, and until every drop of blood drawn with a lash, shall be paid by another drawn by the sword, as was said three thousand years ago, so still it must be said "The judgments of the Lord are true and righteous altogether."

The audience, hushed, stirred, saw that the bronze statue of Freedom now crowned the dome of the Capitol. Not States Rights, but human rights; not civil war alone, but in some respects a religious war . . . and Mr. Lincoln, setting in the gold of Biblical prophecy the gem of wisdom that the past four years had brought him, said:

With malice toward none; with charity for all; with firmness in the right, as God gives us to see the right, let us strive on to finish the work we are in; to bind up the nation's wounds; to care for him who shall have borne the battle, and for his widow and his orphan—to do all which may achieve and cherish a just and lasting peace, among ourselves, and with all nations.

Seeing Mr. Lincoln, Greeley grumbled that "his face was haggard with care and seamed with thought and trouble"; the President looked "care-ploughed, tempest-tossed and weather-beaten," yielding a clue to why ten days after his second inauguration Mr. Lincoln conducted a Cabinet meeting in his bedroom. But an inexhaustible passion to end the war and win the peace drove the President to City Point; and even that habitual worry-wart, Stanton, approved Mr. Lincoln's presence there, wiring him: "If you are on the ground there will be no pause."

With Charleston again in Union hands as a result of Sherman's march into the Carolinas, Stanton planned a great celebration at Sumter. At noon on the fourteenth of April, he telegraphed the President at City Point, Anderson would "raise & plant" upon the ruins of Sumter "the same United States flag which floated over the Battlements of that fort during the rebel assault & which was lowered & saluted by him and the small force of his command, when the works were evacuated." Almost boyishly enthusiastic, Stanton had decided that the flag-raising must be "saluted by one hundred guns from Sumter," which was two for one for the salute when the flag had been lowered, and in addition there would be "a National salute from every fort & rebel battery that fired upon fort Sumter." General Sherman would direct the ceremonies, the naval forces would be invited to participate, and the Reverend Henry Ward Beecher would give the public address. A good-natured dispute arose between the Secretary of War and the President over whether April thirteenth, the day of surrender, or the fourteenth, the day of evacuation, was the more appropriate to celebrate, and Mr. Lincoln finally conceded there was "little or no difference" between the dates. But on the evening of April fourteenth Mr. Lincoln would attend a play at Ford's Theater. It made that difference.

On March twenty-seventh Grant and Sherman reached City Point to confer with the President. The red-headed, nervous, segar-puffing Sherman, a hero to the North after his conquest of Atlanta and march to the sea, wasn't the least concerned that he would be away from his army a few days. He was not an indispensable man, Sherman assured the President; he had left a competent general in command. Perhaps Mr. Lincoln remembered his first meeting with Uncle Billy on another March day in 1861; Sherman never forgot it:

> . . . John [Sherman, Senator from Ohio] then turned to me and said, "Mr. President, this is my brother, Colonel Sherman, who is just up from Louisiana. He may give you some information that you want." "Ah!" said Mr. Lincoln, "how are they getting along down there?" I said, "They are getting along swimmingly —they are preparing for war," "Oh, well!" said he, "I guess we'll manage to keep house." I was silenced, said no more to him, and remember that I broke out on John, d—ning the politicians generally, saying, "You have got things in a hell of a fix, and

you may get them out as best you can," adding that the country
was sleeping on a volcano that might burst forth at any minute,
but that I was going to St. Louis to take care of my family, and
would have no more to do with it. . . .

The President confirmed what Sherman had already observed:
"Men are blind and crazy." The damned-fool South, starting a
war it was bound to lose! There had been another meeting after
the Union disaster at First Bull Run when Sherman had begged
the President not to give him a "superior command" for which
he was temperamentally unsuited. Mr. Lincoln nodded, then
ignored the advice. Sherman's early failures in Kentucky, his
strange hallucinations over the movements of an enemy that did
not exist, the newspaper charges that he was unbalanced to the
point of insanity—these were old tales now; later at Shiloh and
Vicksburg and Missionary Ridge, Sherman had gained confidence
and polish in command and then the country knew—Sherman
was crazy all right, crazy like a fox. He came to City Point in
March, 1865, believing that "every attempt to make war easy and
safe will result in humiliation and disaster." No one in Georgia
or South Carolina accused him of not practicing what he preached.

But Grant had been Sherman's great mentor—Grant, the squint-
eyed, thoughtful, undramatic little man who reduced the science
of war to four words: "When in doubt, fight." Grant simply had
kept coming on, confounding his critics and his enemies; and if
occasionally he drank, he never failed for a clear head when he
needed one. Stuck during the early months of the war in the
mudhole called Cairo, Illinois, Grant had wished he could go
east and command a brigade of cavalry in the Army of the
Potomac. No one appeared willing to let Grant fight, so he began
to force his own opportunities at Belmont in Missouri, at Paducah
in Kentucky, at Henry and Donelson on the Tennessee, and there
all at once he was on the cover of *Harper's Weekly*—"Uncondi-
tional Surrender" Grant, a national hero! Then at Shiloh he came
within a wink of a terrible disaster; the North, shocked by his

fearful losses, wondered if his middle name might not be "Surprise," since surely the Confederates had caught him flat-footed at Shiloh; and stung by the abusive criticism he was on the point of leaving the army when Sherman stormed into his tent. Grant couldn't quit! So they called him "Surprise" Grant—well, he could take this advice from "Crazy" Sherman: "You could not be quiet at home for a week when armies were moving."

Grant stayed and Vicksburg followed and suddenly he stood apart—the best general of the lot—able to see through outmoded rules of war, to abandon a base of supplies and live on the country, to thrust his army between two Confederate armies and whip them both. Seeing him tipped back on a campstool, chewing a cigar, absorbed in his own cogitations, subordinate officers understood why his field orders were clear, concise, almost flawlessly simple. He knew how "to feed a fight" by moving troops quickly to where they were needed; as a boy and now as a general some psychological quirk prevented him from ever taking a backward step; and in battle soldiers said of him, proudly: "Ulysses don't scare worth a damn."

Lincoln watched this man, protected him—when a jealous superior wanted to dump him after Donelson, when a politically powerful general tried to wrest command from him at Vicksburg. The President, borrowing books on military history and theory from the Library of Congress, had been cogitating also—about McClellan, McDowell, Pope, Burnside, Hooker, Meade, the generals to whom he entrusted his magnificent Army of the Potomac and saw it stalemated or wasted at every point. Mr. Lincoln was unwilling to behold in Lee a military miracle; rather, unlike Lee, his own generals lacked the will to success. When after Antietam the overcautious McClellan appeared helplessly stalled once more, the President wrote one of the great letters of the war. Without West Point training, without combat experience, he relied on the ingredient for victory that he considered essential—old-fashioned horse sense:

As I understand, you telegraph Gen. Halleck that you cannot subsist your army at Winchester unless the railroad from Harper's Ferry to that point be put in working order. But the enemy does now subsist his army at a distance nearly twice as great from railroad transportation as you would have to do without the railroad last named. He now wagons from Culpeper C. H. which is just about twice as far as you would have to do from Harper's Ferry. He is certainly no more than half as well provided with wagons as you are. I certainly should be pleased for you to have the advantage of a railroad from Harper's Ferry to Winchester, but it wastes all the remainder of autumn to give it to you; and, in fact ignores the question of *time*, which cannot, and must not be ignored. . . .

There was much more in a similar vein, hitting at the root of why McClellan failed; of why Pope, with his headquarters in the saddle (where, a Confederate wit observed, his hindquarters belonged) could not win on loud talk; of why Burnside bumbled at Fredericksburg by not quickly crossing the Rappahannock over the fords nature had provided for him; of why Hooker, planning a strategic masterpiece at Chancellorsville, lacked the nerve to commit the troops that might have won; of why Meade, stopping Lee dead at Gettysburg, permitted him to escape with his army. The will to success wasn't strong enough in any of them; they lost within their minds and hearts before the battles started; and when Grant kept proving that he wanted to fight, to win, to finish the war and go home to his family, Lincoln called him to Washington.

That was in March, a year ago. With characteristic simplicity the general wrote in the register at Willard's: "U. S. Grant and son, Galena, Ill." Then he called during a reception at the White House, quite unprepared to have the East Room burst out with cries of "Grant! Grant! Grant!" or to find the throng surging and swaying and crowding around him "until alarm was felt for the safety of the ladies" or to be prodded by the resourceful

Seward into standing on a sofa so that all could catch a glimpse of him. Horace Porter, an aide to Grant, heard the President cry, "Why, here is General Grant!" It was a moment of deep significance, Porter reflected, when Mr. Lincoln strode forward and grasped Grant's hand:

> . . . Standing face to face for the first time were the two illustrious men whose names will always be inseparably associated in connection with the war of the rebellion. Grant's right hand grasped the lapel of his coat; his head was bent slightly forward, and his eyes upturned toward Lincoln's face. The President, who was eight inches taller, looked down with beaming countenance upon his guest. Although their appearance, their training, and their characteristics were in striking contrast, yet the two men had many traits in common, and there were numerous points of resemblance in their remarkable careers. Each was of humble origin, and had been compelled to learn the first lessons of life in the severe school of adversity. Each had risen from the people, possessed an abiding confidence in them, and always retained a deep hold upon their affections. Each might have said to those who were inclined to sneer at his plain origin what a marshal of France, who had risen from the ranks to a dukedom, said to the hereditary nobles who attempted to snub him in Vienna: "I am an ancestor; you are only descendants."

Asked later to dinner by the President, the general declined, politely but firmly: "I have become tired of this show business." But Mr. Lincoln understood this fellow Illinoisian who, as Porter commented, "had sprung from the common people to become one of the most uncommon of men." When Grant insisted on bringing Sheridan east to command his cavalry, Mr. Lincoln remarked that Sheridan was "rather a little fellow." Quietly Grant replied: "You will find him big enough for the purpose." Many Union generals for years after the war shuddered every time they beheld Stanton's stern visage on a one-dollar treasury note, but the Secretary of War didn't fluster Grant. The President was content: he had selected the right man to raise to the rank of lieutenant general and place in command of armies numbering more than half a million men. So he sent Grant off to win the war and Lee fell back through the Wilderness and Spotsylvania, rallied at the brutal slaughter of Cold Harbor, then was drawn into the siege of Petersburg with Richmond hanging in the balance, while Sherman took Atlanta and hacked Georgia and South Carolina from the Confederacy.

Against this background aboard the *River Queen* at City Point on March twenty-seventh they would meet for their first and only conference, these three Western men. To the north flashed the light on the lookout tower where lay the flats of Bermuda Hundred; beyond, was Harrison's Landing, whence McClellan had encamped after his futile, mismanaged campaign on the Peninsula; and to the westward lay Petersburg where Grant's fine, well-fed army of one hundred thirty thousand seasoned troops opposed Lee's ragged, hungry fifty thousand Confederates. What Horace Porter reported of the interview Grant told him afterward:

> . . . It began by his [Grant] explaining to the President the military situation and prospects, saying that the crisis of the war was now at hand, as he expected to move at once around the enemy's left and cut him off from the Carolinas, and that his only apprehension was that Lee might move out before him and evacuate Petersburg and Richmond, but that if he did there would be a hot pursuit. Sherman assured the President that in such a contingency his army, by acting on the defensive, could resist both Johnston* and Lee till Grant could reach him, and that then the enemy would be caught in a vise and have his life promptly crushed out. Mr. Lincoln asked if it would not be possible to end the matter without a pitched battle, with the attendant losses and suffering; but was informed that that was a matter not within the control of our commanders, and must rest necessarily with the enemy. Lincoln spoke about the course

---

* General Joseph E. Johnston, commanding the tattered remnant of the Army of Tennessee, now in North Carolina.

which he thought had better be pursued after the war, and expressed an inclination to lean toward a generous policy. In speaking about the Confederate political leaders, he intimated, but he did not say so in express terms, that it would relieve the situation if they would escape to some foreign country. . . .

On the twenty-eighth Sherman left City Point, and Grant departed next morning. Mr. Lincoln intended to remain a few days, hoping for the end. "I think we can send him some good news in a day or two," Grant told Horace Porter.

22

"Kingdom Comin'"

NEXT evening Lincoln wrote Stanton with good-humored chagrin: "Last night at 10:15, when it was as dark as a rainy night without a moon could be, a furious cannonade, soon joined in by a heavy musketry-fire, opened near Petersburg and lasted about two hours. The sound was very distinct here, as also were the flashes of the guns upon the clouds. It seemed to me a great battle, but the older hands here scarcely noticed it, and, sure enough, this morning it was found that very little had been done." The following day there were two telegrams from Grant, and Mr. Lincoln realized that between the two dispatches the general had moved his headquarters "about one mile." Then on April first Sheridan smashed at Five Forks, overwhelming Lee's right. On Sunday, April second, Grant threw a two-pronged assault against Petersburg.

It was a beautiful Sunday. The air was warm and buoyant and the new foliage of the trees sparkled in the sun. In Richmond, Jefferson Davis attended morning services in St. Paul's Church. A messenger came quietly down the aisle and handed Mr. Davis a note from Lee. The blow had fallen—Grant was overrunning Petersburg, Lee was falling back, Richmond was doomed. The President went at once to his office, assembled the heads of the departments and bureaus "as far as they could be found," and

279

arranged to transfer the government to Danville, where he expected Lee and the army to join him.

Jefferson Davis had known for days that the end was near. About a week before he had urged Varina to leave, meeting her protest with the firm declaration that there was only one way now she could help—"by going yourself and taking our several children to a place of safety." He would not let her keep the several barrels of flour she bought. "The people want it," he said, "and you must leave it here." He gave her a pistol and taught her how to load, aim, and fire it. Their parting had been an agony to Varina, and the President "almost gave way, when our little Jeff begged to remain with him, and Maggie clung to him convulsively." What had happened to the Confederacy in four years of war was quickly revealed once they lost sight of Richmond— the worn-out locomotive broke down and Varina and the children sat, forlorn and helpless, through the cold, damp night. Yet they were luckier than many who could not flee.

For them, Richmond was a trap—their own Libby Prison grown around them. Slowly, fearfully, they had sensed the change, not just from the time when Grant appeared, but before that—long before. One of the great reporters of the war, George Alfred Townsend, who wrote for the New York *Herald*, drew a telling portrait of how Richmond, once proud, once gay, lost her soul to a fetish so that she became more symbol than city:

> . . . Not until the battle of Bull Run, when the dead and mangled came by hundreds into the town, did anyone discover the consequences of Richmond's new distinction; but by this time the Rebel government had absorbed Virginia, and was master of the city. Thenceforward Richmond was the scene of all terrors, the prey of all fears and passions. Campaign after campaign was directed against her; she lived in the perpetual thunder of cannon; raiders pressed to her gates; she was a great garrison and hospital only, besieged and cut off from her own provinces; armies passed through her to the sound of drums, and returned to the

creak of ambulances. She lost her social prestige, and became a barrack-city, filled with sutlers, adventurers, and refugees, till, bearing bravely up amid domestic riot and horrible demoralization—a jail, a navy-yard, a base of operation—she grew pinched, and base, and haggard . . .

Richmond, the Valhalla of a withering dream—beaten by blockade, by cotton nobody wanted so that a war for slavery could endure, by worthless treasury notes, by battles won without any hope of final victory, by empty bellies. For it was true, what the Northern papers had reported—on another April second, two years ago, a thousand women had gathered in Capital Square. They had marched down Cary Street, down Main Street, breaking into stores for bread, for clothing. Speeches by Governor Letcher, by Congressmen, and at last by Jefferson Davis had dispersed the mob and Richmond papers had ignored the bread riot—but it had occurred, the spirit and pride had broken. And even then Richmond had been more symbol than city for there were other if smaller, uprisings—in Augusta and Columbus and Milledgeville, Georgia; in Salisbury, North Carolina; in Mobile, Alabama. Governor Zebulon B. Vance of North Carolina was not alone in opening his mail and reading uneasily: ". . . the time has come that we the comon people has to have bread or blood & we are bound boath men & women to hav it or die in the attempt." Call Mr. Lincoln a buffoon, but the Northern people were standing by him, and they were eating well. Call the support of the ridiculous, bumbling, vulgar Lincoln (as Robert Kean, head of the War Bureau, would in his diary for March, 1863) "the most extraordinary spectacle the world has ever produced"; but flour in Richmond sold for $28 a barrel, bacon for $1.25 a pound, a coat for $120, wood for $15 a cord and a salary of $3000 went about as far as $700 would have gone in 1860.

Richmond—Valhalla! Now on the second of April, 1865, with the President rallying his government to flight, Richmond lived out its role, becoming the grief-maddened Brünnhilde, building her pyre upon the James instead of the Rhine, and sending her ravens to notify the god of fire—"Draweth near in the gloom the twilight of the gods." From six miles east of Richmond, as the city burned that Sunday, Colonel E. M. Boykin of the Seventh Georgia still could scarcely believe what he beheld: "Women, their arms filled with goods plundered from warehouses, their hair hanging about their ears, were rushing one way, while a current of the empty-handed surged in a contrary direction." Smoke hung like a pall over the city, and through it swept huge eddies of flames and sparks. In the river the ironclad *Virginia* "burst like a bombshell." From the heights of Manchester, Colonel Boykin glanced back at this city incredibly "undergoing pillage at the hands of its own mob, while the tramp of a victorious army could be heard at its gates." A magazine or depot near the center of town had been fired and the bursting shells and boxes of ammunition "gave the appearance of a thundercloud with lightning playing through it." Steamers and gunboats burned at the navy yard.

To Phoebe Yates Pember, matron in Chimborazo Hospital, a "night of horror" followed; across the James the bridges burned, and by that glow the *Patrick Henry* could be seen, settling low in the water. Judith Brockenbrough McGuire remembered the house shaking, the windows rattling as the ammunition depots exploded; and she remembered, too, the people rushing up and down the streets, the vehicles flying along with those who could escape. Baggage wagons, carts, drays, ambulances—anything that could move would do. Next morning Thomas C. DeLeon gaped as "great blazing planks and rafters" whirled still "over the shrivelling buildings." Uneasily, DeLeon thought: "Should the wind shift, that fire would devour the whole city." A few men looked on "in dismayed apathy"; and then the Union troops took charge: "If the fire could not be stayed at any particular point, a squad entered each house and bore its contents to a safe distance; then a guard was placed over it." The sense of astonishment lingered in DeLeon's reminiscences: "What we received from the enemy that day was aid—protection—safety!"

A fretful Stanton wired Lincoln at City Point not to expose himself, for the Secretary knew the President: he would be running off to see Grant in Petersburg. In a gay spirit, on the evening of the third, Mr. Lincoln telegraphed Stanton not to worry: "Thanks for your caution; but I have already been to Petersburg." And lest his Secretary breathe too easily, the President added: "It is certain now that Richmond is in our hands, and I think I will go there to-morrow. I will take care of myself."

Admiral David Porter made the journey with Mr. Lincoln. The President was animated.

"Thank God," he told Porter, "that I have lived to see this! It seems to me that I have been dreaming a horrid dream for four years, and now the nightmare is gone. I want to see Richmond!"

Near the landing a group of Negroes was digging with spades. An old man of about sixty looked up, put his hands to his eyes, then dropped his spade and sprang forward.

"Bress de Lord," he cried, "dere is de great Messiah! I knowed him as soon as I seed him. He's bin in my heart fo' long yeahs, an' he' cum at las' to free his chillun from deir bondage. Glory, Hallelujah!"

The old fellow fell upon his knees and kissed the President's feet. The others followed his example.

Greatly embarrassed, Mr. Lincoln said: "Don't kneel to me. That is not right. You must kneel to God only, and thank Him for the liberty you will hereafter enjoy. I am but God's humble instrument; but you may rest assured that as long as I live no one shall put a shackle to your limbs, and you shall have all the rights which God has given to every other citizen of this Republic."

To Porter it seemed as though Mr. Lincoln's face "lit up with a divine look . . . He really seemed of another world." The

Negroes at last were persuaded to rise, and, joining hands, burst into a hymn.

Now, Porter realized, "the streets seemed to be suddenly alive with the colored race. They seemed to spring from the earth. They came, tumbling and shouting, from over the hills and from the waterside, where no one was seen as we had passed." Some darted forward, trying to touch the President. Some turned somersaults. Some yelled, some danced, and in their efforts to express their joy Porter believed that "half of them acted as though half demented." Yet shout and sing and dance they would, the prophecy fulfilled:

> De massa run? ha, ha!
> De darkey stay? ho, ho!
> It mus' be now de kingdom comin'
> An' de year ob Jubilo!

Mr. Lincoln managed finally to make himself heard once more: "My poor friends, you are free—free as air. You can cast off the name of slave and trample on it; it will come to you no more. Liberty is your birthright. God gave it to you as he gave it to others, and it is a sin that you have been deprived of it for so long. . . . Don't let your joy carry you into excesses. Learn the laws and obey them; obey God's commandments and thank Him for giving you liberty, for to Him you owe all things."

Mr. Lincoln moved on, everywhere surrounded by crowds, so that, Porter said, "we did not move a mile an hour." At Libby Prison voices cried, "We will pull it down." The President replied: "No, leave it for a monument." The day grew uncomfortably warm, the streets dusty, and, Porter imagined, Mr. Lincoln "would have given up the presidency for a glass of water." Windows were raised, faces looked out, all to Porter with "eager curiosity—nothing more"; but to Mrs. McGuire those who greeted Mr. Lincoln represented "the low, lower, lowest of creation." A man shouted: "Abraham Lincoln, God bless you! You are the poor man's friend!" A girl brought him a bouquet of roses.

"Thirty-four guns announced the arrival of President Lincoln," J. B. Jones, a clerk in the Confederate War Department, noted in his diary. "He flitted through the mass of human beings in Capitol Square, his carriage drawn by four horses, preceded by outriders, motioning the people, etc. out of the way, and followed by a mounted guard of thirty. The cortege passed rapidly, precisely as I had seen royal parties ride in Europe." Richmond's population was perhaps twenty thousand, of which half were Negroes. Between Main Street and the canal, Jones estimated, some seven hundred houses had been lost in the fire. Yet grim though Lincoln may have found this sight, the day otherwise was "bright and beautiful." General Lee's family remained in the city. Rumors contradicted each other—one that Lee had won a great battle at Amelia Court House, another that thousands of South Carolinians and Mississippians had thrown down their arms "giving [Jones chronicled] such information to the enemy as betrayed our weak points." And Jones contended:

> The cheers that greeted President Lincoln were mostly from the negroes and Federals comprising the great mass of humanity. The white citizens felt annoyed that the city should be mostly held by negro troops. If this measure were not unavoidable, it was impolitic if conciliation were to be the purpose. . . .
>
> This morning [April 5] thousands of negroes and many white females are besieging the public offices for provisions. I do not observe any getting them, and their faces begin to express disappointment.
>
> It is said all the negro men, not entering the army, will be put to work, rebuilding bridges, repairing railroads, etc.

The President visited the home of Jefferson Davis. Thomas Thatcher Graves, an aide-de-camp to General Godfrey Weitzel, in charge of the Union occupation, remembered that Mr. Lincoln

> . . . was shown into the reception-room, with the remark that the housekeeper had said that that room was President Davis's office. As he seated himself he remarked, "This must have been President Davis's chair," and, crossing his legs, he looked far off

with a serious, dreamy expression. At length he asked me if the housekeeper was in the house. Upon learning that she had left he jumped up and said, with a boyish manner, "Come, let's look at the house!" We went pretty much over it. . . . As we came down the staircase General Weitzel came, in breathless haste, and at once President Lincoln's face lost its boyish expression as he realized that duty must be resumed. . . .

Later Mr. Lincoln visited the State House; but there is no record that he stopped at the First Baptist Negro Church where, Reporter Townsend contended, Massachusetts chaplains already were expounding "the gospel of John Brown to gaping audiences of wool, white-eyeball and ivory." What the experience meant to Mr. Lincoln he expressed to General Weitzel:

"Let the people down easy."

Old Judge John A. Campbell, who had told Jefferson Davis weeks ago that the jig was up, remained in Richmond to find some basis for bringing Virginia back into the Union. Accompanied by a Mr. Meyer, the judge and the President met twice, and on both occasions Charles A. Dana, as Assistant Secretary of War, wrote sprightly reports on the proceedings for Stanton. Lincoln set three conditions for Virginia's readmission to the Union: the national authority must be restored, slavery abandoned forever, and hostile forces disbanded. Dana informed Stanton that both Campbell and Meyer admitted slavery was now "defunct"; and that Lincoln, when pressed to give some assurances of amnesty, had replied he "would save any repentant sinner from hanging." Lincoln's lighthearted mood came out in another remark, for he believed that "Sheridan seemed to be getting Virginia soldiers out of this war faster than this legislature could think." Dana's letters to Stanton were filled with interesting chitchat. "It is not true," he wrote on April fifth, "that Jeff. Davis sold his furniture before leaving." That evening the theater reopened. On the sixth he reported that the Union feeling in Richmond was not half so sincere as General Weitzel thought; but two days later, he said of those who remained in Richmond: "They are sincerely conscious that they are whipped." Already Dana discounted Lee and the Army of Northern Virginia as a significant factor in future negotiations. Grant, however, was not making that mistake.

On April fourth, when Mr. Lincoln visited desolate and defeated Richmond, Lee still believed that he could pull his forces together and give Grant a fight; if he could get to Danville he had a chance of joining with Joe Johnston's troops in North Carolina.

The dreadful shock of defeat at Five Forks and the breakthrough at Petersburg had worn off; again Lee's mind made plans, his heart filled with hope. Days before, foreseeing an emergency like this, he had instructed Richmond to send supplies to Amelia Court House.

Lee rode on, clinging to the future, steeling himself against any thought of what must be happening inside tormented Richmond. He closed his mind as well to what the flood waters of the Appomattox River could portend. On April fourth he reached Amelia Court House.

There were no supplies.

23

Rather a Thousand Deaths

IF LEE were not already a legend—all that remained of the Cause, the dream of Southern empire and independence— the next five days would have made him one. Against incredible discouragements he pitted a brave heart. From day to day, often from hour to hour, the odds turned more heavily against him and still he struggled on—undaunted, unbreakable. Seeing him, hungry soldiers with gums sore and bloody from chewing parched corn braced up and cheered; hearing his voice, troops almost too weary to carry their muskets fought skirmishes as vicious as any the war produced. As the disasters mounted, as Federal cavalry and infantry cut off one escape route after another, as desperately needed supply trains were captured and hunger approached starvation, as irresistibly the tattered remnant of the Army of Northern Virginia was squeezed into the little pocket of Appomattox Court House with Yankees blocking front, flanks, and rear, officers turned anguished faces to him and muttered: "We'll fight on." It was not duty but love that inspired those last loyal legions; it was no longer the South but Lee and God to whom they offered their lives.

Lee—gallant, heroic Lee! On a Sunday during the bitter siege of Petersburg, the poet Sidney Lanier watched Lee sleeping at a church service; an enemy shell burst within a few hundred yards of where the general slumbered, yet not a muscle stirred; a bird flew into a tree overhead, piping its small, blissful song, and Lanier

288

believed that "the present earth floated off through the sunlight and the antique earth returned out of the past and some majestic god sat on a hill sculptured in stone presiding over a terrible yet sublime contest of human passions." Wrote John Esten Cooke, novelist turned warrior: "Other men reveal their weakness on nearer acquaintance—Lee only revealed his greatness." And at Gettysburg, when the three bloody days ended in Pickett's frightful defeat, a cavalryman heard him moan: "Too bad! *Too bad!* Oh! Too BAD!" But quickly Lee regained his self-control; and as Pickett's shattered troops reeled by, he called: "Don't be discouraged.... It was my fault this time.... All good men must hold together now." In the midst of that disorderly retreat, seeing a lieutenant raise a stick to a balky horse, he cried: "Oh, don't do that! I once had a foolish horse and I found gentle measures so much the best."

Lee, man and legend. Now short by less than a week, four full years of struggle and tears had shaped both. At the end had come Grant, the one antagonist who wouldn't be beaten—Grant, the man of the go-ahead West, the man who kept growing because he came from a land where all life was growth and wide horizons—Grant, part legend himself. Each, really, had fought in a different war—Grant, the modern man, in a war that had touched the entire nation; and Lee, the Virginian, in a war within that larger conflict.

How much did Lee remember? After only eight days in Richmond, during those first weeks following Sumter when he had toiled day and night to defend a tragically unprepared Virginia against certain invasion, he had written Mary: "The war may last ten years." He had resisted the giddy-heads who shouted for "carrying the war into Africa" through some such precipitate act as an invasion of Maryland, and Mrs. Chesnut had reported some who grumbled: "At heart Robert E. Lee is against us."

But then as now at heart Lee was with God rather than against anyone; and if heaven as he conceived of it existed principally in

Virginia, then weakness and strength were born of the same passionate conviction. His first command took him into pro-Unionist western Virginia where Confederate forces had been demoralized by a sharp defeat at Rich Mountain. Weeks of endless rain, sickness, green troops all conspired against him; he was too much the gentleman to deal brusquely with inept, insubordinate officers; and newspapers, eager to portray the son of noble old "Light Horse Harry" as a hero, invented victories where no battles had occurred. When at Cheat Mountain he suffered a costly failure, the excuse he gave Mary was entirely in character: ". . . the Ruler of the Universe willed otherwise and sent a storm to disconcert a well-laid plan, and to destroy my hopes." A Tennesseean put another face on the story, growling: "Never were men more sick of Virginia or Virginians."

So Lee, leaving Richmond as an avenging hero, returned a military goat. Next he was placed in charge of coastal defenses from the Carolinas to Florida and soon was writing home that he had been sent on "another forlorn hope expedition." Through sheer intensity of personal will he achieved miracles and yet these months away from Virginia had acid moments that etched into his conscience misgivings about the South. Something was deeply wrong. "It is very hard to get anything done," one letter told Mary; another complained that the people of the South "should be humbled and taught to be less boastful, less selfish, and more devoted to right and justice to all the world"; and to his daughter Annie he could not conceal his scorn for those content "to nurse themselves and their dimes" while leaving "the protection of themselves and families to others." Meanwhile at Henry and Donelson an obscure Union general named Grant had begun to emerge; but Lee could see only one valid lesson in these distant disasters—the Southern people needed to rely more on God.

Did Lee remember, pressed now into the pocket of Appomattox Court House by that obscure general? By September, 1862, Lee also had emerged—defender of Richmond against McClellan on the Peninsula, against Pope at Second Manassas. That September disordered Federal columns fell back on Washington, and the capital, poorly defended, dangled like a ripe plum; but Lee faced an innate weakness of his army: "My men had nothing to eat." Other weaknesses, chiefly within himself, he did not recognize and would never recognize. He saw Lincoln too much as a fool, a weakling, a knave rather than as a man with a faith as sublime as his own; and so he failed to grasp that in holding the Border States Lincoln had won the first phase of a war in which the foe was to be strangled to death. How characteristic of Lee that on assuming command of the Army of the Peninsula his first act was to rename it the Army of Northern Virginia. Thus he defined his whole purpose, his sacred duty, his contempt for "these people" who opposed *his* war.

And how characteristic, with Pope reeling back on Washington, for Lee to act with that same contempt for his adversaries. Congressional elections approached and should shatter Lincoln's political power and so, by invading Maryland, all of Lee's instincts and convictions (almost invariably, they were the same) would be fulfilled. He would carry the war *away* from Richmond—his first purpose, always; he would give the people of Maryland a chance to throw off the Federal yoke; he would feed his soldiers and fodder his horses; and he would give such encouragement to the peace movement in the North that the war would end before his beloved Virginia was bled into exhaustion. He urged President Davis to propose peace "when it is in our power to inflict injury" and so "enable the people of the United States to determine at their coming elections whether they will support those who favor the prolongation of the war, or those who wish to bring it to a termination, which can be but productive of good to both parties without affecting the honor of both." Long before the discovery of a copy of his Secret Order No. 191 wrapped around two cigars gave McClellan the chance to force the bloody, drawn battle at Antietam, the greater blows had fallen. Lee had found precious little loyalty to the South in the mountains of Maryland; and Mr. Lincoln already had drafted an announcement of his intention to issue the Emancipation Proclamation.

Lee carried his war back into Virginia and twice more before the summer of 1863 became the dogged, audacious, unyielding defender of Richmond—against Burnside at Fredericksburg, against Hooker at Chancellorsville. And yet what had he won? Private John Dooley felt heartsick at how Lee's hair and beard were turning gray, and Private Dooley had merely to look upon war-torn Virginia after another autumn and winter to understand why: "The fences are burned, the meadows trampled down, the cattle all gone and the harvests unharvested; proud homesteads in ruins, the masters on the war trail and the old couple and daughters sit mournful and comfortless around expiring embers."

Did Lee remember, with surrender only hours away, how from afar in the late spring of 1863 Grant again had threatened his purpose? Summoned to Richmond, Lee left his hungry, ragged, shoeless army and met with President Davis and the Cabinet. Should Lee detach troops to help the besieged Pemberton against Grant at Vicksburg? Forsake Virginia? Never! He would strike into Pennsylvania, feed and clothe his army in that abundant land, and throw such a scare into the North that the Peace Democrats (with help from the Copperheads, where they differed) would rid the country of Lincoln. Later in a letter to President Davis he confessed his fear: Confederate resources diminished constantly, those of the North steadily augmented, and if a peace with reasonable concessions could be secured, this was no time for making "nice distinctions" between "those who declare for peace unconditionally and those who advocate it as a means of restoring the Union." After all, those who wished peace in the North must make some concessions too, he reasoned, appending this rather remarkable paragraph:

> Should the belief that peace will bring back the Union become general, the war will no longer be supported, and that, after all, is what we are interested in bringing about. When peace is pro-

posed to us, it will be time enough to discuss its terms, and it is not the part of prudence to spurn the proposition in advance, merely because those who wish to make it believe, or affect to believe that it will result in bringing us back to the Union. We entertain no such apprehensions, nor doubt the desire of our people for a distinct and independent national existence will prove as steadfast under the influence of peaceful measures as it has shown itself in the midst of war . . .

To suspend hostilities on one basis while discussing peace on another posed a dilemma that Mr. Davis didn't attempt to resolve. Somehow if there had been no Sumter, no blockade, no King Cotton toppled off his throne, no Emancipation Proclamation, no Cockney woman shouting through the streets of London that "Lincoln's been and gone and done it," no loyal Border States, no war in the West, no emergence of an American conscience that would make of the African what Helen had been to ancient Greece, Lee might have approached reality. But all of these forces had been unleashed, and Lee invaded Pennsylvania and was stopped at Gettysburg and the following day Vicksburg surrendered to Grant.

So Lee came back once more to Virginia, and with another spring the stumpy little man, who for so long had been making noises in the wings of this grand stage of the war, arrived at Culpeper to take command of all the Union armies. Sherman predicted: "The fur will fly." And Lee, grasping the whole truth at last, told Jefferson Davis: ". . . this war presents to the European world but two aspects, a contest in which one party is contending for abstract slavery and the other against it. The existence of vital rights involved does not seem to be understood or appreciated. As long as this lasts, we can expect neither sympathy nor aid. Nor can we expect the policy of any government towards us to be governed by any other consideration than that of self-interest. Our safety depends on ourselves alone. If we can defeat or drive the armies of the enemy from the field, we shall have peace."

Surrender also could bring peace . . . but on April eighth General William N. Pendleton had found Lee about noon resting along the side of the old stage road that ran from Richmond through Appomattox Court House to Lynchburg. Awkwardly Pendleton had explained that a group of officers had met the evening before. The situation looked hopeless. Perhaps surrender was the wise course.

"Surrender?" Lee asked, sharply. "I have too many good fighting men for that!"

That was yesterday.

For weeks Lee had tried to remember a face. Years before during the war in Mexico they had met: he was certain of that. Yet he could recall nothing of Grant—how he looked or walked or talked. Awake, restless, Lee judged that the time must be about one o'clock in the morning. A new day—April 9, 1865. Palm Sunday.

Although here in the mountains the oaks were tasseling, a white frost probably would cover the ground at daybreak. In the chill darkness Lee's sleepless mind reviewed the correspondence of the past two days between Grant and himself. The first letter had been delivered at night on the seventh, and there were two stories connected with it.

The story Lee didn't know was this: On the sixth at Saylor's Creek the Federals had captured seven thousand Confederates in a bruising battle, among them Ewell, one of Lee's oldest and best corps commanders. Ewell had talked freely, claiming that the Cause had been lost from the time Grant crossed the James River and that a responsible government would have sued for terms "while they still had a right to claim concessions." Now, in Ewell's judgment, the Confederate authorities "had no right to claim anything," and for every man killed somebody must take responsibility for an act "little better than murder." Grant next day had reached the village of Farmville on the south side of the Appomattox River. Union forces now fought on both sides of the river and Sheridan raced to cut off Lee at Appomattox. What

Ewell had said was repeated to Grant, and it affected him deeply. "The result of the last week must convince you of the hopelessness of further resistance," he wrote Lee. He felt it his duty, Grant said, "to shift from myself the responsibility of any further effusion of blood" and therefore he was asking Lee to surrender. With darkness Union troops still poured through Farmville, highspirited, cheering Grant, brandishing torches, swinging muskets in the air, singing "John Brown's Body". . . the pressure Grant could build up to crush Lee completely would have been obvious to a schoolboy.

But Lee knew nothing of Union troops on *both* sides of the river, nor did "Old Pete" Longstreet, the trusted old "war horse" who had fought with Lee since the Peninsula and who had joined his commander in a cottage about three and a half miles from Farmville. Both Lee and Longstreet still had only one idea—to reach Johnston's army through Danville or by crossing the watershed between the Appomattox and the James to push on via Lynchburg. Sometime after nine Grant's letter was delivered, Lee read it carefully, then handed it to "Old Pete."

"Not yet," Longstreet said.

Lee nodded. He replied to Grant at once; he would not admit that his situation was hopeless, then said: "I reciprocate your desire to avoid useless effusion of blood, & therefore before considering your proposition, ask the terms you will offer on condition of its [the army's] surrender." Grant wrote again next morning, but with the two armies moving and skirmishing the answer did not reach Lee until after nightfall. Grant set only one condition: "that the men and officers surrendered shall be disqualified from taking up arms against the Government of the United States until properly exchanged." He would meet Lee—or to spare Lee, if he did not care to come in person, would "designate officers to meet any officers you may name"—at a point "agreeable to you."

"How would you answer that?" Lee asked a member of his staff.

"I would answer no such letter."

"Ah, but it must be answered."

Lee left himself two "outs" in replying to Grant. He had not, he wrote, proposed "surrender" but simply had asked "the terms of your proposition." And: "To be frank, I do not think the emergency has arisen to call for surrender." Within those conditions, as far as Grant's proposal tended to restore peace, "I shall be pleased to meet you at 10 A.M. tomorrow on the old stage road to Richmond between the picket lines of the two armies." On the other hand, if Lee cut his way through Grant's lines before then, there would be no meeting.

But the hope was slim. Now, tossing in the darkness, Lee heard the younger officers, as keyed up as he, stirring outside. Lee arose, chose a fresh uniform and fastened a handsome sword with a sash of red silk. Once more, picking up a pair of fine gray gauntlets, he wished that he could recall at least one feature of Grant's face.

General Pendleton beheld Lee with astonishment. Why was he dressed so fancily?

"I have probably to be General Grant's prisoner and thought I must make my best appearance," Lee answered.

Around small campfires staff officers mixed meal and water and at least secured a little warmth if not much nourishment from this skimpy gruel. Lee ate no breakfast that morning.

About three o'clock Lee walked over to the artillerists, urging them to get a little rest. Daylight crept bitterly across the mountains, obscuring them in fog. Toward five, about half a mile west of the village, the fighting resumed. Sometime after eight a report came from General John B. Gordon. Federal troops, concealed in a woods, had fought Gordon's corps "to a frazzle"; Gordon could do nothing against the bluecoats unless "heavily supported by Longstreet." But "Old Pete" at that moment was holding off two Federal corps in the rear. Lee couldn't mistake the hopelessness of the Confederate position. The Army of Northern Virginia—the hungry, surrounded, outnumbered remnant of it that endured—faced annihilation.

"There is nothing left me to do but to go and see General Grant," Lee said. His spirit rebelled; he had to say it: "I would rather die a thousand deaths!"

So, too, would the members of his staff. Was it right to surrender the army in the field? What would history say? Lee understood their grief, their terrible yearning to fight on.

"How easily I could be rid of this, and be at rest!" he muttered, caught up in the same emotions. "I have only to ride along the line and all will be over!"

It was so easy, so simple, and yet . . . and yet . . .

"What will become of the women and the children of the South if we are not here to protect them?" his conscience asked.

The legend of Lee approached its crowning moments. "Old Pete" Longstreet asked a blunt question. By sacrificing the Army of Northern Virginia could the South gain elsewhere? Lee shook his head. Then, grumbled Longstreet, the situation answered itself. But General E. Porter Alexander protested. Let the men take to the woods, escape to their homes, fight as the governors of their states directed.

"Two-thirds of us would get away," Alexander insisted. "We would be like rabbits and partridges in the bushes and they could not scatter to follow us."

Lee demurred. As "Christian men" they had no right to think only of themselves. What would be the effect of Alexander's plan upon the country? "Already it is demoralized by four years of war," Lee said sadly. "If I took your advice, the men would be without rations and under no control of officers. They would be compelled to rob and steal in order to live. They would become mere bands of marauders, and the enemy's cavalry would pursue them and overrun many sections they may never have occasion to visit. We would bring on a state of affairs it would take the country years to recover from. You young fellows might go to bushwhacking, but the only dignified course for me would be to go to General Grant and surrender myself and take the consequences of my acts."

Alexander felt "ashamed" of his suggestion.

Lee rode toward the rendezvous point on the old stage road. Catching sight of the general, soldiers burst into cheers. The general nodded, smiled briefly, but within himself there was only the heartsickness. Poor, tattered army—poor, broken country! Ahead jogged the officer bearing a white flag, grim symbol of defeat and humiliation.

Presently a courier arrived with a letter from Grant. "As I have no authority to treat on the subject of peace the meeting proposed for 10 A.M. today could lead to no good," Grant wrote, explaining his absence. Nor could he accept Lee's surrender except on one basis: "By the South laying down their arms they will hasten that most desirable event, save thousands of human lives, and hundreds of millions of property not yet destroyed."

No verbal message from Grant—just *this*. Lee began dictating a reply. A courier from Longstreet whipped his horse down the road. A road had been found over which the army could escape!

Stoically, Lee continued dictating: "I now request an interview in accordance with the offer contained in your letter of yesterday . . ." He signed the note and ordered it delivered to Grant's courier. Soon another message from Longstreet acknowledged a mistake—no path of escape existed.

The danger now was that the Federals, poised for an assault, might not suspend hostilities until Grant could be reached. Confederate nerves were anything but serene that morning and Major General George A. Custer—he was then only twenty-five—came close to precipitating a new war by telling Longstreet: "Sheridan and I are independent of Grant today, and we will destroy you if you don't surrender at once."

"Old Pete" ripped out furiously at this brash young man, who "violated the decencies of military procedure" and ended in a roar: "Now, go and act as you and Sheridan choose and I will teach you a lesson you won't forget! Now go!"

Sheridan, less aggressive, still doubted if he possessed the authority to suspend hostilities and preferred to put the question to

General George Meade. Colonel Theodore Lyman, who served on Meade's staff, described the equally tense moment that resulted:

... At 10:30 came, one after the other, two Negroes, who said that some of our troops entered Lynchburg yesterday; and that Lee was now cut off near Appomattox Court House. This gave us new wings! An aide-de-camp galloped on, to urge [General Andrew A.] Humphreys to press the pursuit, and all waggons were ordered out of the road, that the 6th Corps might close in immediately on his rear. Away went the General again, full tilt, along the road crowded by the infantry, every man of whom was footing it, as if a lottery prize lay just ahead! A bugler trotted ahead, blowing to call the attention of the troops, while General [Alexander S.] Webb followed, crying "Give way to the right! Give way to the right!" Thus we ingeniously worked our way, amid much pleasantry. "Fish for sale!" roared one dough-boy. "Yes," joined in a pithy comrade, "and a tarnation big one, too!" The comments on the General were endless. "That's Meade." "Yes, that's him." "Is he sick?" "I expect he is; he looks kinder wild!" "Guess the old man hain't had much sleep lately."

The heavy artillery firing we had earlier heard, now had suddenly ceased, and there was a perfect stillness—a suspicious circumstance that gave us new hope. Somewhat before noon we got to General Humphreys, some five miles east of the Court House and at the very head of his men. He reported that he had just struck the enemy's skirmish line, and was preparing to drive them back. At that moment an officer rode up and said the enemy were out with a white flag. "They shan't stop me!" retorted the fiery H.; "receive the message but push on the skirmishers!" Back came the officer speedily, with a note. General Lee stated that General [Edward O. C.] Ord had agreed to a suspension of hostilities, and he should ask for the same on this *end* of the line. "Hey! what!" cried General Meade, in his harsh, suspicious voice. "I have no authority to grant such suspension. General Lee has already refused the terms of General Grant. Advance your skirmishers, Humphreys, and bring up your troops. We will pitch into them at once!" But lo! here comes now General [James W.] Forsyth, who had ridden through the Rebel army, from General Sheridan (under a flag), and who now urged a brief suspension. "Well," said the General, "in order that you may get back to Sheridan, I will wait till two o'clock, and then, if I get no communication from General Lee, I shall attack!" So back went Forsyth, with a variety of notes and dispatches. We waited, not without excitement, for the appointed hour. Meantime, Negroes came in and said the Rebel pickets had thrown down their muskets and gone leisurely to their main body; also that the Rebels were "done gone give up." . . .

While Meade strained to pitch into the Confederates once more, Lee rested on a pile of fence rails and a blanket under an apple tree. Noon approached; in occupied Richmond church services were ending. In accordance with President Lincoln's instructions to "let the people down easy" the only restriction imposed on Sabbath worship forbade any public prayer for Jefferson Davis; but triumphantly, Mrs. McGuire noted in her diary, "Thank God, our private prayers are free from Federal authority."

The same hard core of rebellion nagged Lee. He was clearly worried, embarrassed by the wait, suspicious of what it might portend. Longstreet rode up to join Lee, still boiling at his interview with that upstart Custer. At about a quarter past twelve hoofbeats along the road announced the arrival of Grant's courier. Watching the rider, Longstreet turned to Lee and burst out:

"General, unless he offers us honorable terms, come back and let us fight it out."

Lee said nothing. Grant's letter apologized for the delay; Lee's communication had just reached him—11:50 A.M.—and he was pushing forward at once to meet Lee.

What was to follow, as Charles Francis Adams observed, became "the most creditable episode in all American history—an episode without a blemish, imposing, dignified, simple, heroic. . . . Consider the possibilities; think for a moment of what that day might have been; you will then see cause to thank God for much."

24

The Two Countrymen

GRANT had spent the night at a farmhouse some distance to the rear of his army. Fighting a sick headache, he had bathed his feet in hot water and had sat up almost until daylight putting mustard plasters on his wrists and the back of his neck. Lee's letter, asking for a meeting on the old stage road but setting his two "outs," added to Grant's depression.

"It looks as if Lee still means to fight," he grumbled.

At four o'clock on the morning of Palm Sunday Horace Porter found the general "pacing up and down in the yard, holding both hands to his head."

With daylight Grant's "soldierly instincts" rebelled at the suggestion that he ride in a covered ambulance. Since he had to go around Lee's army to reach the head of his own columns, Lee's final letter, offering to surrender, did not reach him until ten minutes to twelve.

"The pain in my head seemed to leave me the moment I got Lee's letter," he told Porter.

He started immediately to meet Lee. Once, "cutting across lots," he almost rode into the Confederate left flank, and there seemed a chance he might become a prisoner in Lee's line instead of Lee in his—"a circumstance," commented Porter, that "would have given rise to an important cross-entry in the system of campaign bookkeeping."

About one o'clock Grant approached the little village of Appomattox Court House. A single street with a half dozen houses comprised the whole of the place. Here the old stage road between Richmond and Lynchburg climbed a slight rise; beyond the village the country dipped again into a broad valley. Lee's soldiers and wagon trains covered the lower ground; the Union cavalry, Fifth Corps, and part of Ord's command held the high ground. Grant's glance fell upon Little Phil Sheridan.

"How are you, Sheridan?" Grant asked.

"First rate, thank you. How are you?"

Grant pointed up the road. "Is Lee here?"

"He is at that brick house waiting to surrender to you."

"Well, then," Grant said, "we'll go over."

Upon reaching Appomattox Court House, Reporter Sylvanus Cadwallader recalled, he found the soldiers of both armies "ready to renew the contest on short notice." Officers galloped "in all directions," colors "were flying," and the scene "had more the appearance of a grand review of troops, than of two contending hosts." Grant confessed that his troops were "very much excited, and expressed their view that this was all a ruse employed to enable the Confederates to get away," but, he added, "I had no doubt about the good faith of Lee." The dwelling selected for the meeting belonged to Wilmer McLean, who formerly had lived at Manassas Junction where the battle of First Bull Run had been fought and who declared afterward that the war began in his back yard and ended in his front. It was a fine old house with a high wooden porch facing the street; a hall from front to back separated two large rooms, each with a front and rear window and two doors opening on the hall. Lee's large gray horse "Traveller," its bridle off, grazed in the grass. Grant mounted the steps, and entered quickly. Lee arose and Grant extended his hand.

"General Lee," he said.

They shook hands.

"What General Lee's feelings were I do not know," Grant wrote afterward. "As he was a man of much dignity, with an impassable face, it was impossible to say whether he felt inwardly glad that the end had finally come, or felt sad over the result, and was too manly to show it. Whatever his feelings, they were entirely concealed from my observation; but my own feelings, which had been quite jubilant on the receipt of his letter, were sad and depressed. I felt like anything rather than rejoicing at the downfall of a foe who had fought so long and valiantly, and had suffered so much for a cause, though that cause was, I believe, one of the worst for which a people ever fought, and one for which there was the least excuse. I do not question, however, the sincerity of the great mass of those who were opposed to us."

Horace Porter was struck by the contrast of the two generals as they sat facing each other:

... General Grant, then nearly forty-three years of age, was five feet eight inches in height, with shoulders slightly stooped. His hair and full beard were nut-brown, without a trace of gray in them. He had on his single-breasted blouse of dark-blue flannel, unbuttoned in front and showing a waistcoat underneath. He wore an ordinary pair of top-boots, with his trousers inside, and was without spurs. The boots and portions of his clothes were spattered with mud. He had worn a pair of thread gloves of a dark-yellow color, which he had taken off on entering the room. His felt "sugar-loaf," stiff-brimmed hat was resting on his lap. He had no sword or sash, and a pair of shoulder-straps was all there was about him to designate his rank ...

Lee, on the other hand, was six feet and one inch in height, and erect for one of his age, for he was Grant's senior by sixteen years. His hair and full beard were a silver-gray, and thick, except that the hair had become a little thin in front. He wore a new uniform of Confederate gray, buttoned to the throat, and a handsome sword and sash. . . . His top-boots were comparatively new, and had on them near the top some ornamental stitching of red silk. . . . On the boots were handsome spurs with large rowels. A felt hat which in color matched pretty closely that of his uniform, and a pair of long, gray buckskin gauntlets, lay beside him on the table. . . .

Grant spoke first. "I met you once before, General Lee, while we were serving in Mexico, when you came over from General Scott's headquarters to visit Garland's brigade, to which I then belonged. I have always remembered your appearance, and I think I should have recognized you anywhere."

"Yes," Lee answered. "I know I met you on that occasion, and I have often thought of it, and tried to recollect how you looked, but I have never been able to recall a single feature."

Grant chatted on "about old army times." At daybreak they had been enemies; now they had met as countrymen, and Grant admitted, as though still self-conscious at the memory, "I almost forgot the object of our meeting." Reminded by Lee that perhaps they should return to the purpose of the interview, Grant said he proposed only that Lee's army should lay down their arms and not take them up for the remainder of the war unless "duly and properly exchanged." Again Grant "fell off" into "conversation about matters foreign to the subject which had brought us together" and again Lee set him back on the track. Then, calling for writing materials, Grant set down his terms, not knowing what words he would use but having clearly in mind the intention of sparing Lee and his army "unnecessary humiliation":

Appomattox C. H., Va.,
Ap'l 9th, 1865

Gen. R. E. Lee,
Comd'g C.S.A.

Gen.: In accordance with the substance of my letter to you of the 8th inst., I propose to receive the surrender of the Army of N. Va. on the following terms, to wit: Rolls of all the officers and men to be made in duplicate. One copy to be given to an officer designated by me, the other to be retained by such officer or officers as you may designate. The officers to give their individual paroles not to take up arms against the Government of the United States until properly exchanged, and each company or regimental commander sign a like parole for the men of their commands. The arms, artillery, and public property to be parked and stacked, and turned over to the officer appointed by me to receive them. This will not embrace the side-arms of the officers, nor their private horses or baggage. This done, each officer and man will be allowed to return to his home, not to be disturbed by the United States authority so long as they observe their paroles and the laws in force where they may reside.

Very respectfully,

U. S. Grant,

Lt.-Gen.

Porter recorded the little things Lee did to relieve his tension when Grant's letter was handed him. He pushed aside the books and two brass candlesticks on the table. He wiped his steel-rimmed spectacles, crossed his knees, adjusted his glasses carefully, then took up the draft of the terms. He caught the omission of the word "exchanged" and with Grant's permission inserted it in pencil. Coming to the sentence that permitted officers to retain their side arms, private horses, and baggage, his eyes grew suddenly warm.

"This will have a very happy effect upon my army," he said.

Grant inquired if Lee had any further suggestions before the letter was copied.

Lee paused. He had met a countryman, not an antagonist—in this triumph, Grant had risen to a shining hour. Yes, Lee said, there was one suggestion:

"The cavalrymen and artillerists own their own horses in our army. Its organization in this respect differs from that of the United States. I should like to understand whether these men will be permitted to retain their horses."

Federal officers exchanged glances; Lee had set his "country" apart from theirs; the spell for a moment wavered. Grant remarked that the terms as written would not permit that concession. Lee reread the closing part of the letter; keenly disappointed, he said: "No, I see the terms do not allow it; that is clear." Grant spoke quickly, recapturing the spell:

"Well, the subject is quite new to me. Of course I did not know that any private soldiers owned their animals; but I think we have fought the last battle of the war,—and I sincerely hope so, —and that the surrender of this army will be followed soon by that of all the others; and I take it that most of the men in the ranks are small farmers, and as the country has been so raided by the two armies, it is doubtful whether they will be able to put in a crop to carry themselves and their families through the next winter without the aid of the horses they are now riding, and I will arrange it in this way: I will not change the terms as now written, but I will instruct the officers I shall appoint to receive the paroles to let all the men who claim to own a horse or mule to take the animals home with them to work their little farms."

To Porter, General Lee was "anything but a demonstrative man," but he could not conceal his relief and appreciation.

"This will have the best possible effect upon the men," he said. "It will be very gratifying, and will do much toward conciliating our people."

The spell remained; the stumpy, rough-dressed Grant and the older, dignified Lee had reached a solution as gentlemen, as friends. Hereafter Lee would always retain an image of the man with the nut-brown beard; hereafter the Westerner and the Virginian would share the common victory of Appomattox.

Waiting for Lee's reply to be drafted, General Sheridan said to Colonel Marshall of Lee's staff: "This is very pretty country."

"I haven't seen it by daylight," Marshall replied wryly.

Lee pointed out to Grant that he had a thousand Federal prisoners for which he had no provisions. "I have, indeed," he added, "nothing for my own men." He had telegraphed to Lynchburg, he explained, and asked for rations to be sent on by rail. The eyes of the Federal officers turned on Sheridan, who had captured these supply trains the night before. Grant interposed quickly,

asking how many men remained with Lee, and when the Southerner could not say exactly, Grant asked: "Suppose I send over
25,000 rations, do you suppose that will be a sufficient supply?"

"Plenty, plenty," Lee said. "An abundance."

Lee's letter accepting Grant's terms of surrender was brief. He
signed it and received the letter from Grant. The time was then
approaching four in the afternoon. Grant explained that he was
without a sword because he had come directly from the field; Lee
requested that Meade be notified of the capitulation so that hostilities would not be resumed; the generals shook hands.

Lee came onto the porch. Federal officers sprang to their feet,
saluted, and Lee returned the courtesy. He slapped his gauntlets
against his hands three times, and in a voice filling with emotion
called: "Orderly! Orderly!" His horse was brought and he
mounted. Others heard his sigh. Grant, appearing on the porch,
stopped, took off his hat, waited in silence. Federal officers lifted
their hats.

Without a word, Lee raised his own hat. He turned his horse and
rode away.

Joy ran wildly through the Union army, but Grant, hearing that
his troops had commenced firing a salute of a hundred guns to
celebrate the victory, ordered it stopped instantly. Colonel Theodore Lyman remembered that at about five o'clock the news
reached Meade's headquarters and then:

> . . . Such a scene followed as I can never see again. The soldiers
> rushed, perfectly crazy, to the roadside, and there crowding in
> dense masses, shouted, screamed, yelled, threw up their hats and
> hopped madly up and down! The batteries were run out and
> began firing, the bands played, the flags waved. The noise of the
> cheering was such my very ears rang. And there was General
> Meade galloping about and waving his cap with the best of them!
> Poor old Robert E. Lee! His punishment is too heavy—to hear
> those cheers, and to remember what he once was! . . .

A different wildness broke out at the McLean house. Now, reported Horace Porter, the

> . . . relic-hunters charged down upon the manor-house, and began to bargain for the numerous pieces of furniture. Sheridan paid the proprietor twenty dollars in gold for the table on which General Grant wrote the terms of surrender, for the purpose of presenting it to Mrs. Custer, and handed it over to her dashing husband, who galloped off to camp bearing it on his shoulder. [It is now in the Smithsonian Institution.] Ord paid forty dollars for the table at which Lee sat, and afterward presented it to Mrs. Grant, who modestly declined it, and insisted that Mrs. Ord should become its possessor. [It is now in the Chicago Historical Society.] General Sharpe paid ten dollars for the pair of brass candlesticks; Colonel Sheridan, the general's brother, secured the stone inkstand . . . A child's doll was found in the room, which the younger officers tossed from one to the other, and called "the silent witness." . . .

"Cane bottomed chairs," War Correspondent Cadwallader recalled, "were ruthlessly cut to pieces; the cane splits broken into pieces a few inches long, and parceled out among those who swarmed around. Haircloth upholstery was cut from chairs, and the sofa was also cut into strips and patches and carried away."

Meanwhile Lee rode back to his army, three-quarters of a mile northeast of the Court House—the longest ride of his life. Whole lines of men rushed down to meet him. They crowded around. They tried to shake his hand. "General, say the word and we'll go in and fight 'em yet," cried a veteran.

Lee started to speak. "Men, we have fought through the war together." He saw tears in the faces turned toward him. "I have done the best I could for you," he said. He struggled against his emotion, then murmured: "My heart is too full to say more."

Voices cried, "God bless you, Uncle Robert. God help you, General!"

A general growled, "Blow, Gabriel, blow! My God, let him blow, I am ready to die!"

Alone later in an apple orchard, Lee gave in to his feelings. "He paced backward and forwards like a caged lion," recalled Lieutenant Colonel W. W. Blackford; he seemed "in one of his savage moods"

> . . . when it was safer to keep out of his way; so his staff kept to their tree except when it was necessary to introduce the visitors. Quite a number came; they were mostly in groups of four or five and some of high rank. It was evident that some came from curiosity, or to see General Lee as friends in the old army. But General Lee shook hands with none of them. . . . When he would see Colonel Taylor coming with a party towards his tree he would halt his pacing and stand at "attention" and glare at them with a look which few men but he could assume. They would remove their hats entirely and stand bareheaded . . . while General Lee sometimes gave a scant touch to his hat in return and sometimes did not even do that. I could not hear what passed, but the interviews were short. . . .

The news traveled down the road toward Charlottesville, and a Confederate cavalryman, raising a clenched fist, cried out the Southern protest:

"If General Lee has had to surrender his army, there is not a just God in heaven!"

A wire from Grant told Stanton: "General Lee surrendered the Army of Northern Virginia this afternoon on terms proposed by myself."

But Washington was dark and damp when the news trickled through. The President, returning that Palm Sunday from City Point, learned of Lee's surrender from Stanton.

Mr. Lincoln smiled and went to bed.

25

"While God Is Marching On!"

AT DAYBREAK in Washington next morning an artillery battery on Massachusetts Avenue, behind Lafayette Square, awakened the citizens of the capital. They leaped out of beds that rocked. They rushed to windows cracked by the concussion of the cannon's salvo. Dank, dreary, rain-drenched streets reflected a bleak dawn. But newsboys were already hawking the extra they would read at breakfast: SURRENDER OF LEE AND HIS WHOLE ARMY! "We may now expect," Washington was told by the press, "to hear at any moment of the surrender of Johnston and his army, and most of the scattered remnants of the Confederate military organization throughout the South will follow as soon as the news of the capitulation of their military chief is known."

Just a week ago Washington had celebrated to the point of jubilant exhaustion the fall of Richmond. Now the events at Appomattox came almost as an anticlimax. But the government departments and most businesses closed down for the day; soon the streets filled with hurrahing, happy people; from the Navy Yard a group tramped through the mud and rain, hauling two howitzers down Pennsylvania Avenue; church bells tolled; and everywhere the great songs of the war were sung—"The Battle Hymn of the Republic" and "Kingdom Coming" more than any others. One difference marked this rainy April day from the celebration of last Monday. Honest Old Abe—Father Abraham—Abe, the Great Emancipator was back at the White House!

The crowds kept coming to the Executive Mansion, calling for the President, cheering, refusing to disperse when word was sent that Mr. Lincoln could not leave the important work awaiting him. Twice the President made brief, good-humored appearances at the window—with, naturally, his son Tad sharing in the lime-light by popping up beside his father bearing a captured Rebel flag. At each sight of the President the people went wild. Hats sailed through the air. Bands blared. Faces turned red with screech-ing. Once Mr. Lincoln said he had consulted with the Attorney General and had secured a legal opinion that one prize of war the South had appropriated had been fairly recaptured. That was the song "Dixie," and when the laughter and applause subsided, Mr. Lincoln added: "I now request the band to favor me with its performance." The band struck up "Dixie," threw in "Yankee Doodle" for good measure, and the President said: "Now give three good hearty cheers for General Grant and all under his com-mand." When the huzzahs quieted, the President suggested: "Three more cheers for our gallant Navy."

When Mr. Lincoln appeared the second time, he "supposed in consequence of the glorious news" there would be some more general demonstration "when I will be expected, I presume, to say something." And he said, with an obvious twinkle, "Every-thing I say, you know, goes into print." The crowd laughed and applauded. "If I make a mistake," the President continued, "it doesn't merely affect me nor you but the country. I, therefore, ought at least try not to make mistakes." Voices cried: "You have made no mistakes yet!" Mr. Lincoln said: "If, then, a general demonstration be made tomorrow evening, and it is agreeable, I will endeavor to say something, and not make a mistake, without at least trying carefully to avoid it."

No mind in America was more keenly aware than Mr. Lincoln's of the hard tasks ahead. He could not speak lightly or quickly. The nation had come to depend on him in a manner that was unique. He was set apart from his party—and certainly from the radical wing of it—because he had become now a symbol to the people. He had understood so well the common aspirations of the masses—the free masses—that he had given articulation to their conscience, dimension to their faith. And yet it was not for this gift alone that the people trusted him. They knew how quick he always had been to grant a pardon to an erring soldier; they had read the conclusion of his Second Inaugural. Justice for all with mercy for all . . . this was the image of the Union, reunited, as he had conceived it. It was deep in him now, this conviction that right could not compromise with wrong, that God did not consort with Satan, that freedom could not live with slavery. The South had claimed a legal right, an economic right, a human right, but without the institution of slavery, how could any of these arguments have arisen? America could not escape history. "In *giving* freedom to the *slave*," Lincoln had said, "we *assure* freedom to the *free*—honorable alike in what we give, and what we preserve." Therein had rested the essence of the war, the nation's trial before the bar of humanity; and he had said, writing in prose a ballad of America: "We shall nobly save, or meanly lose, the last, best hope of earth."

So the war became the epic of a people, and behind the guns, the diplomacy, the exigent maneuvers of the politicians, had existed and would always exist this deeper struggle of conscience— not the conscience of New England or of the West or of the South, but of a nation, unified by a merciful heart, a just mind. This single truth Mr. Lincoln had known before Sumter, and during the bleak days when there had seemed no end to the bloodletting; and now, after Appomattox, his faith remained as unshaken as it ever had been: "The people, under Providence, will set all right." Right as opposed to evil. For God must be the Partner. To Him alone was any man's homage due; to Him alone, as he had told the Negroes in Richmond, should any man kneel.

No, he could not speak lightly or quickly. And within himself he was deeply troubled by a dream one night before leaving City

Point. He had heard sobs, but the mourners were invisible; he had believed he was in the White House, wandering from room to room, but no living person had been in sight; everywhere the dwelling had been lighted, he had recognized familiar objects, and always the unseen, mournful sobbing had surrounded him; alarmed, he had reached the East Room and there had stood a catafalque with a corpse wrapped in funeral vestments. "Who is dead in the White House?" he had demanded of a guard beside the catafalque. And above the strident weeping of the people the soldier had answered: "The President; he was killed by an assassin!"

A strangely mystical man, Mr. Lincoln; he could name the chapters in the Bible in which dreams were mentioned—sixteen in the Old Testament, he believed, and four or five in the New. Through four years in the White House, he told a Cabinet meeting, a dream of "floating away on some vast and indistinct expanse, toward an unknown shore" had preceded every important event or disaster. Only his family and his friends knew this side of the President; he was unlike anyone else they knew—impelled, perhaps inspired, in what he said and thought and did.

And in this spirit Mr. Lincoln toiled carefully over his remarks for the demonstration.

The large audience that gathered before the White House to hear him overflowed onto Pennsylvania Avenue. At the sight of the President, a witness said, "There was something terrible in the enthusiasm." Mr. Lincoln's face had lost the peakedness of a fortnight before. Yet his manner was sober and earnest and those who came to hear a rousing speech in celebration of Lee's surrender were quickly surprised. A few brief sentences brought Mr. Lincoln to the problems of reconstruction, a subject "fraught with great difficulty." The plan that had been applied in Louisiana impressed him as offering sound principles to follow. The question of whether the seceded states "are in the Union or out of it" seemed to Mr. Lincoln a bad one for it was simply a "basis for controversy, and good for nothing at all." He said of the seceded states: "Finding themselves safely at home, it would be utterly immaterial whether they had ever been abroad." On the matter of the elective franchise for the colored man the President admitted that he would prefer "that it were now conferred on the very intelligent, and on those who serve our cause as soldiers."

Listening, John Wilkes Booth reputedly muttered to his dull-witted friend, David Herold: "That means nigger citizenship. Now, by God, I'll put him through!" But Mr. Lincoln had more to say:

> Some twelve thousand voters in the heretofore slave-state of Louisiana have sworn allegiance to the Union, assumed to be the rightful political power of the State, held elections, organized a State government, adopted a free-state constitution, giving the benefit of the public schools equally to black and white, and empowering the Legislature to confer the elective franchise upon the colored men. Their Legislature has already voted to ratify the constitutional amendment recently passed by Congress, abolishing slavery throughout the nation. These twelve thousand persons are thus fully committed to the Union, and to perpetual freedom in the state—committed to the very things, and nearly all the things the nation wants—and they ask the nation's recognition, and its assistance to make good their committal. . . .

What would happen if these now loyal Louisianans were rejected? Mr. Lincoln answered:

> . . . We in effect say to the white man, "You are worthless, or worse—we will neither help you, nor be helped by you." To the blacks we say "This cup of liberty which these, your old masters, hold to your lips, we will dash from you, and leave you to the chances of gathering the spilled and scattered contents in some vague and undefined when, where, and how." If this course, discouraging and paralyzing both white and black, has any tendency to bring Louisiana into practical relations with the Union, I have, so far, been unable to perceive it. If, on the contrary, we recognize, and sustain the new government of Louisiana

the converse of all this is made true. We encourage the hearts, and nerve the arms of the twelve thousand to adhere to their work, and argue for it, and proselyte for it, and fight for it, and feed it, and grow it, and ripen it to a complete success. The colored man too, in seeing all united for him, is inspired with vigilance, and energy, and daring, to the same end. Grant that he desires the elective franchise, will he not attain it sooner by saving the already advanced steps toward it, than by running backward over them? . . .

To the very large extent that Mr. Lincoln placed the nobility of his ideas above flag-waving he perhaps spoiled the occasion for many, who found the outlet they wanted in the brief remarks by Senator James Harlan of Iowa, soon to become the Secretary of the Interior.

What, Harlan asked, should be done with "these brethren of ours?"

"Hang 'em!" roared the crowd.

But Harlan argued that was wrong; the masses in the seceding states must be treated as innocent; all would work out well if the future was entrusted to the President, and his audience cheered boisterously. What Mr. Lincoln wanted he explained in a letter to General James H. Van Alen three days later: "A Union of hearts and hands as well as of States."

Wars end raggedly. Broken homes, broken dreams, broken bodies, lives that must find new direction, bitterness, hatred, minds unable to accept defeat, all remain when the great unifying passion that begins a war reaches its breaking point. North and South, after Lee's surrender, when the final collapse of Confederate resistence had become inevitable (Johnston asked Sherman for terms on April fourteenth), weary soldiers tramped the dusty roads home, wondering what they would find. Johnny Reb, who had gone off in high fettle as a "Lincoln Killer" desperately hoping he could get into a fight before the war was over, far too often returned to fields overgrown with weeds, to a Pa and Ma who looked shrunken and pinched from the hunger that had been the enemy on the home front, and a kind of dreary, fearful, uncertain lassitude hung on the air. The war had cost the South heavily.

Mrs. Chesnut heard the news in Chester, South Carolina: "Just now Mr. [Clement] Clay dashed up stairs, pale as a sheet. 'General Lee has capitulated.' I saw the news reflected in Mary Darby's face before I heard him. She staggered to the table, sat down, and wept aloud. Mr. Clay's eyes were not dry. Quite beside herself, Mary shrieked: 'Now we belong to Negroes and Yankees.'" The bitterness crept through in many ways: "We hear they have all grown rich. Genuine Yankees can make a fortune trading jack knives!" But there was deep pride too: "The plucky way our men bear up is beyond praise. No howling! Our poverty is made a matter of laughing. We deride our penury. Of the country, we try not to speak at all."

Young Kate Stone, who had been driven from her home when Grant besieged Vicksburg, heard the news in Tyler, Texas. "A crushing blow," she sobbed. Into her journal she poured the universal grief of the South:

> I cannot bear to hear them talk of defeat. It seems a reproach to our gallant dead. If nothing else can force us to battle on for freedom, the thousands of grass-grown mounds heaped on mountainside and in every valley of our country should teach us to emulate the heroes who lie beneath and make us clasp closer to our hearts the determination to be free or die. "When the South is trampled from the earth—Her women can die and be free." I say with my whole soul:
>
> > Shame to the traitor-heart that springs
> > To the faint, soft arms of Peace,
> > Though the Roman eagle shook his wings
> > At the very gates of Greece.

Seventeen-year-old Emma Florence LeConte, who lived through the terrorizing night when Sherman's troops burned Columbia, South Carolina, remembered the once brave dream:

The troops are coming home. One meets long-absent, familiar faces on the streets, and congregations once almost strictly feminine are now mingled with returned soldiers. . . . For four years we have looked forward to this day—the day when the troops would march home. We expected to meet them exulting and victorious. That was to be a day of wildest joy, when the tidings of peace should reach us, and the thought of that time used to lighten our hearts and nerve us to bear every trial and privation. Then we determined, after our independence was acknowledged and the time came for Gen. Lee to disband his army, to go on to Richmond to see the glorious sight, to see the hero take leave of his brave victorious men. The army is disbanded now—oh! Merciful God!—the hot tears rush into my eyes and I cannot write.

Old Edmund Ruffin could not endure the destruction of his dream and one day took his life; but Robert Barnwell Rhett not only was determined to survive the chaos of 1865 but was sneering a quarter of a century later that to say the Confederacy was overwhelmed by superior numbers alone was simply "an agreeable sop to Southern pride." Brains rather than brawn had decided the war, in Rhett's judgment. "Eliminate the good sense and unselfish earnestness of Mr. Lincoln," wrote Rhett, "and the great ability and practical energy of Seward and Adams, and of Stanton and Chase from the control of the United States; conceive a management of third-rate and incompetent men [Rhett's estimate of Davis and his Cabinet] in their places—will any one doubt that matters would have ended differently?" Between the suicide and the penitent secessionist was a large group who spoke of starting life anew in a foreign country, and Mexico and Brazil seemed to exert a special appeal.

Quietly Robert E. Lee returned to Richmond. "He came unattended, save by his staff—came without notice, and without parade," Mrs. McGuire noted in her diary; "but he could not come unobserved; as soon as his approach was whispered, a crowd gathered in his path, not boisterously, but respectfully, and increased as he advanced to his home on Franklin Street, between 8th and 9th, where, with a courtly bow to the multitude, he at once retired to the bosom of his beloved family."

Lee was dead tired and did not care to talk about the war. "I could have taken no other course save without dishonor," he said on a rare occasion when he did express himself. One Sunday at services in St. Paul's Church he set an example for other worshipers:

> It was communion day, and when Dr. Minnegerode was ready to administer the holy communion, a Negro in the church arose and advanced to the communion table. He was tall, well-dressed and black. This was a great surprise and shock to the communicants, and for several moments they retained their seats in solemn silence, and did not move . . . Dr. Minnegerode was evidently embarrassed.
>
> General Robert E. Lee . . . ignoring the actions and presence of the Negro, arose in his usual dignified and self-possessed manner, walked up the aisle to the chancel rail, and reverently knelt down to partake of the communion, and not far from the Negro. . . .

Others went forward to the communion table . . . the South would need Lee in returning to "the faint, soft arms of Peace." He wrote Beauregard, glad he was not one of those planning on leaving the country: "I think the South requires the aid of her sons now more than at any period of her history" and he defined "true patriotism" as doing an act exactly the contrary at one period to the act of a man at another "and the motive that impels them— the desire to do right—is precisely the same." To a clergyman who had preached a bitter, anti-Union sermon, Lee said: "Doctor, there is a good old Book which I read, and you preach from, which says, 'Love your enemies, bless them that curse you, do good to them that hate you, and pray for them which despitefully use you.'"

On Good Friday, April fourteenth, John Wilkes Booth shot

Mr. Lincoln. When the news of the President's assassination reached Columbia, young Emma Florence LeConte "*flew* home and for the first time in oh, so long, I was trembling and my heart beating with excitement." The girl thought: "If it is *only* true! . . . The man we hated has met his proper fate." In Tyler, Texas, young Kate Stone rejoiced: "All honor to J. Wilkes Booth, who has rid the world of a tyrant and made himself famous for generations." But Mrs. Chesnut could speak only of "this foul murder" and fear the "worse miseries" it would bring down upon the South.

That morning Mr. Lincoln held a Cabinet meeting. The President spoke of the dream that so often haunted him, and someone said, trying to laugh off the incident, "At any rate it cannot presage a victory or defeat this time, for the war is over."

Grant had reached Washington and attended the Cabinet meeting.

"What terms did you make for the common soldier?" the President asked.

"I told them," Grant replied, "to go back to their homes and families, and they would not be molested, if they did nothing more."

Frederick W. Seward, attending the meeting for his ailing father, recalled that "Mr. Lincoln's face glowed with approval."

Earlier the Cabinet had debated if "the leaders in treason" should go entirely unpunished, and the President was asked if he would be sorry to see them escape from the country.

"Well, I would not be sorry to have them out of the country," he said, "but I should be for following them up pretty close, to make sure of their going."

Mr. Lincoln had said, in his First Inaugural, "You cannot fight always; and when, after much loss on both sides, and no gain on either, you cease fighting, the identical questions, as to terms of intercourse, are again upon you." At this point the country had now arrived. Stanton brought to the meeting a long roll of paper with an outline of how Federal functions of government were to be revived in the seceding states, and once Mr. Lincoln remarked:

"We can't undertake to run State governments in all these Southern States. Their people must do that—though I reckon that at first some of them may do it badly."

As the meeting broke up, Mr. Lincoln agreed to receive Sir Frederick Bruce, the new British Minister, in the Blue Room of the White House at two o'clock the following afternoon. But next morning, at twenty-two minutes past seven, the President died.

So the one man who more than any other had believed in national character and national conscience now belonged to the ages. He was neither for the North nor against the South; he was for the country as "the last, best hope of earth." The illusion of individuality never trapped him. Justice for all with mercy for all. . . . no man could be free otherwise. Clearly, beautifully, he recognized the epic vision of America. He saw beyond Illinois. He saw beyond Virginia. With time, with patience, America would fulfill its mission; no legal argument, no armies in the field must be stronger than the decency of government and the dignity of man. Mr. Lincoln's America, the Truth that opposed the Great Rebellion, could not be achieved in a generation. Yet as America grew, as its wealth increased, as its moral fiber toughened, as it resisted the sophistry that New England or the West or the South could be set apart or above human aspiration, as it resolved that no man of any color ever could be made the forgotten son of God, as it looked forward to a day when no one would ask a Negro to die on a battlefield to protect liberties and opportunities his children could not enjoy, then, and only then, would Mr. Lincoln's War end. And Mr. Lincoln's America documented this emotion and this purpose; in the age in which he lived the people sang:

In the beauty of the lilies Christ was born across the sea,
With a glory in His bosom that transfigures you and me;
As He died to make men holy, let us die to make men free,
While God is marching on!

And that was the epic vision for which an epic war was fought.

NOTES ON THE SOURCES

BIBLIOGRAPHY

INDEX

Notes on the Sources

Sources, given in full in the Bibliography, are cited only by short title. The following sources are cited as:

Chesnut	Chesnut, *A Diary from Dixie*
Crawford	Crawford, *The Genesis of the Civil War*
C.W.	Basler, *The Collected Writings of Abraham Lincoln*
Davis	Davis, *The Rise and Fall of the Confederate Government*
DeForest	DeForest, "Charleston Under Arms"
Doubleday	Doubleday, *Reminiscences of Fort Sumter and Moultrie in 1860–61*
Grant	Grant, *Personal Memoirs*
Leech	Leech, *Reveille in Washington, 1860–1865*
Lewis	Lewis, *Captain Sam Grant*
Nichols	Nichols, *The Disruption of American Democracy*
O.R.	*War of the Rebellion ... Official Records of the Union and Confederate Armies*
Plain People	Wiley, *The Plain People of the Confederacy*
RTLP	*The Robert Todd Lincoln Papers*
Secret History	Pollard, *Life of Jefferson Davis with a Secret History of the Confederacy*
War Years	Sandburg, *Abraham Lincoln: The War Years*

PROLOGUE

Snider quotation: Snider, *The American Ten Years War*, 14-5. Lincoln quotations: *C.W.,* II, 267; II, 132; IV, 438.

Part I. Christmas Week, 1860

1. "WE DID IT GLORY TO GOD"

Adams on Seward: Adams, *Education,* 104. Moran on Seward: Wallace and Gillespie, *Journal of Benjamin Moran,* I, 546, 548. Seward in England: Hendrick, *Lincoln's War Cabinet,* 27-8. Medill on Seward: Bancroft, *Life of Seward,* I, 531.

An excellent study of the complex forces dominating the Republican National Convention is Hesseltine's *Lincoln and the War Governors,* 17-53. Convention telegrams to Lincoln: *RTLP* and *Chicago History,* I, 250, 254. Halstead on Convention: Halstead, *Caucuses,* 121-23, 261. Lincoln instructs supporters: *C.W.,* IV, 34.

Adams on Civil War: Adams, *Education,* 98-9. Seward's New England Dinner Speech: *Harper's Weekly,* January 5, 1861. Seward and the Radicals: Williams, *Lincoln and the Radicals,* 6, 20.

2. "GOD WILL KEEP LINCOLN RIGHT"

Opening anecdotes: Villard, *Lincoln on the Eve of '61,* 3-4, 6-7, 30-1. Ridicule of Lincoln: Anderson, *A Border City,* 15-6. Herndon on Lincoln: Herndon and Weik, *Life of Lincoln,* 254, 266-67, 273, 280, 292, 342, 344.

Lincoln's Springfield speech of 1854 was repeated in Peoria on October 16, and it is from this text, the only one published, that the quotations are taken; the speech in its entirety is in *C.W.,* IV, 247-83, and an abbreviated, interpretive version appears in *The Living Lincoln,* edited by Angle and Miers, 160-79.

Lincoln to Herndon on Stephens's Mexican War speech: *C.W.,* I, 48. Stephens and his health: Von Abele, *Alexander H. Stephens,* 135. Stephens's speech to the Georgia Legislature: McPherson, *Political History,* 20-5. Stephens's letter to Lincoln: *RTLP* and Mearns, *The Lincoln Papers,* II, 339-40. Lincoln's reply: *C.W.,* IV, 160. Conclusion to the debates with Douglas: *C.W.,* III, 315.

On Lincoln's character: Villard, *Lincoln on the Eve of '61,* 36, 39-41.

Lincoln to Peter H. Sylvester: *C.W.*, IV, 160. *Greeley on secession:* New York *Tribune*, December 17, 1860.

3. THE REVOLT OF THE ANCIENTS

Charleston during Christmas week: *Chesnut*, I, 3. See also Rhett, *Charleston, An Epic of the Carolinas*, 219-20; Grayson, *The Hireling and the Slave*, 42; Parrington, *Main Currents*, II, 95; and *DeForest*, 489-90, 491.

Doubleday's account of life in Fort Moultrie: *Doubleday*, 14-5, 16, 17, 18-20, 26, 31-2, 33, 41-2, 43-4, 47, 49, 50-1, 57. Gist's correspondence with the Southern governors: Nicolay and Hay, *Abraham Lincoln*, II, 306-14. Charleston at time of secession: Rhodes, *History of the United States*, III, 115-21; *DeForest*, 494; Charleston *Mercury*, November 8, 1860.

Quotations attributed to Rhett: *Secret History*, 45, and *War Years*, I, 5. Story of Ruffin and the John Brown pikes: *Chesnut*, 93. See also Fitzhugh, *Sociology for the South*, 175; and for an analysis of the full attack on Jefferson's philosophy that was vital in shaping the mind of a Rhett and a Ruffin, an excellent study is Wish, *George Fitzhugh, Propagandist of the Old South*, 94-112.

Charleston's mood at time of Buell's visit: *DeForest*, 488, 489, 491, 495. Buell's instructions to Anderson: *O.R.*, I, 90. See also *Chesnut*, 3, and *De Bow's Review*, December 1860, 702, 710.

4. CRANKS AND PROPHETS

The letters quoted in this section are in *RTLP* or were in the magnificent collection of Oliver R. Barrett; see also Mearns, *The Lincoln Papers*, I, 327; II, 333-34, 347, 359, 370; and Sandburg, *Lincoln Collector*, 65-7.

5. THE ORACLE AND THE COPPERHEADS

Quotations from the New York *Tribune:* December 18, 21, and 25, 1860; see also Durden's *James Shepherd Pike*, 38-41, and Potter's *Lincoln and His Party in the Secession Crisis*, 51-7. Auburn Prison straw vote: Sandburg, *Lincoln Collector*, 228. Greeley's letter to Lincoln: *RTLP;* Mearns, *The Lincoln Papers*, II, 349-50; and Dunlap, "President Lincoln and Editor Greeley," *Abraham Lincoln Quarterly*, June 1948, 94-7. Seward at Astor House: *Harper's Weekly*, January 5, 1861.

Greeley on Fernando Wood: New York *Tribune*, January 8, 1861; all of the quotations attributed to Wood are drawn from the Mayor's recommendation "to the Honorable the Common Council" for the secession of New York City, January 6, 1861, and may be found in McPherson, *Political History*, 42-4. Draft Riot incident: Werstein, *July, 1863*, 116. Spread of peace sentiment: Rhodes, *History of the United States*, III, 172-73.

6. LEE'S LONELY DEBATE

Lee's early opposition to secession: Jones, *Life and Letters*, 115-18, 120-21, and Craven, *To Markie*, 58-9. Attack on McFee: Cash, *The Mind of the South*, 100.

Rooney Lee at Harvard: Adams, *Education*, 57-8. Peale on the South: Wilson, *Collected Essays*, 5. Cash on the South: *The Mind of the South*, 107-10.

Helper quote: *The Impending Crisis*, 16. Antislavery sentiment, 1820-37: Cohn, *Life and Times of King Cotton*, 82-3. Racialistic literature: Wish, *George Fitzhugh*, 33, 42. For B. Stringfellow, *Negro Slavery No Evil*, 16; for T. Stringfellow, *Scriptural and Statistical Views*, 81-3.

Schlesinger's edition of Olmsted's *The Cotton Kingdom* has been quoted: 32, 35, 214-15, 284-85, 310, 366, 455; the unquoted letter in the *Times* appeared January 12, 1854 (Schlesinger, 614n) and like all of Olmsted's travel letters appeared under the nom de plume of "Yeoman." Slave ship and ophthalmia: Cohn, *Life and Times of King Cotton*, 31.

7. THE MAN WHO JOURNEYED THROUGH HELL

See *Grant*, 584, for slavery as cause of war; for James Truslow Adams on the West, see *The March of Democracy*, 338, and for Anthony Trollope's reactions, see *North America*, 400.

Grant in Galena: Stitt, *War Papers*, 274. Previous experiences: *Grant*, 106-07; *Lewis*, 346, 354; "Grant and the Frémonts," *St. Louis Republican*, August 24, 1885. Galena portrait between arrival and secession: Garland, *Ulysses S. Grant*, 149; *Lewis*, 376, 382, 386; *Grant*, 109, 110; Richardson, *A Personal History*, 175-76.

Brian Waters edited *Mr. Vessey of England;* see specifically 119, 121, 122-23, 127. An excellent account of the visit of the Prince of Wales to Chicago is in *Chicago History*, II, 199-200; see also Englehardt,

Journal of . . . Visit, and N. A. Woods, *The Prince of Wales in Canada and the United States.*

Lincoln's speech in Wisconsin: *C.W.,* III, 472, 473, 479, 480, 478. Letter to Lyman Trumbull: *C.W.,* IV., 162. Land Grant College Act: Schmidt, *The Liberal Arts College,* 154. In *Herman Melville,* 199, Lewis Mumford dates the revival of *Moby Dick* as occurring "only since 1914."

8. THE EVIL OF WHITENESS

Emerson quote: *Journals,* VIII, 339. For Parrington: *Main Currents,* II, 312, 347. For Garrison: *William Lloyd Garrison,* III, 88. Webster on abolitionism: Webster, *Works,* V, 357. For victory of the extremists in the Compromise of 1850, see Russel, "What Was the Compromise of 1850?" *Journal of Southern History,* August, 1956.

Mrs. Chesnut's reactions to *Uncle Tom's Cabin: Chesnut,* 122, 199-200; 347, 21. Other examples of Southern sensitivity to evils of slavery: Anderson, *Brokenburn,* 8; Stampp, *The Peculiar Institution,* 353; Olmsted, *The Cotton Kingdom,* 269, 277-78. Publishing background of *Uncle Tom's Cabin: Chicago History,* II, 354-56, 358-59; also Furnas, *Goodbye to Uncle Tom,* 44; Rhodes, *History of the United States,* I, 278, and Wilson, *Division and Reunion,* 181. John Brown at Pottawatomie: Nichols, *Bleeding Kansas,* 113-14, 245-46.

9. BORDER CITY

See Anderson, *A Border City,* 1-3, 5, 13-4, 18, 19, 21-2, 24-5, 29-31, 164 for background, role of Schurz in election, and last slave auction. Dr. Sappington comments on Claib Jackson: Monaghan, *Civil War on the Western Border,* 19. President Truman on his mother: *Memoirs,* I, 220.

Mark Twain's fictionalized "The Private History of a Campaign that Failed" is included in Twain, *The American Claimant and Other Stories and Sketches.* Quotations from Wecter: Wecter, *Sam Clemens of Hannibal,* 100. The thesis of the two intellectual Souths is ably defended by Parrington.

10. OLD BUCK BLOCKS THE GAME

Mrs. Gwin on President Buchanan: *Nichols,* 438. Lammond's advertisement: *Leech,* 23. Pollard on Buchanan: *Secret History,* 56-7. Lincoln on Douglas: *C.W.*, II, 382-83. A penetrating study of the Democratic campaign of 1860 is in *Nichols*, 334-67. Shrinkage of Southern economy: Ramsdell, *Behind the Lines*, 7-8, 10-20. Keitt on Buchanan: *Secret History*, 58.

Buchanan to Floyd on "millstones tied about our necks": *Philadelphia Weekly Press*, August 11, 1881. Buchanan's message to Congress: *Messages and Papers of the Presidents*, V, 626-27, 630, 636.

11. A FRETFUL CHRISTMAS

Judge Campbell, on the breakdown of Southern faith in due process of law, as quoted in this and the previous chapter, will be found in *Southern Historical Society Papers*, 42: 18-9, 24-5. Propositions submitted to Committee of Thirty-three: McPherson, *Political History*, 53-5. Washington background: *Leech*, 8.

Portraits of Jefferson Davis and Andrew Johnson: *Secret History*, 68, 69-70, 74. Seward on Crittenden Compromise: Hendrick, *Lincoln's War Cabinet*, 136. Profile of Scott: *Leech*, 1; *War Years*, I, 29. Seward and his attitude on slavery: Hendrick, *Lincoln's War Cabinet*, 244-46, and *Galaxy Magazine*, II, 257. Mrs. Chesnut's comment on sensitivity to smallpox: *Chesnut*, 3. Seward to Lincoln on Cabinet appointments: *C.W.*, IV, 164.

12. TALE OF TWO CITIES

Removal of Federal forces from Moultrie to Sumter: *Doubleday*, 61-9. Anderson's letter: *O.R.*, I, 2; see also Williams, *Lincoln Finds a General*, I, 20.

Letter from Anderson to Floyd: *O.R.*, I, 3. Holt on Floyd: Wilson, *Atlantic Monthly*, XXVI, 471, and Hendrick, *Lincoln's War Cabinet*, 248-50. Correspondence between commissioners and Buchanan: *O.R.*, I, 120-28, and McPherson, *Political History*, 29. Scott to Floyd: *O.R.*, I, 112. Scott to Floyd and Lincoln: Nicolay, *Lincoln's Secretary*, 46-7. Cabinet meeting, evening, December twenty-eighth: *Nichols*, 430-31. Black recants on his resignation: Black, *Essays and Speeches*, 14. Scott writes Buchanan: *O.R.*, I, 112. Floyd apologizes for resignation: *Nichols*, 432. Buchanan replies to commissioners: McPherson, *Political History*, 29-32. Scott warns Buchanan: *O.R.*, I, 119.

Charleston's reactions: *DeForest*, 493, 497, and *Chesnut*, 4. Anderson becomes a hero: Starr, *Bohemian Brigade*, 10-11; *Doubleday*, 88; New

York *Times*, January 4, 1861; New York *Tribune*, January 6, 1861; *Harper's Weekly*, January 26, 1861.

Medill writes Lincoln: *RTLP*, and Mearns, *The Lincoln Papers*, II, 359-60, 363. Douglas and Crittenden telegraph Georgians: Rhodes, *History of the United States*, III, 245, and *Nichols*, 440. Buchanan and New Year's reception: *O.R.*, I, 120-25; *Nichols*, 433; *Leech*, 24. Seward's two-timing: Wilson, *Atlantic Monthly*, XXVI, 465-67; Hendrick, *Lincoln's War Cabinet*, 253-55.

13. LINCOLN AS A. LINCOLN KNEW HIM

Lincoln to Lyman Trumbull on Seward: *Chicago History*, I, 370-71, and *C.W.*, IV, 151-52, 164. Lincoln and Simon Cameron: *C.W.*, IV, 165-68; Hendrick, *Lincoln's War Cabinet*, 51-9, 107-08; Thomas, *Abraham Lincoln*, 232-34. Lincoln and the Crittenden Compromise: *C.W.*, IV, 155, 157, 158, 162-63, 163-64; Bancroft, *Life of Seward*, II, 10, and Thomas, *Abraham Lincoln*, 235-36.

Part II. Sumter Day, 1861

14. WHERE YELLOWHAMMERS SANG

Olmsted on Montgomery, *The Cotton Kingdom*, 382; DeLeon on Montgomery, *Four Years in Rebel Capitals*, 23-7; Pollard on bloodless February coup, *Secret History*, 87-9; Mrs. Chesnut on Montgomery, *Chesnut*, 5, 8, 10-11, 19, 21-2, 23; also Peyton, *The American Crisis*, I, 114.

Reactions to Jefferson Davis: *Chesnut*, 6, 20; *Secret History*, 102-03, 106; Younger, *Inside the Confederate Government*, xxxi; Freeman, *R. E. Lee*, I, 517-18. Background on Davis: Strode, *Jefferson Davis*, 3, 26, 41-2, 95, 118-19, 126, 141. At Transylvania: Schmidt, *The Liberal Arts College*, 122. Davis and slaves: Stampp, *The Peculiar Institution*, 171-72. Davis and Douglas as opponents: *Davis*, I, 45, and Rowland, *J. D. Constitutionalist*, V, 44-5. Following resignation: New York *Tribune*, January 11, 1861, and *Davis*, II, 228-31.

Dated "Steamship Star of the West, New York, Jan. 12," Captain J. McGowan's report appeared in the New York *Tribune*, January 14, 1861; see also *Harper's Weekly*, January 26, 1861, and *Doubleday*, 102-04.

15. THE SOUTH GIRDS FOR WAR

Stephens's role in shaping Confederacy: Von Abele, *Alexander H. Stephens*, 191-95; also *Chesnut*, 65. Davis in war mood: *Davis*, I, 198, and Rowland, *J. D. Constitutionalist*, V, 48. For a full account of Lee's conversation with Cosby on leaving Texas, see Freeman, *R. E. Lee*, I, 425-26.

Rhodes, *History of the United States*, III, 322, discusses slavery provisions in Confederate Constitution; for Davis on slavery, see *Davis*, I, 78.

Harry Macarthy's "The Bonnie Blue Flag" was published in New Orleans by A. E. Blackamar & Brother. Johnny Reb's humble background: *Plain People*, 36, 45, 50. Nat Turner's uprising: Stampp, *The Peculiar Institution*, 132-35, 380-81. See also Wiley, *Life of Johnny Reb*, 16-7. "De bone fight none" is in *Plain People*, 86. Henry Clay Work's "Kingdom Coming" was published 1862 in Chicago by Root & Cady.

"The War Spirit in Charleston" appeared in the New York *Tribune*, January 14, 1861. Background on Beauregard: Williams, *P. G. T. Beauregard, Napoleon in Gray*, 1-50; also *Chesnut*, 31. *Mercury* quote: issue of March 5, 1861.

16. "EVERYTHING WILL COME OUT ALL RIGHT"

Lincoln's visit to stepmother: Coleman, *Abraham Lincoln and Coles County*, 199, 206. Lincoln en route to Washington: Thomas, *Abraham Lincoln*, 238-44, and *Chesnut*, 19. Washington in 1861: Riddle, *Recollections*, 7-9. Lincoln's interview with Peace delegates: Chittenden, *Recollections*, 71-6, and *Leech*, 37-9.

Crawford on Lincoln and Buchanan: *Davis*, I, 263-66. Lincoln's Inaugural: Thomas, *Abraham Lincoln*, 245, 247; *War Years*, I, 122-23; New York *Tribune*, March 5 and 12, 1861; *Chesnut*, 12; *Davis*, I, 257. Lincoln at ball: Adams, *Education*, 107. Letter from Anderson: Nicolay and Hay, *Abraham Lincoln*, II, 376-79. Seizure of other forts: McPherson, *Political History*, 27-8. Testing Cabinet's position: Randall, *The Civil War and Reconstruction*, 232-36, and Nicolay and Hay, *Abraham Lincoln*, II, 378-79. Lee's refusal of a Confederate command: Freeman, *R. E. Lee*, I, 433-34. Speeches in Virginia Convention: McPherson, *Political History*, 6.

Seward's letter on Confederate Commission: Rowland, *J. D. Constitutionalist*, V, 86, 89. His conversations with Campbell: *Davis*, I, 267-69; Rhodes, *History of the United States*, III, 339; Hendrick, *Lincoln's War Cabinet*, 166-67. Blair's interview with Lincoln: *Crawford*, 363; Hendrick, *Lincoln's War Cabinet*, 164; Thomas, *Abraham Lincoln*, 251-52.

Wives and children evacuated from Sumter: *Harper's Weekly*, February 23, 1861. Beauregard and the defenses of Charleston: Williams, *P. G. T. Beauregard, Napoleon in Gray*, 52-4, and Rowland, *J. D. Constitutionalist*, V, 60. Gossip: *Chesnut*, 28-33. Seward's further duplicity: *Davis*, I, 270.

17. FATEFUL WEEKS

St. Louis remains loyal: Anderson, *A Border City*, 43-4, 46, 58-60; also *Journal and Proceedings of the Missouri State Convention, 1861.* Lyon and the fight for the Arsenal: Anderson, *A Border City*, 67, 71-3; Catton, *This Hallowed Ground*, 30.

Charleston as Doubleday experienced it: *Doubleday*, 109, 114, 126-27, 130-31. Fox at Sumter: *Doubleday*, 131-32; *RTLP*, and Mearns, *The Lincoln Papers*, II, 501-02; Williams, *Lincoln Finds a General*, I, 38-9. Lamon and Hurlbut at Sumter: Thomas, *Portrait for Posterity*, 29-30; *War Years*, I, 191, 192; *O.R.*, I, 196-98; Williams, *Lincoln Finds a General*, I, 40-2. Scott advises Lincoln: Mearns, *The Lincoln Papers*, 476-78, and *C.W.*, IV, 279. James L. Hill writes Lincoln: Mearns, *The Lincoln Papers*, II, 484-85. Lincoln decides to supply Sumter: *C.W.*, IV, 301.

DeLeon sees Davis in Montgomery: *Four Years in Rebel Capitals*, 25. Davis on Fox and Lamon: *Davis*, I, 272. On Douglas: *Ibid.*, 292. Indifference of British to Cotton Diplomacy: Cohn, *Life and Times of King Cotton*, 122-23, 131. Civil war resembles religious war: Fuller, *Grant and Lee*, 32.

Responsibility for Sumter: Ramsdell, *Journal of Southern History*, II, 285; Angle, "The Changing Lincoln," in Ander's *John M. Hauberg Historical Essays*, 11-2; Potter, *Lincoln and His Party in the Secession Crisis;* Rowland, *J. D. Constitutionalist*, V, 61; Ballard, *Military Genius of Abraham Lincoln*, 36; *Davis*, I, 276. Seward and Campbell: *Ibid.*, 273.

18. FATEFUL DAYS

Seward offers to be President: *C.W.*, IV, 316-18; Angle and Miers, *The Living Lincoln*, 393-94; Thomas, *Abraham Lincoln*, 252-54; Hendrick, *Lincoln's War Cabinet*, 174-78.

Commissioners telegraph Pickens: *Crawford*, 391. Mrs. Gilman on Charleston: Jones, *Heroines of Dixie*, 17. Anderson cannot remove laborers: *Crawford*, 375. Doubleday writes wife: *RTLP*, and Mearns, *The Lincoln Papers*, II, 513-14. Captain Chester on defenses: *Battles and Leaders*, I, 65. Incident of *Rhoda B. Shannon: Crawford*, 375-77. Anderson's correspondence with Washington: *Ibid.*, 391-92.

Porter-Seward-Welles fiasco: *O.R.*, I, 1, 254, IV, 112; *Crawford*, 382-83, 412-15; *Davis*, I, 284-85; Welles, *Diary*, I, 24-5; Hendrick, *Lincoln's War Cabinet*, 178-82. Harvey telegram: *O.R.*, I. 1, 187; Hendrick, *Lincoln's War Cabinet*, 183-84; Nicolay and Hay, *Abraham Lincoln*, IV, 32. Charleston reaction: *Crawford*, 392; *Chesnut*, 32. Mr. Chew complicates the issue: *O.R.*, I, 291; Williams, *Lincoln Finds a General*, I, 43-4; *Crawford*, 395. Campbell and Seward: *Davis*, I, 277. Ambulances ordered ready: Moore's *Rebellion Record*, I, 21. Charleston prepares to fight: *Chesnut*, 34-5; New York *Times*, April 10, 1861; Charleston *Mercury*, April 9, 1861; Moore's *Rebellion Record*, I, 21-2.

Montgomery reacts: *Davis*, I, 290-92. Rhett criticizes Davis: *Battles and Leaders*, I, 99. Pickens writes Davis: Rowland, *J. D. Constitutionalist*, V, 62. Negotiations between Montgomery and Charleston: *Crawford*, 421-22, and Moore's *Rebellion Record*, I, 23. Federal fleet off Charleston: *Crawford*, 416-18. Mr. Lincoln on April tenth: *C.W.*, IV, 326.

Chesnut meets with Anderson: *Crawford*, 423-24; *Davis*, I, 288; Moore's *Rebellion Record*, I, 23, 25. Lincoln on slave or wife: *C.W.*, II, 405.

Rowan refuses to take in *Pawnee: Crawford*, 417. Anderson gives alarm: *Doubleday*, 142. Captain Chester describes first shot: *Battles and Leaders*, I, 66.

19. "FREEDOM IS SAVED"

The seven dispatches here quoted appear in the Philadelphia *Inquirer* for April 13, 1861; subsequent details are taken from the *Inquirer* for April 15.

First dispatch: Chester, in *Battles and Leaders,* I, 66; *Chesnut,* 36; Tuttle, in *War Sketches and Incidents,* 18; New York *Times* quoted in Moore's *Rebellion Record,* I, 62; Croffut and Morris, *Military and Civil History,* 18.

Second dispatch: *Chesnut,* 36; Jones, *Heroines of Dixie,* 19; Chester, in *Battles and Leaders,* I, 66; Emory, in *Annals of the War,* 776; Crozier, *Yankee Reporters,* 42; Moore's *Rebellion Record,* I, 58, 61-2; Croffut and Morris, *Military and Civil History,* 39.

Third dispatch: Chester, in *Battles and Leaders,* I, 69; *Chesnut,* 36; Moore's *Rebellion Record,* I, 26; Chicago *Tribune,* April 15, 1861; Croffut and Morris, *Military and Civil History,* 42-54; Anderson, *A Border City,* 75; Crozier, *Yankee Reporters,* 46-7, 49-50.

Fourth dispatch: Jones, *Heroines of Dixie,* 19; Chester, in *Battles and Leaders,* I, 68; *Crawford,* 417-18; Nicolay and Hay, *Abraham Lincoln,* IV, 70.

Fifth dispatch: Chester, in *Battles and Leaders,* I, 70-1; Moore's *Rebellion Record,* I, 62; Nicolay and Hay, *Abraham Lincoln,* IV, 72.

Sixth dispatch: Miers, *When the World Ended,* 86; Moore's *Rebellion Record,* I, 67-70.

Seventh dispatch: Moore's *Rebellion Record,* I, 62.

Afterward: Croffut and Morris, *Military and Civil History,* 32; Moore's *Rebellion Record,* I, 26; Emory, in *Annals of the War,* 776; Philadelphia *Inquirer,* April 15, 1861; Chicago *Tribune,* April 15, 1861. Douglas story: New York *Tribune,* October 31, 1864.

20. "WE ARE COMING, FATHER ABRAHAM!"

Draper story: Cannon, *Personal Reminiscences,* 19-20. Douglas goes westward: Milton, *Abraham Lincoln and the Fifth Column,* 26-7. St. Louis sermon: Anderson, *A Border City,* 127-30. Cavalry advertisement: Beach, *The First New York Cavalry,* 9-10. Connecticut-Chicago-editorials-Brook Farm: Croffut and Morris, *Military and Civil History,* 45; Kimbell, *History of Battery "A,"* 13-4; Moore's *Rebellion Record,* I, 64-6; Gordon, *Brook Farm to Cedar Mountain,* 13. Grant at Galena rally: *Grant,* 116-17; *Lewis,* 397; Richardson, *A Personal History,* 178-79. Massachusetts Fourth: Stephenson, *Civil War Papers,* II, 537-39. Lee refuses Union command: Lee, Jr., *Life and Letters,* 27-8; Nicolay and Hay, *Abraham Lincoln,* IV, 98; Freeman, *R. E. Lee,* 435-37; Miers, *Robert E. Lee,* 4-10, 27.

Negative reactions to Lincoln: Moore's *Rebellion Record,* I, 67-8.

Baltimore riot: Emory, in *Annals of the War*, 777-84. British reaction: Moore's *Rebellion Record*, I, 228, 230; Wallace and Gillespie, *Journal of Benjamin Moran*, I, 802, 804; Hutton, "Lincoln Through British Eyes," *Abraham Lincoln Quarterly*, June, 1944, 63-92.

Part III. Palm Sunday, 1865

21. AT CITY POINT

Welles on Lincoln: Welles, *Diary*, II, 264. Press comment on health: Kimmel, *Mr. Lincoln's Washington*, 174. Passage of Thirteenth Amendment: Thomas, *Abraham Lincoln*, 495-96. Dana's evaluation: Dana, *Recollections*, 174, 180. Lincoln on the state of the Union: *C.W.*, V, 527 and VIII, 140, 152. Lincoln's Second Inaugural: *C.W.*, VIII, 333. Stanton's correspondence with Lincoln: *O.R.*, I, XLVI, 3, 332, and *C.W.*, VIII, 375-76.

Sherman and Lincoln: Sherman, *Memoirs*, I, 167-68, 193, II, 408. Grant and Lincoln: *Ibid.*, I, 256; Miers, "He Reduced War to Four Words," *Saturday Review*, July 9, 1955; *C.W.*, V, 460, and Angle and Miers, *The Living Lincoln*, 505; Porter, *Campaigning with Grant*, 19-20, 21, 22-3. Interview at City Point: *Ibid.*, 423-24, 426.

22. "KINGDOM COMIN' "

Lincoln to Stanton: *C.W.*, VIII, 377-78.

Richmond falls: *Davis*, II, 656; Varina Davis, *A Memoir by His Wife*, 11, 575-78; Townsend, *Rustics in Rebellion*, 274; Ramsdell, *Behind the Lines*, 47, 49, 50; *Plain People*, 49; Younger, *Inside the Confederate Government*, 42-3; Boykin, *Falling Flag*, 12-3; Jones, *Heroines of Dixie*, 393; DeLeon, *Four Years in Rebel Capitals*, 361-62.

Lincoln in Richmond: *C.W.*, VIII, 385; Porter, *Incidents and Anecdotes*, 293ff.; Graves, in *Battles and Leaders*, IV, Pt. 2, 727-28; Townsend, *Rustics in Rebellion*, 277; Dana, *Recollections*, 271; Jones, *A Rebel War Clerk's Diary*, II, 469-71; Rhodes, *History of the United States*, V, 133; *O.R.*, XLVI, Pt. 3, 574-75, 594, 619, 655.

23. RATHER A THOUSAND DEATHS

Lee as a legend: Lanier quoted in Armes, *Stratford on the Potomac*, 5; Cooke, *Robert E. Lee*, 371; Alexander, in *Battles and Leaders*, III, 366-67.

Lee and the war: *Chesnut*, 58; Lee, Jr., *Life and Letters*, 58-66; Durkin, *John Dooley*, 70; Miers, *Robert E. Lee*, 31-2, 39-44, 47, 98, 144-45; Freeman, *R. E. Lee*, IV, 110n.

Grant and Lee, exchange of first letters: *Grant*, 552-54; Porter, *Campaigning with Grant*, 458-61; Longstreet, *Manassas to Appomattox*, 610; Freeman, *R. E. Lee*, IV, 103-05, 112.

Decision to surrender: Freeman, *R. E. Lee*, IV, 119-30; Alexander, *Military Memoirs*, 604-05, 609; *O.R.*, XLVI, 3, 664; Freeman, *Lee's Lieutenants*, III, 734-36; Agassiz, *Meade's Headquarters*, 356-57; Longstreet, *Manassas to Appomattox*, 628.

24. THE TWO COUNTRYMEN

Grant goes to Court House: *Grant*, 553-4; Porter, *Campaigning with Grant*, 462-63, 466, 468, 469-70; Thomas, *Three Years with Grant*, 326.

The surrender: *Grant*, 555-56, 557-8; Porter, *Campaigning with Grant*, 473-74, 475, 477-80; Freeman, *R. E. Lee*, IV, 138-9; Miers, *Robert E. Lee*, 187-90.

Afterward: *Grant*, 559; Agassiz, *Meade's Headquarters*, 358; Porter, *Campaigning with Grant*, 486-87; Thomas, *Three Years With Grant*, 330; Owen, *In Camp and Battle*, 387; Blackford, *War Years*, 292-93; Freeman, *Lee's Lieutenants*, III, 144-45.

25. "WHILE GOD IS MARCHING ON!"

Washington receives the news: *Leech*, 381-2; Kimmel, *Mr. Lincoln's Washington*, 181-82; Washington *Daily National Republican* and Washington *Daily National Intelligencer*, April 11, 1865; *C.W.*, VIII, 393-95.

The mystical Lincoln and his last public address: Lamon, *Recollections*, 114-18; Seward, *Reminiscences*, 254-55; *C.W.*, VIII, 399-404, 413.

Southern reaction: *Chesnut*, 520-21; Anderson, *Brokenburn*, 334; Miers, *When the World Ended*, 98-9; *Confederate Veteran*, XIII, 360, and Jones, *Lee*, 400. Reaction to assassination: Miers, *When the World Ended*, 92-3; Anderson, *Brokenburn*, 333; *Chesnut*, 522.

Bibliography

NEWSPAPERS AND PERIODICALS

Abraham Lincoln Quarterly, The
Atlantic Monthly, The
Charleston Mercury
Chicago History
Chicago News and Tribune
Confederate Veteran, The
De Bow's Review
Galaxy Magazine
Harper's Weekly
Journal of Southern History
New York Times
New York Tribune
Philadelphia Inquirer
Philadelphia Weekly Press
Saturday Review
Southern Historical Society Papers
St. Louis Republican
Washington Daily National
   Intelligencer
Washington Daily National
   Republican

BOOKS AND OTHER SOURCES

Adams, Henry. *The Education of Henry Adams.* New York: The Modern Library, 1938.

Adams, James Truslow. *The March of Democracy.* New York: Charles Scribner's Sons, 1932.

Agassiz, George R. (ed.). *Meade's Headquarters, 1863–1865, Letters of Theodore Lyman.* Boston: The Atlantic Monthly Press, 1922.

Alexander, Edward Porter. *Military Memoirs of a Confederate.* New York: Charles Scribner's Sons, 1907.

Ander, O. Fritiof (ed.). *The John M. Hauberg Historical Essays.* Rock Island: Augustana Book Concern, 1954.

Anderson, Galusha. *The Story of a Border City During the Civil War.* Boston: Little, Brown and Company, 1908.

Anderson, John Q. (ed.). *Brokenburn: The Journal of Kate Stone, 1861–1868.* Baton Rouge: Louisiana State University Press, 1955.

Angle, Paul M. *Created Equal? The Complete Lincoln-Douglas Debates of 1858.* Chicago: The University of Chicago Press, 1958.

—— (ed.). *The Lincoln Reader*. New Brunswick: Rutgers University Press, 1947.

——. "The Changing Lincoln." See O. Fritiof Ander, *The John M. Hauberg Historical Essays*.

Angle, Paul M., and Earl Schenck Miers (eds.). *The Living Lincoln*. New Brunswick: Rutgers University Press, 1955.

Annals of the War. Philadelphia: The Times Publishing Company, 1879.

Appleton's Cyclopaedia of American Biography. 6 vols. New York: D. Appleton and Company, 1898.

Armes, Ethel. *Stratford on the Potomac*. Greenwich, Conn.: William Alexander Jr. Chapter, United Daughters of the Confederacy, 1928.

Ballard, Colin R. *The Military Genius of Abraham Lincoln*. Cleveland and New York: The World Publishing Company, 1952.

Bancroft, Frederic. *Life of William H. Seward*. 2 vols. New York: Harper & Brothers, 1900.

Basler, Roy P., and others (eds.). *The Collected Writings of Abraham Lincoln*. 8 vols. New Brunswick: Rutgers University Press, 1953.

Battles and Leaders. See Johnson and Buel, below.

Beach, William H. *The First New York (Lincoln) Cavalry*. New York: The Lincoln Cavalry Association, 1902.

Black, Jeremiah Sullivan. *Essays and Speeches*. New York: D. Appleton and Company, 1885.

Blackford, W. W. *War Years with Jeb Stuart*. New York: Charles Scribner's Sons, 1946.

Boykin, E. M. *The Falling Flag*. New York: E. J. Hale & Sons, 1874.

Cannon, LeGrand B. *Personal Reminiscences of the Rebellion*. New York: Burr Printing Company, 1895.

Cash, W. J. *The Mind of the South*. New York: Anchor Books, 1954.

Catton, Bruce. *This Hallowed Ground*. New York: Doubleday and Company, 1956.

Chesnut, Mary Boykin. *A Diary from Dixie*. Ben Ames Williams, ed. Boston: Houghton Mifflin Company, 1949.

Chester, James, "Inside Sumter in '61." See *Battles and Leaders,* I.

Chittenden, Lucius C. *Recollections of President Lincoln and His Administration*. New York: Harper & Brothers, 1895.

Clemens, Samuel L. *The American Claimant and other Stories and Sketches, by Mark Twain (pseud.)*. New York: Harper and Brothers, 1917.

Cohn, David L. *The Life and Times of King Cotton.* New York: Oxford University Press, 1957.

Coleman, Charles H. *Abraham Lincoln and Coles County, Illinois.* New Brunswick: Scarecrow Press, 1955.

Commager, Henry Steele (ed.). *The Blue and the Gray.* Indianapolis: The Bobbs-Merrill Company, 1950.

Cooke, John Esten. *A Life of General Robert E. Lee.* New York: D. Appleton and Company, 1875.

Craven, Avery. *The Coming of the Civil War.* Chicago: The University of Chicago Press, 1957.

―――― (ed.). *To Markie.* Cambridge: Harvard University Press, 1938.

Crawford, Samuel W. *The Genesis of the Civil War.* Hartford, Conn.: C. L. Webster and Company, 1887.

Croffut, William A., and John M. Morris. *The Military and Civil History of Connecticut During the War of 1861–65.* New York: Ledyard Bill, 1868.

Crozier, Emmet. *Yankee Reporters, 1861–65.* New York: Oxford University Press, 1956.

Dana, Charles A. *Recollections of the Civil War.* New York: D. Appleton and Company, 1898.

Davis, Jefferson. *The Rise and Fall of the Confederate Government.* 2 vols. New York: D. Appleton and Company, 1881.

Davis, Varina Howell. *Jefferson Davis, Ex-President of the Confederate States of America. A Memoir by His Wife.* 2 vols. New York: Belford Company, 1890.

[DeForest, J. W.]. "Charleston Under Arms," *The Atlantic Monthly,* VII.

DeLeon, Thomas C. *Four Years in Rebel Capitals.* Mobile: Gossip Printing Company, 1890, 1892.

Dictionary of American Biography. 20 vols. New York: Charles Scribner's Sons, 1928–1944.

Doubleday, Abner. *Reminiscences of Forts Sumter and Moultrie in 1860–61.* New York: Harper and Brothers, 1876.

Dunlap, Lloyd A., "President Lincoln and Editor Greeley," *The Abraham Lincoln Quarterly,* June, 1948.

Durden, Robert Franklin. *James Shepherd Pike: Republicanism and the American Negro, 1850–1882.* Durham: Duke University Press, 1957.

Durkin, Joseph T. (ed.). *John Dooley, Confederate Soldier.* Washington D.C.: Georgetown University Press, 1945.

Eisenschiml, Otto. *Why the Civil War?* Indianapolis: The Bobbs-Merrill Company, 1958.

Emerson, Ralph Waldo. *Complete Works.* 12 vols. Boston: Houghton, Mifflin Company, 1903-21.

Emory, Frederic, "The Baltimore Riots." See *Annals of the War.*

Englehardt, Sir John Gardiner D. *Journal of H. R. H. The Prince of Wales' Visit to America.* London: Privately Printed [1860?].

Fitzhugh, George. *Sociology for the South.* Richmond: A. Morris, 1854.

Freeman, Douglas Southall. *Lee's Lieutenants: A Study in Command.* 3 vols. New York: Charles Scribner's Sons, 1944.

————. *R. E. Lee.* 4 vols. New York: Charles Scribner's Sons, 1951.

Fuller, J. F. C. *Grant and Lee.* Bloomington: Indiana University Press, 1957.

Furnas, J. C. *Goodbye to Uncle Tom.* New York: William Sloane Associates, 1956.

Garland, Hamlin. *Ulysses S. Grant: His Life and Character.* New York: Doubleday and McClure Company, 1898.

Garrison, William Lloyd. The Story of His Life Told by His Children. 4 vols. Boston: Little Brown and Company, 1885-89.

Gordon, George H. *Brook Farm to Cedar Mountain.* Boston: James R. Osgood and Company, 1883.

Grant, U. S. *Personal Memoirs.* E. B. Long, ed. Cleveland and New York: The World Publishing Company, 1952.

Graves, Thomas Thatcher, "The Occupation of Richmond." See *Battles and Leaders,* IV.

Grayson, William J. *The Hireling and the Slave.* Charleston: J. Russell, 1854; San Francisco: McArthur and Company, 1856.

Greeley, Horace. *The American Conflict.* 2 vols. Hartford: O. D. Case & Company, 1864.

Halstead, Murat. *Caucuses of 1860: A History of the National Conventions of the Current Presidential Campaigns.* Columbus, Ohio: Follet, Foster & Company, 1860.

Harwell, Richard B. *Confederate Music.* Chapel Hill: The University of North Carolina Press, 1950.

————. *The Confederate Reader.* New York: Longmans, Green and Company, 1957.

————. *Songs of the Confederacy.* New York: Broadcast Music, Inc., 1951.

Helper, Hinton Rowan. *Compendium of the Impending Crisis of the South.* New York: A. B. Burdick, 1860.

Hendrick, Burton J. *Lincoln's War Cabinet.* Boston: Little, Brown and Company, 1946.

Herndon, William H. and Jesse W. Weik. *Life of Lincoln.* Cleveland and New York: The World Publishing Company, 1942.

Hesseltine, William B. *Lincoln and the War Governors.* New York: Alfred A. Knopf, 1948.

Horn, Stanley F. (ed.). *The Robert E. Lee Reader.* Indianapolis: The Bobbs-Merrill Company, Inc., 1949.

Hutton, Graham, "Lincoln Through British Eyes," *The Abraham Lincoln Quarterly,* June, 1944.

Johnson, Allen. *Stephen A. Douglas: A Study in American Politics.* New York: The Macmillan Company, 1908.

Johnson, Robert Underwood, and Clarence Clough Buel (eds.). *Battles and Leaders of the Civil War.* 6 vols. New York: The Century Company and D. Van Nostrand Co., 1884–1888.

Jones, J. B. *A Rebel War Clerk's Diary.* 2 vols. Philadelphia: J. B. Lippincott & Co., 1866.

Jones, John William. *Life and Letters of Robert Edward Lee, Soldier and Man.* Washington D.C.: The Neale Publishing Company, 1906.

Jones, Katherine M. *Heroines of Dixie.* Indianapolis: The Bobbs-Merrill Company, Inc., 1955.

Journal and Proceedings of the Missouri State Convention, 1861.

Kimbell, Charles B. *History of Battery "A" First Illinois Light Artillery Volunteers.* Chicago: Cushing Printing Company, 1899.

Kimmel, Stanley. *Mr. Lincoln's Washington.* New York: Coward-McCann, Inc., 1957.

Lamon, Ward Hill. *Recollections of Abraham Lincoln, 1847–1865* Chicago: A. C. McClurg & Company, 1895.

Lee, Capt. Robert E., Jr. *Recollections and Letters of General Robert E. Lee.* New York: Doubleday, Page & Company, 1924.

Leech, Margaret. *Reveille in Washington, 1860–1865.* New York: Harper & Brothers, 1941.

Lewis, Lloyd. *Captain Sam Grant.* Boston: Little, Brown and Company, 1950.

Lincoln, Robert Todd, Papers. Unpublished: Library of Congress.

Longstreet, James. *From Manassas to Appomattox: Memoirs of the Civil War in America.* Philadelphia: J. B. Lippincott Company, 1896.

[McGuire, Judith Brockenbrough]. *Diary of a Southern Refugee During the War, by a Lady of Virginia.* New York: E. J. Hale & Son, 1867.

McPherson, Edward. *The Political History of the United States of America During the Great Rebellion.* Washington D.C.: James J. Chapman, 1882.

Maurice, Sir Frederick (ed.). *An Aide-de-Camp of Lee, being the Papers of Colonel Charles Marshall.* Boston: Little, Brown and Company, 1927.

Mearns, David C. *The Lincoln Papers.* 2 vols. Garden City: Doubleday & Company, 1948.

Messages and Papers of the Presidents. 11 vols. Washington D.C.: 1907.

Miers, Earl Schenck. *Robert E. Lee, A Great Life in Brief.* New York: Alfred A. Knopf, 1956.

———. *When the World Ended: The Diary of Emma Florence LeConte.* New York: Oxford University Press, 1957.

———. "He Reduced War to Four Words," *Saturday Review,* July 9, 1955.

Miller, Francis Trevelyan (ed.). *The Photographic History of the Civil War.* 10 vols. New York: The Review of Reviews Company, 1911.

Milton, George Fort. *Abraham Lincoln and the Fifth Column.* New York: The Vanguard Press, 1942.

Monaghan, Jay. *Civil War on the Western Border, 1854–1865.* Boston: Little, Brown and Company, 1955.

Moore, Frank (ed.). *The Rebellion Record: A Diary of American Events.* 11 vols. New York: G. P. Putnam, 1861–1863 and D. Van Nostrand, 1864–1868.

Mumford, Lewis. *Herman Melville.* New York: Harcourt, Brace and Company, 1929.

Nevins, Allan. *The Ordeal of the Union.* 2 vols. New York: Charles Scribner's Sons, 1947.

———. *The Statesmanship of the Civil War.* New York: The Macmillan Company, 1953.

Newman, Ralph, Otto Eisenschiml, and E. B. Long. *The Civil War.* 2 vols. New York: Grosset & Dunlap, Inc., 1956.

Nichols, Alice. *Bleeding Kansas.* New York: Oxford University Press, 1954.

Nichols, Roy Franklin. *The Disruption of American Democracy.* New York: The Macmillan Company, 1948.

Nicolay, Helen. *Lincoln's Secretary.* New York: Longmans, Green and Company, 1949.

Nicolay, John G., and John Hay. *Abraham Lincoln: A History.* 10 vols. New York: Century Company, 1890.

Official Records. See *War of the Rebellion,* below.

Olmsted, Frederick Law. *The Cotton Kingdom.* 2 vols. London: Sampson Low & Co., 1861. See also Arthur M. Schlesinger, *The Cotton Kingdom.*

Owen, William Miller. *In Camp and Battle with the Washington Artillery.* Boston: Ticknor & Company, 1885.

Parrington, Vernon L. *Main Currents in American Thought.* 3 vols. New York: Harcourt, Brace and Company, 1927.

Peyton, John Lewis. *The American Crisis, or Pages from the Note-Book of a State Agent During the Civil War.* London: Saunders, Otley & Company, 1867.

Pollard, Edward A. *Life of Jefferson Davis With a Secret History of the Confederacy.* Philadelphia: National Publishing Company, 1869.

Porter, David D. *Incidents and Anecdotes of the Civil War.* New York: D. Appleton and Company, 1898.

Porter, Horace. *Campaigning with Grant.* New York: The Century Company, 1897.

Potter, David M. *Lincoln and His Party in the Secession Crisis.* New Haven: Yale University Press, 1942.

Ramsdell, Charles W. *Behind the Lines in the Southern Confederacy.* Baton Rouge: Louisiana State University Press, 1944.

Randall, James G. *The Civil War and Reconstruction.* Boston: D. C. Heath & Company, 1937.

Rhett, Robert Barnwell, "The Confederate Government in Montgomery." See *Battles and Leaders,* I.

Rhett, Robert Goodwyn. *Charleston, An Epic of the Carolinas.* Richmond: Garrett and Massie, Inc., 1940.

Rhodes, James Ford. *History of the United States from the Compromise of 1850.* 7 vols. New York: Harper and Brothers, 1895.

Richardson, Albert Deane. *A Personal History of Ulysses S. Grant.* Hartford: American Publishing Company, 1868; San Francisco: R. J. Trumbull and Company, 1868.

Riddle, Albert G. *Recollections of War Times.* New York: G. P. Putnam, 1895.

Rowland, Dunbar (ed.). *Jefferson Davis Constitutionalist, His Letters, Papers and Speeches.* 10 vols. Jackson: Mississippi Department of Archives and History, 1923.

Russel, Robert D., "What Was the Compromise of 1850?" *Journal of Southern History,* August, 1956.

Sandburg, Carl. *Abraham Lincoln: The War Years.* 4 vols. New York: Harcourt, Brace & Company, 1939.

———. *Lincoln Collector.* New York: Harcourt, Brace & Company, 1949.

Schlesinger, Arthur M. (ed.). *The Cotton Kingdom.* New York: Alfred A. Knopf, 1953. See also Frederick Law Olmsted, *The Cotton Kingdom.*

Schmidt, George P. *The Liberal Arts College.* New Brunswick: Rutgers University Press, 1957.

Seward, Frederick W. *Reminiscences of a War-Time Statesman and Diplomat, 1830–1915.* New York: G. P. Putnam, 1916.

Sherman, William T. *Memoirs.* 2 vols. New York: D. Appleton and Company, 1875.

Snider, Denton J. *The American Ten Years War, 1855–1865.* St. Louis: Sigma Publishing Company, 1906.

Stampp, Kenneth M. *The Peculiar Institution.* New York: Alfred A. Knopf, 1956.

Starr, Louis M. *Bohemian Brigade.* New York: Alfred A Knopf, 1954.

Stephenson, Luther. "Three Months' Service in 1861 with the 4th Regiment M. V. M.," *Civil War Papers.* 2 vols. Boston: Printed for the Commandery, 1900.

Stern, Philip Van Doren. *An End to Valor.* Boston: Little, Brown and Company, 1958.

Stitt, Thomas L. "Who Put Down the Rebellion," *War Papers read before the Indiana Commandery.* Indianapolis: Military Order of the Loyal Legion, 1898.

Stringfellow, B. F. *Negro Slavery No Evil.* Boston: 1855.

Stringfellow, Thornton. *Scriptural and Statistical Views in Favor of Slavery.* Richmond: J. W. Randolph, 1856.

Strode, Hudson. *Jefferson Davis, American Patriot.* New York: Harcourt, Brace and Company, 1955.

Swanberg, W. A. *First Blood.* New York: Charles Scribner's Sons, 1958.

Thomas, Benjamin P. *Abraham Lincoln.* New York: Alfred A. Knopf, 1952.

———. *Portrait for Posterity.* New Brunswick: Rutgers University Press, 1947.

——— (ed.). *Three Years with Grant as Recalled by War Correspondent Sylvanus Cadwallader.* New York: Alfred A. Knopf, 1955.

Thorp, Willard (ed.). *A Southern Reader.* New York: Alfred A. Knopf, 1955.

Townsend, George Alfred. *Rustics in Rebellion.* Chapel Hill: The University of North Carolina Press, 1950.

Trollope, Anthony. *North America.* New York: Alfred A. Knopf, 1951.

Truman, Harry S. *Memoirs,* I: "Years of Trial and Hope, 1946–1952." Garden City: Doubleday and Company, 1956.

Tuttle, J. M., "Personal Recollections of 1861." See *War Sketches and Incidents.*

Villard, Henry. *Lincoln on the Eve of '61.* New York: Alfred A. Knopf, 1941.

Von Abele, Rudolph. *Alexander H. Stephens.* New York: Alfred A. Knopf, 1946.

Wallace, Sarah Agnes, and Frances Elma Gillespie, (eds.). *The Journal of Benjamin Moran, 1857–1865.* 2 vols. Chicago: Chicago University Press, 1949.

War of the Rebellion . . . Official Records of the Union and Confederate Armies. 128 vols. Washington, D.C., 1880–1901.

War Sketches and Incidents. Des Moines: P. C. Kenyon, 1893.

Waters, Brian (ed.). *Mr. Vessey of England.* New York: G. P. Putnam's Sons, 1956.

Webster, Daniel. *Writings and Speeches.* 18 vols. Boston: Little, Brown and Company, 1903.

Wecter, Dixon. *Sam Clemens of Hannibal.* Boston: Houghton Mifflin Company, 1952.

Welles, Gideon. *The Diary of Gideon Welles, Secretary of the Navy under Lincoln and Johnson.* 3 vols. Boston: Houghton, Mifflin Company, 1911.

Werstein, Irving. *July, 1863.* New York: Julian Messner, 1957.

Wiley, Bell Irwin. *Life of Johnny Reb.* Indianapolis: The Bobbs-Merrill Company, Inc., 1943.

———. *The Plain People of the Confederacy.* Baton Rouge: Louisiana State University Press, 1944.

Williams, Kenneth P. *Lincoln Finds a General.* 4 vols. New York: The Macmillan Company, 1949–1956.

Williams, T. Harry. *Lincoln and the Radicals.* Madison: The University of Wisconsin Press, 1941.

———. *P. G. T. Beauregard, Napoleon in Gray.* Baton Rouge: Louisiana State University Press, 1954.

Wilson, Edmund (ed.). *The Collected Essays of John Peale Bishop.* New York: Charles Scribner's Sons, 1933–48.

Wilson, Henry, "Jeremiah S. Black and Edwin M. Stanton," *Atlantic Monthly,* XXVI.

Wilson, Woodrow. *Division and Reunion.* New York: Longmans, Green and Co., 1910.

Wish, Harvey. *George Fitzhugh, Propagandist of the Old South.* Baton Rouge: Louisiana State University Press, 1943.

Woods, Nicholas Augustus. *The Prince of Wales in Canada and the United States.* London: Bradbury and Evans, 1861.

Younger, Edward (ed.). *Inside the Confederate Government: The Diary of Robert Garlick Hill Kean.* New York: Oxford University Press, 1957.

Index

Note: Military personnel not designated as (C.S.A. or C.S.N.) fought with the national armed forces.

ABOUT THE AUTHOR

Earl Schenck Miers was born in Brooklyn, New York, in 1910. A graduate of Rutgers University, he was first an associate editor of university publications at Rutgers and then, after two years as editor at the Westminster Press, became director of the Rutgers University Press in 1944. Subsequently he was an editor for both Alfred A. Knopf, Inc., and The World Publishing Company. Mr. Miers' distinguished editorial career, which he abandoned to devote his full time to writing, is matched by his eminence as a writer and historian, notably of the Civil War period. Among his books are *The Living Lincoln,* edited with Paul M. Angle, *The Web of Victory, Robert E. Lee, The General Who Marched to Hell,* and *Gettysburg,* with Richard A. Brown. Mr. Miers is also well known as a writer of children's books and of books dealing with publishing and academic life. He lives in Edison, New Jersey, with his wife and three children.

This book was set in Granjon and Caslon types
by The Haddon Craftsmen. The paper is
Perkins and Squier Company's RRR Wove Antique
made by P. H. Glatfelter Company.
It was printed and bound at the press of
The World Publishing Company.
Typography and design are by Larry Kamp.